THE ROMAN OPTION

Also by William Oddie

Dickens and Carlyle: the Question of Influence

*What Will Happen to God? Feminism and the
Reconstruction of Christian Belief*

*After the Deluge: Essays towards the
Desecularization of the Church (ed.)*

*The Crockford's File: Gareth Bennett and the
Death of the Anglican Mind*

*The Everyman Paperback Edition of Apologia pro
Vita Sua by John Henry Newman*

THE ROMAN OPTION

Crisis and the realignment of English-speaking Christianity

WILLIAM ODDIE

HarperCollins*Publishers*

HarperCollins*Religious*
Part of HarperCollins*Publishers*
77– 85 Fulham Palace Road, London w6 8jb

First published in Great Britain
in 1997 by HarperCollins*Religious*

1 3 5 7 9 10 8 6 4 2

Copyright © 1997

William Oddie asserts the moral right to be identified as the author of this work

A catalogue record for this book is
available from the British Library

ISBN 000 628064 1 (hardback)
ISBN 000 628065 x (paperback)

Printed and bound in Great Britain by
Caledonian International Book Manufacturing Ltd, Glasgow

Christopher Morgan: *Father Geldard, looking to the long term, hasn't the Roman option effectively been slapped down this morning by the [Catholic] Bishop in East London, when he said it would be absurd folly for Anglicans to join Rome on this issue?*

Peter Geldard: *If people use this issue alone to make such a decision, that, quite rightly, is not the motive for making that change. But the Roman Catholic Church is a very generous body and a very charitable body. That's the way we must interpret her actions ... when in 1976 she allowed [American Christians] who realized their sacramental life was now in jeopardy ... to retain their Anglican gifts and their Anglican heritage and yet to come under the auspices of the Roman Catholic Church. This option must be examined: a lot of people are talking about something they don't yet know or understand ...*
BBC Radio 4, *Sunday* programme, 15 November 1992

If that 'spell' which Newman thought prevented Anglo-Catholics from recognizing the true reality of the Church in England has finally been broken, he would hope that the Roman Catholic authorities will now look as sympathetically as possible at the practicality of establishing, as has been done in the United States, a special rite within the Roman Catholic Church for former Anglicans.

When the possibility of an Anglican Uniate Church was mooted in 1876, Newman could only welcome any 'means of drawing to us so many good people, who are now shivering at our gates'.
Father Ian Ker, *Daily Telegraph*, 18 November 1992

CONTENTS

PREFACE

This book is not the one I began to write early in 1993. It was evident to me then that we were witnessing an important moment in the history of the English Church, one which had implications far beyond these shores. What I did not realize then was how long drawn out the process would prove to be. I had supposed in my simple way that five years after the decision to ordain women in the Church of England, we would have a fairly clear idea of the broad lines of a final settlement whereby communities of those of the Catholic mind within the Church of England might be received into the Roman Catholic Church without wholly losing what Pope Paul VI had called Anglicanism's 'worthy patrimony'. At the same time I thought we would be much further along the road towards the other necessary – indeed natural – outcome in a broad process of 'realignment', the union of various strands of the English Reformed tradition around a transformed Church of England.

Most of those who might be thought likely to make such journeys would by then, I supposed, have been in a position to decide to set out if they had not already arrived. But events did not take the course that many – with good information – supposed they would. What, five years on, has become increasingly evident is not only that this historical process is incomplete, but that it has hardly begun. The Catholic bishops have not seen the end of dramatic developments in the Church of England to which it will be their apostolic duty to make a worthy pastoral response, just as the bishops of the Church of England have achieved only the early stages of the process which began with the November Synod of 1992.

Thus, a book which began with the simple intention of describing the origins of an Anglican exodus (which early in the new millennium would, I supposed, be more or less complete) has become instead an attempt to understand what actually happened as a way of unlocking some kind of understanding of what lies ahead over the coming decades.

This is a more perilous undertaking. Writing about events while they are still unfolding cannot be done with the same kind of perspective and balance as would be possible if they were in some sense complete, at least theoretically. Apart from anything else, the kind of factual detail available to the historian is not yet accessible. My original intention to give a detailed factual account of how the process worked out has given way to a more impressionistic approach, since even what the process is has not yet wholly emerged. Personal experiences are still at the stage of formation. Statistics are as yet patchy and unreliable (in some parts of the Catholic Church they appear hardly to exist) and I have therefore used them as little as possible. The impressions of those closely involved cannot be quoted in the same way as they could if the events in which they are still involved were complete and their life's work done. Bishops and priests in particular cannot for the most part be named as sources, since without my reassurance of their anonymity their impressions would have had to be less than frankly expressed.

So I cannot acknowledge the help of those I would most like to thank: they know who they are, and how much my book owes to what they have told me so that the truth may be known. Much of the most important information in this book was not intended to see the light of day, at least not yet. But it has seemed to me vital that it should be better understood now why the decisions which have been taken were taken, and that they were not the only decisions which could have been taken. My message, in part at least, is that events might have unfolded otherwise: to that extent, this book borders on what the school of historical writing recently exemplified in a volume entitled *Virtual History* terms 'counterfactual' – the history that might have been. 'What might have been', however, is a gloomy song; it is much more important to understand what yet might be.

Despite the impossibility of publicly thanking most of those I have consulted, I must thank certain individuals for their kindness, while insisting that no inferences can be made that they are the source of information about events in which they were or remain involved. Cardinal

Basil Hume in Westminster, Cardinal Bernard Law in Boston, Bishop Clarence Pope in Fort Worth, and Bishop Alan Clarke in Norwich, kindly saw me in the book's early stages; so, then and later, did the former Bishop of London, Father Graham Leonard. In a different way the Revd Dr Ian Ker has been an unfailing source of guidance. Father Ker is well known as the leading authority on that greatest of all English converts, John Henry Newman, under whose protective shadow all subsequent conversions from Canterbury to Rome have taken place; he has also taken a scholarly interest in the process of conversion itself, and I am grateful for his judgement on my conclusions as they developed. My conclusions, however, are my own; wherever they are ill judged, they are not to be laid at his door.

A few words about the book's subtitle are necessary: the word 'English-speaking' might be thought to imply that I have attempted a survey of the entire English-speaking world. My focus has been particularly on events in England, but has taken account (in places extensively) of how closely developments in America have been connected with these events. But they have had their repercussions, too, elsewhere, wherever Anglicanism has followed the flag. I have not referred directly to developments in Canada, New Zealand and Australia, or even in Wales, Scotland and Ireland; I have used the word 'English-speaking', nevertheless, to convey that I am well aware (unlike some Englishmen) that England is not the only country where Anglicanism is practised. It is the centre, however, of one of many interconnecting circles: understand the process here, and the lessons will have their implications elsewhere.

*

There are, when writing about a subject involving such perilous questions as women's ordination and the validity of Anglican Orders, a number of terminological pitfalls. I have attempted to avoid occasions of gratuitous offence, not always an easy matter. Thus, many Roman Catholics, mostly from old habit rather than polemical instinct, avoid the use of the word 'priest' when describing Anglican clergy. Similarly, Anglican clergy of the Catholic mind never describe themselves as clergymen or ministers, and may even be offended if others do so. The variations exist in the use of the term 'Catholic'. I have used both Anglican and Catholic usage indiscriminately and mean no offence to anyone. There are similar difficulties in knowing how to describe ordained women. To write of 'women priests' without any qualifying indication can be interpreted as implying that women can validly be ordained to the priesthood. I cannot write as though this were my view, but I do not wish to be unpleasant. To write of 'women "priests"' or 'priestesses' is simply offensive. I have adopted the neutral usage of the late Dr Gareth Bennett and hyphenated them, thus: women-priests; I hope that this will do the trick.

INTRODUCTION

This could be a big moment of grace, it could be the conversion of England for which we have prayed all these years. I am terrified now we are going to turn round and say we do not want these newcomers. We have prayed for Christian unity and now it could be happening: a realignment of English Christianity so as to bring us closer together, in two blocs, instead of lots of blocs.
Basil, Cardinal Hume, February 1993

Basil does tend to go over the top rather; we had to claw him back from the edge of the precipice.
Crispian Hollis, Bishop of Portsmouth, Eastertide 1993

We ... cannot expect that the issues and concerns of the present time can be resolved quickly ... For our part, we must proceed patiently, and with prayer.
Pastoral letter from the Archbishops and Bishops of England and Wales, Fourth Sunday of Easter, 1993

What are the English bishops afraid of?
Joseph, Cardinal Ratzinger, Eastertide 1993

ON NOVEMBER 11, 1992, the General Synod of the Church of England voted to ordain women to its priesthood. It was the climax of a bitter and prolonged struggle. It had been in 1975 – the year after the first American Anglican women-priests were illicitly ordained by rebel bishops in Philadelphia – that the Synod had first voted (though narrowly) in favour of the proposition that there were 'no fundamental objections' to such a step.

A few well-informed commentators had predicted the final outcome in England, though to the very end it was a close-run thing. But the consequences, as they unfolded over the weeks and months that followed, had been foreseen by nobody. They turned out to be quite different from what had happened in America. Events on both sides of the Atlantic remained intimately connected, nevertheless. American radicals had funded and otherwise nurtured the campaigners for women's ordination in England; in the same way, English and American traditionalists had become close over the years. It was not to be expected that as the matter approached a kind of resolution, events in the mother Church would be without their effect on the other side of the Atlantic.

THE COMPROMISE UNRAVELS

The Church of England's final decision was a shattering blow to those who had opposed it for so long, many of whom had come to suppose that it could be indefinitely postponed by the use of sophisticated synodical tactics. The effect of the vote was immediately felt beyond the narrow confines of the Church of England: by nightfall not only the Cardinal Archbishop of Westminster but the Pope in Rome had expressed their disquiet. English Christianity now moved for some months into uncharted and precipitous territory. It was a region of mists and sudden strange alarums, in which none of the old landmarks could any longer be relied upon. The London *Times* columnist William Rees-Mogg wrote magisterially of 'the unwinding of the original compromise which combined Protestant and Catholic elements in a single state church': a 'realignment of English Christianity' was widely surmised to be under way by commentators no less weighty, who included Cardinal Hume, the head of the Catholic Church in England and Wales.

When the mists cleared, it was discerned that the old scenery had altered, in some places violently and in others hardly at all. It was like some ancient landscape through which a major road scheme – longed for by many, resisted fiercely by others – had been driven, almost invisible from some vantage points but changing everything nevertheless by the mere fact of its existence. The six months that followed the historic vote had seen a period of dramatic activity within both the Church of

England and the English Roman Catholic Church, from which emerged, in both Churches, agendas whose consequences would take at least a generation to unfold.

In the Church of England, the immediate crisis had been contained by a previously unimaginable stratagem: the invention of a new kind of itinerant or 'flying' bishop – officially known as Provincial Episcopal Visitors or PEVs – to minister to parishes which now refused to have anything to do with their own diocesan bishop. This was widely (and correctly) understood as a desperate measure. It was prompted partly by the fact that some dioceses had become ungovernable, and partly by the real fear that Rome would soon offer imaginative proposals for the reception into the Catholic Church of much if not most of the Catholic tendency within Anglicanism (together with a good deal of its cultural and liturgical inheritance).

Another major change had to wait a little longer, for the new legislation to become active: the shift in the collective character of the Anglican clergy that began to take place with the ordination of the first women-priests. Five years after the decision, there were 900 full time stipendiary women clergy in the parishes, and another 806 in chaplaincies or unpaid ministry – around 15 per cent of the total ministry of the Church of England. The official figures for full time clergy who had resigned in protest and taken the compensation to which they were entitled was 422, rather less than half the equivalent figure for the women who replaced them, though there were numerous unofficial estimates which cast doubts on the official figures: these had, according to some disaffected clergy, been 'massaged', and some claims of the numbers who had resigned were as high as 700: but even the official figure was well over double that officially projected before November 1992. One statistic was undeniable: after five years there were still no women-bishops, because this had been expressly excluded by the enabling legislation in order to minimize the vote against it. The exclusion of women-bishops from the legislation may well have ensured victory for the cause of women-priests, though at a price: in effect, the Church of England had established for women a different and second-class priesthood, one incapable of promotion to the episcopate.

It was not, of course, a situation that could last. Everyone understood the political logic of the situation: that in the end there would have to be women-bishops. But few were willing at the time to contemplate the inevitable consequence: that is, a new crisis, possibly deeper than the first. This would be unleashed by a declaration by the flying bishops that they are no longer in communion with the other bishops of the Church of England, thus not only causing the original damage limitation operation to unravel but creating a new and (without even more flexibility than has already been shown) infinitely more intractable crisis.

THE UNDERLYING ISSUE

But why was there a crisis in the first place? That was the question many asked then and continue to ask. What has been the issue between the supporters and the opponents of women-priests? Ultimately, it went well beyond the narrow question of whether or not women could be or should be ordained to the priesthood. This was something the Movement for the Ordination of Women (MOW) could never grasp: their opponents had to run the gauntlet of accusations ranging from simple sexual hang-ups to rampant misogyny: but gender was only incidentally what the struggle had been about.

The underlying issue was not a new one. What most commentators forgot as the consequences of the November vote began to make themselves felt was how close the Church of England had already been to a crisis of precisely this kind, one involving a perceived threat to the integrity of Anglican sacramental life, a crisis, too, in which – though rather differently – 'the realignment of English Christianity' was intimately bound up. The Anglican-Methodist reunion scheme of nearly a quarter of a century earlier had been in many ways a dress rehearsal for what was finally to happen when, after a struggle equally passionate but greatly more prolonged, the Anglo-Catholic wing of the Church of England was finally and irreversibly defeated over an issue which it correctly saw as threatening its very existence.

Nearly all the fundamental elements of the crisis of 1992 were there in 1968. A scheme had been proposed for the reunion of the English Methodist Church with the Church of England. It was a scheme in which not only dissident Anglo-Catholics but also – though privately – senior Roman Catholics had perceived a threat to Anglican-Roman Catholic relations; one, too, in which there had been a perception (by no less a luminary than the Papal Legate, Rome's official representative in London), that perhaps at some stage special ecclesial arrangements might have to be made for disaffected Anglicans of the Catholic mind.

Both crises were about far more than their immediate occasion: in the end, the question they really posed was whether – to quote William Rees-Mogg's analysis of the crisis over women-priests – 'the original compromise which combined Protestant and Catholic elements in a single state church' could any longer, with integrity, be maintained.

For MOW achieved more in November 1992 than it had intended: it had changed the balance of power within Anglicanism, not simply between male and female or even between liberal and conservative but also between Protestant and Catholic. And just as a scheme for union between Anglicans and Methodists had been defeated for a generation by a concerted political alliance co-ordinated by Anglo-Catholics, so the ultimate and definitive political defeat of Anglo-Catholicism finally created the conditions under which such a scheme (this time involving most mainline English Protestant churches) could at last easily surmount the obstacle of a two-thirds vote in the General Synod.

WHAT IS A PRIEST?

It has been one of the great paradoxes of Anglican life over the last forty years: that the search for Christian unity has repeatedly been – with the one exception of the movement for women's ordination – the greatest cause of internal schism. This has certainly been true within the Church of England itself, and to a lesser but still important extent within the Churches of the Anglican diaspora. The record shows that the overwhelming instinct of Anglicanism (except in such exotic manifestations as the province of Papua-New Guinea) has been towards union with other Churches of the Reformation rather than with Rome, if a choice had to be made between the two.

And of course a choice always *did* have to be made (though it was always officially claimed by the Anglican authorities that they wanted unity with all comers). The reason was simple enough. In practice, the reformed Churches did not accept priesthood in any recognizably Catholic sense. Any scheme acceptable to the Protestant Churches had to be an effective denial of a sacramental priesthood: at the very least it had to be sufficiently ambiguous to allow of that interpretation. Thus, in 1968, one objection to the Anglican-Methodist Unity scheme was that by its nature it had to embody the fundamental Methodist belief, expressed in Methodism's Deed of Union, that an ordained minister's 'priesthood' does not and cannot differ in kind from that of a layman. In the words of the leader of the opposition to the scheme, Dr Graham Leonard (then Suffragan Bishop of Willesden in London), 'It is hard to avoid the conclusion that those elements of the Church of England which express its Catholic nature and heritage are to be modified or regarded as expendable; while those which witness chiefly to the reformed element in its tradition are to be preserved unscathed.'

However this perception might be denied, that was the way most Anglicans of the Catholic mind had to regard the matter: the integrity of Anglican sacramental life was under threat. But most of the Anglican clergy did not hold this view at all. Anglo-Catholic clergy thought of themselves as priests of the universal Church; many insisted on the title 'Father'. But most of the Anglican clergy emphatically did not see their orders in the same way as Roman Catholic priests saw theirs. They did not consider that ordination had effected in them a change which was fundamental and permanent, in theological language one which was 'ontological': their real view was much closer to that of the Methodists – that ordination conferred a human commission to minister in a particular way. Ever since the Reformation, for most English-speaking Christians the word 'priest' had meant an ordained Roman Catholic; and despite the changes wrought in the Anglican mind by Tractarianism and then by the more militant Anglo-Catholicism of the late nineteenth and twentieth centuries, that was the way, deep down, most of them still thought.

When in 1969 the Anglican-Methodist scheme came before the joint Convocations of Canterbury and York, it narrowly fell; but only because the almost insurmountable fence of a 75 per cent vote of approval had been erected against it. In the Convocation of Canterbury, it was approved by 93 per cent in the House of Bishops but by only 67 per cent in the Lower House (in the Convocation of York, this result was repeated: success for the scheme in the Upper House, failure, though with a 69 per cent vote, in the Lower). It failed again later in the General Synod (which effectively replaced the Convocations in 1970), this time narrowly failing the lower hurdle of a two-thirds vote.

THE PAPAL LEGATE INTERVENES

Essentially, for the Anglo-Catholics, the issues were the same as they were to be in the controversy over women's ordination: the integrity of the sacramental system and the possibility that the path to an eventual reconciliation with Rome might be for ever foreclosed. Shortly after the publication of the final version of the Anglican-Methodist unity scheme, the Roman Catholic theologian Bishop B.C. Butler wrote to the great Anglo-Catholic scholar Dr Eric Mascall, summing up his objections in terms which could have been used verbatim twenty-five years later: the proposed scheme would so radically change the character of Anglicanism that relations between Canterbury and Rome would inevitably be of a different, and more distant, character:

> I fear that the report, if accepted, will give *de jure* rights to Protestantism; and that this will in fact (according to one's point of view), either compromise a position which has hitherto been substantially intact, or give fresh endorsement to a compromise which is already existing. From the point of view of Anglican-RC relations ... I should deplore this. *I need hardly point out to you that sacramental forms which in one context of official doctrine are 'valid' can be invalidated by removal into a different (official) context* [My italics].

The Greek Orthodox Metropolitan Athenagoras made clear that he shared these misgivings over the sacramental viability of the scheme (as both the Russian and the Greek Orthodox were later to do over women's ordination): 'I ... fear,' wrote Athenagoras to Leonard, 'that the special relationship between our two communions will be seen as seriously impaired ... The Methodist minister is in a similar position to an Orthodox sub-deacon; he has received charismata from the Spirit, but he has not received the grace of the priesthood.'

In July 1968, Bishop Leonard and Dr Mascall were invited to discuss the matter privately with the Apostolic Delegate, Archbishop Eugene Cardinale. Leonard needed to know what, if the scheme were to go through, the attitude of Rome might be towards Anglicans who would refuse to participate in the new dispensation (as the Anglicans who rallied under the banner of 'Forward in Faith' were to do in November 1992). Leonard said he thought there would have to be a financial settlement, an idea which was to recur in his thinking as the vote over women's ordination drew close. Archbishop Cardinale contributed another important idea which was to re-emerge a generation later: if, he said, a body of Anglicans were to stand firm in order to maintain the Catholic heritage within Anglicanism, there would, he thought, be no difficulty in allowing them to be in communion with the Roman Catholic Church. He said, too, that he would send a copy of Dr Leonard's pamphlet on the controversy, *To Every Man's Conscience*, to the Pope.

Thus, when the vote over women priests finally took place in November 1992, much that was thought to be unprecedented in the thinking, not only of the Anglican dissidents but also of some influential Roman Catholics, had in fact been long anticipated, though privately. For most of the Anglican bishops the seismic convulsions triggered off by the November vote came as a complete, and very nasty, surprise. They had never understood why the Anglo-Catholics had allowed themselves to become so excited over women-priests (just as earlier they simply had not understood their opposition to reunion with the Methodists); in both cases they had always imagined that once the voting was over and the schemes were in place everyone would soon come to see what a good idea it all was and quickly settle down with their new colleagues. They had regarded the forecasts of internal schism as empty threats made for the purpose of winning synodical votes; they were ill-prepared for what actually happened when the vote was won. Suddenly, it really did begin to look as though the Church of England as it had been since the Elizabethan settlement was in the process of unravelling: and it was all happening in the context of a high-profile public debate conducted in the newspapers. Something drastic would have to be done: but what?

INSIDE THE CATHOLIC GHETTO

The strains and tensions within the English Catholic Church were scarcely less dramatic, though they were, in general, more discreetly expressed. Nevertheless, given the intensity of the media interest, the internal debate within the Catholic Church could not wholly be kept behind closed doors, for all the instinctive secretiveness of English Catholicism. One Bishop in particular had criticized publicly those

Anglican dissidents who hoped for a 'Roman Option' – for some way in which disaffected Anglicans could establish a new Catholic Anglican jurisdiction in communion with the Holy See. But his criticism was also, by implication, an attack on those within the Catholic Church who were naive enough to have become involved in the machinations of these undesirables: he was privately particularly scathing, to both clergy and laity within his own diocese, about the head of the English Catholic Church, Cardinal Basil Hume, Archbishop of Westminster.

By the time the English Catholic bishops met for their traditional meeting in Low Week (the week after Easter week) 1993, an 'outline response' had emerged, the principles of which appeared to contrast starkly with the visionary hopes of many Anglican Catholics. To some extent their disappointment was inevitable; there were too many unknowns for it to have been possible, after only six months, to produce the kind of concrete and detailed package for which they had longed as a storm-tossed mariner longs for a lighthouse. Nevertheless, particularly among those who had been privy to the discussions, led by Cardinal Hume, between a group of representative Anglican dissidents and four Catholic bishops, there was the certain knowledge that the vision which had united the whole group had to some extent been undermined by Catholic antagonisms and insecurities.

But was the vision now dead? Had it really all been a chimera? When the dust had settled, it began to be seen that the beginnings at least of a real 'Roman Option' had after all opened out, one which was not only more substantial than had at first appeared, but which had also within it the possibility for more radical future developments. These could now take place quietly, the Press having in general now adopted the view that the bare letter of the Low Week 'response' was all the Roman Option was going to turn out to be. There was now no hurry; developments could quietly take their course. Potentially the most dramatic of these developments now began to stir in North America, where the first – and still the most radical – moves towards opening up a Roman Option for Anglicans had been installed at the beginning of the eighties.

THE AMERICAN DIMENSION

America was where it all began. Within the Protestant Episcopal Church of the United States (PECUSA), radicals had successfully installed the first body of women-priests in the Anglican communion and traditionalists had negotiated a means whereby dissident congregations could be received into the Catholic Church with their clergy and their Anglican ways intact. Pope John Paul II, in one of the early acts of his reign, authorized for their use a Catholicized but still recognizably Anglican liturgy, the traditional language version of which may well be the most sumptuously beautiful vernacular Mass in existence. The whole package, or 'Pastoral Provision', was supported by an article of canon law later to be part of the basis of the early negotiations in England.

Over a decade later – with the end of the final hope of Anglican traditionalists on the other side of the Atlantic that the Mother Church at least would stand firm over women priests – it soon became clear to those in the know that far-reaching preparations were under way: Episcopalian dissidents and the relevant Catholic authorities in America had radical notions for the development of the Pastoral Provision, plans which went very much further than anything most English Catholic bishops wanted to entertain. This internationalization of the process opened up a new dimension in its growth and development which has almost certainly not yet run its course.

These North American developments, which are (as I shall show) enthusiastically supported in Rome, could be activated at any time during the next decade; or for that matter, the next hundred years: this would – I believe will – have far-reaching results for all those Christian Churches directly or indirectly concerned throughout the English-speaking world.

PREPARING FOR THE REAL CRISIS

In England, the apparent stalling of the 'realignment' in Low Week 1993, far from being the end of the matter, can be seen as creating the necessary conditions for its future development. Instead of laying down a detailed scheme (Rome's usual instinct) the bishops established principles on which they could act pragmatically. It was a very English – almost, one might say a very Anglican – solution. It was also one which its enemies would find hard to shoot down.

This was important. For it was now clear that there existed an element within the Catholic Church which did not want these converts, and which would oppose any measures designed to remove unnecessary obstacles to their reception. The six months that followed the decision to ordain women had been notable for some very public dramatics among Anglicans; everyone had expected that. But English Catholics had always tried to live a quiet life, out of the public eye, offending nobody: the glare of the media had brought to the surface some insistent questions about the future role of the Catholic Church in English life, a subject on which, it emerged, there were passionately held and mutually exclusive opinions.

Thus, the inside story of the dramatic rise and exaggerated fall of the so-called 'Roman Option', between November 1992 and April 1993, constitutes in itself a kind of living X-ray of the internal psychology of Anglicanism and Catholicism in England, at what can be seen as a turning point in the history of both Churches.

WHAT HAPPENED?

But was it really a turning point: had a real and long-term shift in the balance and character of English Christianity really taken place, as some believed: or had it all been a wild dream? That was the question now. Certainly the shift – if shift it was – turned out, in the short term at least, to be less openly dramatic than some commentators had predicted and hoped for. It was real enough, nevertheless: but its effects were contained, first by what some thought the prudence and others (including very senior figures in Rome) the excessive caution of the English Catholic bishops; and second, by the urgent damage limitation operation hastily improvised by the bishops of the Established Church. But the provision of the 'flying bishops' was not a scheme designed for durability; and it remains open to sudden collapse if the earth should subside once more beneath the Church of England's embattled minority, as I predict that it will when women become bishops in the Church of England

When this new crisis supervenes, the English Catholic bishops will once more be faced by a new and imperative pastoral necessity. They have it in their power, this time, to be less cautious and better prepared in their response. The Anglican bishops, for their part, may be less inclined to perpetuate the disunity of their own Church by further attempts to keep the dissidents at all costs in communion with Canterbury, emboldened, perhaps, by the opportunities for a renewed and more focused Anglicanism – one around which English Protestants can at last unite – which another (and larger) exodus of Catholic-minded Anglicans would present.

But first, they need – Catholic and Protestant alike – to consider the lessons of their response to the immediate aftermath of the decision to ordain women. It was a time of boldness and vision; it was also a time of intense insecurity, even fear. It has now become clear that the 'Roman Option' for Anglicans has not (as was at first feared) operated as a mere escape hatch for ritualist troublemakers, nor has choosing it been an obscurantist reaction against change: it was in its origins, on the contrary, a creative movement for the reunion, even in one sense the renewal, of the Catholic tradition in England: this movement should now, I believe, be enabled by the English and Welsh Catholic bishops to run its course.

And this time, the new exodus should be allowed, even encouraged, to depart by the Bishops of the Church of England, unimpeded by soft words and temporary expedients. For the situation has now moved on. The provision of the flying bishops (the three PEVs and, for the London area, the Suffragan Bishop of Fulham, currently and significantly the head of 'Forward in Faith', John Broadhurst) has brought about one important development: the gathering and consolidation of a large and stable constituency of non-jurors, a body of believers who now need a permanent and corporate ecclesial solution for their problem. They will never be happy again within the bounds of New Anglicanism. It is my contention that the bishops of the English Roman Catholic Church not only have it in their power to offer the best available pastoral solution, but that they are are under an historic obligation to do so. The evidence is that the relevant authorities in Rome would support such a solution were it to be offered; and the arguments against doing so seem to me trivial and pettifogging compared with the gains, which as I shall argue would be as substantial for the unity and renewal of the Reformed Churches in England as for the future cohesion and spiritual renewal of the Catholic tradition itself.

INTO ONE FOLD AND UNDER ONE SHEPHERD

This is a continuing story which I have tried to tell in a truthful and balanced way, though I can hardly claim to be dispassionate. One of my qualifications for writing this book, indeed (though I hope there are others), is my entire lack of objectivity. I had for years been part of the movement within the Church of England which had tried to prevent what finally happened, ironically on Armistice Day, 1992. I had been brought into the battle by my first theologically based book, a study of the substance and effects of radical feminist theology (*What will happen to God? Feminism and the reconstruction of Christian belief* (1984)) which was widely read among the dissidents, especially in North America: this led to extensive speaking tours on that continent, mostly addressing Episcopalians but also the so-called 'continuing' Anglicans who had broken away from the American Episcopal Church. I had taken the road to Rome myself some time before the final vote on women's ordination, and was already convinced that for those within the Church of England who were of the Catholic mind there was now, in the end, no other real alternative. I played a small part in getting the initiative that became known as the 'Roman Option' off the ground; I knew many of the personalities, some of them well, who became caught up in it.

This book, therefore, is addressed to several audiences. It is addressed, first, to those Anglicans who believe that there is such a thing as a Universal, or Catholic Church, and who are members of the Anglican Church because they were firmly convinced that Anglicanism was part of it: for classical Anglicanism of that kind is, I believe, no longer a viable option.

Second, it is addressed to those in the Roman Catholic Church in England and Wales (and also in a different way in America) who – for a variety of reasons – are unhappy to contemplate a continuing influx of dissident Anglicans, perhaps doubting their commitment to the faith of the contemporary Catholic Church. I know these dissidents and what their faith is; for many years it was mine. I am also aware, as a convert to Catholicism, how utterly opaque is the Anglican mind in general, and the Anglo-Catholic mind in particular, to my fellow Roman Catholics. To them, I have attempted to explain the real motives of the Anglican dissidents; to Anglican dissidents who feel that the Catholic Church might be a little more effusive in its welcome, I have tried to explain some Catholic difficulties.

I have also in mind a third audience, though I strongly suspect it will not be inclined to listen. One Catholic 'liberal' attacked me in the *Guardian* as 'proving the old adage about over-zealous converts [by] slagging off his erstwhile spiritual home at every turn with the mis-placed enthusiasm of the Spanish Inquisition'. In fact, my most hostile criticisms of the Church of England, in books and in the London *Daily Telegraph*, were written during the eighties as an Anglican priest, and attracted support from many fellow Anglicans throughout the English-speaking world. I remain critical of the Church of England, though now in a rather different way. My Anglican criticism of the Anglican Church was that it had ceased to be Anglican and had become something else. My criticism now is that it has failed to realize the fact, and carries on pretending that nothing of any great moment has occurred. The Church of England should now accept that it has become, and irreversibly, an essentially Protestant Church. It could then achieve a unity it has never known before, and become a national focus of unity for a particular Christian view which is not mine, but which is arguably in many ways more agreeable to the national temper than the Christianity of the historical mainstream.

I hope that I have said enough about myself to pre-empt any accusations that I have undeclared motives in writing this book, or that lurking beneath its surface there is a hidden agenda. My motives and my agenda are plain enough, though I also know enough by now about the polemical habits of one or two fellow Catholic journalists to realize that there is one accusation I need to rebut from the outset. My sympathy with the Anglican dissidents attracted from one of them the charge (as unjust to them as to me) that my position is 'on the extreme right'. This accusation, in Anglican circles, might convey nothing more serious than a taste for Cranmerian English and a vague tendency to vote Conservative. In a Catholic context it is a very much graver charge, implying Lefebvrist and neo-fascist leanings. Let me confess the truth. I have never attended, nor do I desire to attend, the 'Old Mass' (though I think that those who do ought to be accorded more respect); and I have become, if anything, somewhat more left-wing in my political views since becoming a Catholic.

But I do have one very definite and passionate belief. It is that it is now time for the long slow withdrawal of the Christian cause to cease. Anglicanism is no longer the same thing it used to be: but it could become something very much greater than it is. It must come to terms with its new identity as a focus for Protestant Christianity and move forward once more. There are new tensions to overcome and new battles to be fought – particularly in the field of moral teaching – before this can take place: but it is not beyond the bounds of possibility that this desirable outcome could be the greatest achievement of the reign of Dr George Carey, who may well yet prove to be the most underrated Archbishop of Canterbury of the twentieth century.

And it is time for the Catholic Church in England to move out from the ghetto, not to become a 'national church' on the old Anglican model but to assume national responsibilities, to cease to be merely a private chaplaincy for a defensive minority. This does not necessarily mean that having been timorous English Catholics should become unduly aggressive. Cardinal Hume's words, that 'this could be a big moment of grace' were addressed to Catholics in the first place; but his hope for a 'realignment of English Christianity' was that it 'should bring us all closer together, *in two blocs, instead of lots of blocs*': precisely the result which would, I believe, flow from the corporate Roman Option for Anglicans which could and should now be developed.

For there is, I believe, an essential first step for a realignment of the whole of English-speaking Christianity which truly would 'bring us all closer together'. It is the beginning from which all else would flow: that all those of the Catholic mind should now kneel, at last, before the same altar. This means that Anglican Catholics – on both sides of the Atlantic and in both hemispheres – must now accept that Anglo-Catholicism has come to its natural end, that the Oxford Movement is over, that it is right for them to set out at last for the home that has awaited them so long, liberating Anglicanism as they go to be true to what has already become its predominant tradition.

For me, that is not simply my analysis of the present reality: it is also my hope and heartfelt prayer. When I think of all those who still stand where once I stood, of their present condition of ecclesial limbo, and of all the grace I have received since I left them to become a Catholic, my mind returns irresistibly to the final page (which George Eliot said she could not read without tears) of Newman's great classic, the *Apologia pro Vita Sua*. In it, Newman gathers up and bears in memory

> ... those familiar affectionate companions and counsellors, who in Oxford were given to me, one after another, to be my daily solace and relief; and all those others, of great name and high example, who were my thorough friends, and showed me true attachment in times long past ...

And I earnestly pray for this whole company ... that all of us, who once were so united, and so happy in our union, may even now be brought at length, by the power of the Divine Will, into One Fold and under One Shepherd.

Oxford, Solemnity of Corpus Christi, 1997

PART ONE

CHAPTER ONE

'A GIANT STEP FOR WOMANKIND'

... the code of practice indicates the sensitivity with which the legislation will be implemented ... I, fellow bishops and many others will work strenuously to keep space and room in every ministry of the Church for those who ... have difficulty with the ordination of women.
The Bishop of Guildford, proposing the motion, 11 November 1992

The legislation simply phases out the objectors. You may bandy about the words 'provisional' and 'reception' and 'co-existence' as much as you wish ... If there can be no more diocesan bishops opposed ... opponents will be ... left to wither and die.
The Archdeacon of Leicester, opposing the motion, 11 November 1992

The chairman: *Unfortunately, the hall must be evacuated because there is a ... fire alert in the building.*
General Synod debate, 11 November 1992

AFTER THE VOTE, while Synod members were still streaming out of the chamber, the ladies and gentlemen of the media were told that the press conference planned to take place immediately would now be delayed. One speculation was that a new press release was being hastily cobbled together, that the two Archbishops had not expected this result; but nobody really knew.

Outside in Dean's Yard, a triumphant celebration was taking place. Women deacons in clerical collars, some wearing – to a conservative eye – strangely discordant accessories such as ethnic-looking pendants and long dangling earrings, sang jubilant songs and swigged champagne straight from the bottle. Inside the main entrance, Archdeacon George Austin, pale with distress, protested bitterly that if the opponents had won and had celebrated in this way, there would have been no end to the complaints from the women-priests lobby. It was, he commented later, 'a cruel and insensitive demonstration'.

About an hour later, in a small hall inside Church House, the TV news cameras were being set up, and the Lambeth Palace press team were distributing a statement, issued in the name of the two Archbishops. Archbishop Habgood and Archbishop Carey sat side by side on the platform, at a table, answering questions. Would Archbishop Carey write to the Pope, to inform him of the decision? Dr Carey said he would (later the same evening, the Pope made it clear he already knew). Archbishop Carey called for everyone to refrain from doing anything to inflame the situation. Would he care to comment on the demonstrations now taking place in Dean's Yard, which were causing deep offence? Dr Carey looked puzzled. Was there a demonstration? He had heard some singing; but we had to understand that these women's hearts were full of joy after so many years of struggle.

'WHAT BINDS US TOGETHER'

The statement itself conveyed two contradictory undercurrents of feeling about the situation in which the Church of England now found itself. It was clear that the Archbishops anticipated strong feeling, and there is an element of deep nervousness in this interesting text. But there is also a confidence that in the end the Establishment's customary procedures would be able to cope. With the benefit of hindsight, the statement seems somewhat optimistic; even at the time it had about it a curious unreality:

> While for many this result is a source of joy and relief, to others it will bring anguish. We pray that all those who opposed the measure will feel comforted by the great love for them in Christ felt by their fellow Anglicans with different views on this particular matter. What binds us together in God's love as a Church is vastly more important than a disagreement about women's ordination.

But whatever it was that may have tenuously united the two sides until now had come unstuck; there was, it soon became clear, not even a common language: they were like inhabitants of different planets. It was now obvious to everyone that there were some very strong emotions welling up, which were potentially dangerous for the stability of the Church of England; feelings had somehow to be calmed, though it soon emerged that the bishops had not the vaguest idea of how to do it.

In the meantime, however, the Archbishops made their appeal, calling for 'a period of quiet reflection and deep prayer in which emotions are calmed, not further inflamed'. What the Archbishops were afraid of (and their fears were to be amply borne out) was a large-scale refusal to accept the authority of the General Synod. The potential consequences of that were incalculable: for it was in the General Synod that the Church of England as an institution had invested its credibility. If it had moral or juridical authority to do anything, the Church itself had decided that it was from the General Synod that it would derive. The Synod had become its ultimate centre of unity. Now, however, the Church was faced with a very large minority which repudiated synodical authority: the Synod, as John Gummer explained on his resignation from it the following month, had 'arrogated to itself powers to which it has no title and no right'. Any widespread refusal to accept its authority was bound to lead to some disunity, whatever the issue. But here was a disputed synodical decision to do with the central sacrament of unity itself. Charles Moore, the following Eastertide, explained the dilemma:

> Since I don't believe the Synod can make women priests, I do not believe that the women ordained as a result will have the power to make bread into the Eucharist, and so I am not in communion with them, or with the people who ordain them, and being in communion with people is the definition of membership of a Church. Therefore there is schism, and that is the thing above all that bishops should seek to avoid. Dr Carey seems almost to have courted it.

PLAYING FOR TIME

In the immediate aftermath of the vote, Dr Carey and Dr Habgood were still hoping that such feelings would not be widespread. They now solemnly urged 'all members of the Church to abide by the General Synod's decision'; and they added – obviously anticipating reproaches of partisan bias – 'We would be saying exactly the same had the vote gone the other way'. Then they went on to plead for the dissidents to abstain from what they termed 'hasty or ill-considered action'; this would, they said, 'be inappropriate and serve no good purpose'.

The difficulty for Dr Carey and Dr Habgood was that they were addressing a large minority – as much as a third of the Church – which simply did not trust them. Thus, the assurance they now gave the dissidents about their place in the new order was regarded by those to whom it was principally addressed as nothing less than preposterous:

> The role and ministry of those opposed to the legislation is no less greatly valued and secure in the Church today and for the future than it has been hitherto.

For what the dissidents had felt for years was that those of them known to be opposed to women's ordination had been pushed to the margins already.

The tactic of the House of Bishops now, however, emerged with great clarity: to play for time. There had been just such a perilous situation in the American Episcopal Church in 1976. Over thirty of the Church's ninety-odd dioceses had refused to ordain women. There had been talk of breakaway; in the end only a few small 'continuing' Churches had been formed. More than a third of the membership had simply unchurched themselves – they disappeared from the statistics of the Episcopal Church, and reappeared on nobody else's; but who was to say they would not have drifted away in any case?

The point was that the institution had survived intact; and institutional survival was the name of the game. One by one, the dissident American bishops had (with only a few embarrassing exceptions) been replaced by safe men; and the crisis had been contained: though vociferous opposition from the minority continued, this could even be presented as a bonus, with talk of creative tension, Anglican comprehensiveness, and 'theological pluralism' – this last device for holding together those who held incompatible views on fundamental issues became the belle of the ball at the 1988 Lambeth Conference. The important thing for the Church of England now was to hold the ring, handle the malcontents, and hope that apathy and resignation would set in:

There will now be a delay of at least a year before the measure approved by General Synod today can actually become law and take effect. There is, therefore, plenty of time for detailed discussion with those still deeply opposed to the legislation about how their consciences can be safeguarded and their rightful place within the mainstream life of the Church of England maintained. The whole House of Bishops is united in seeking to ensure that there will be no discrimination in selection against those opposed to the ordination of women to the priesthood; that the unity and integrity of the Church of England will be maintained; and that the Bishops, in communion with one another as Bishops of one Church, will continue to provide episcopal oversight and pastoral care for all members of the Church.

Or, as Dr David Jenkins, Bishop of Durham, had put it during the debate in his inimitably convoluted way, 'We know that we must choose to ordain or not to ordain, but we refuse to choose to exclude disagreeing brothers and sisters.' The trouble was that the disagreeing brothers and sisters thought that to override their deeply held feelings and principles on this key question was in itself to exclude them. Dr Jenkins, for his part, had always given the traditionalist clergy in his own diocese the impression that if you disagreed with him, he supposed it could only be because you misunderstood what he had said; to a journalist, after the vote, he simply said he hoped that the opposition would turn out to be a matter of 'huffing and puffing but little blowing down of houses', and that everything would soon settle down.

'JOY GREETS HISTORIC VOTE BUT CHURCH FACES SPLIT'

But everything was not going to settle down. One of the traditionalists' warnings was now swiftly borne out: that by acting unilaterally, the Church of England would turn its back on its historic claim to be a part of the Church Catholic, whose orders were part of its Catholic heritage. The Catholic Church itself now made it clear that though it would still hope for friendly relations with the Church of England, those relations would now necessarily be on a wholly different basis. An official statement from the Vatican described the decision as a 'new and grave obstacle' to unity and emphasized that several Popes had given this warning to various Archbishops of Canterbury and that what had been done was something that even Rome itself did not feel it had the power to do. 'The Catholic Church', its spokesman said, with chilling finality, 'does not feel it has the right to authorize such ordinations.'

Cardinal Basil Hume – often described as being very Anglican in his manner and sympathies – soon made it clear that these alleged tendencies did not extend to matters of theological principle. He was, he said, 'disappointed but not surprised' by the vote. Women's ordination, he went on, was not a question involving such secular considerations as equality or justice; nor could it be decided exclusively because of changed values and attitudes to society. The Cardinal's statement could almost be seen as a direct rebuttal of the argument offered by several speakers in the Synod debate itself, to the effect that women's ordination would give the Church of England credibility 'in the eyes of the world'. Such a development, the Cardinal insisted, could only come when it could be seen to be theologically justified beyond any reasonable doubt: 'A change of such importance has to be in harmony both with Scripture and Tradition, and it must reflect a moral unanimity of believers.' Again, he might have been arguing in the Synod itself a few hours earlier.

It was the perfect twin-track story for the press: 'Vicars in Knickers', inimitably punned *The Sun*; 'A Giant Step for Womankind', was the headline in the *Daily Mail*, beneath the strap-line 'Joy greets historic vote but Church faces split'. The lead story excitedly forecast that 'thousands of the Church of England's most loyal supporters and clergy are preparing to desert it. On some calculations the number of priests could be 3,000, including some bishops.' This figure was based on support for the clerical ginger group Cost of Conscience; but it was clear from the outset that at least half, perhaps as many as two-thirds, of those opposed would stay inside the Church of England for a variety of reasons. That still left a very large number of potential defectors, certainly enough to cause a crisis: not only a spiritual crisis, but – hardly less important in an institution whose investments had recently been so grossly mismanaged – one which was also financial.

The *Mail* also carried a significant story by Bishop Graham Leonard, the former Bishop of London. The message was a familiar one: that the ordination of women was part of a wider rejection of Christian tradition: '... the Church of England has shown in recent years', wrote Dr

Leonard, 'that it thinks it can modify the truths which are revealed by God through Scripture. Such is the case over doctrines such as the Resurrection, and in moral matters such as marriage.'

'THE CHURCH OF ENGLAND IS NO MORE'

From the beginning, among those who had opposed the legislation, there were three reactions, similar but distinct. There were those who were not going to leave, but who would never accept what had happened. There were those who now decided that their departure was only a matter of time. And there was a third group, somewhere between the two, who were going to wait and see what happened. But whether they were going to stay, go, or bide their time, few of these would ever again believe in the integrity – indeed, many now denied the very existence – of the Church of England. The day after the vote, women members of Synod from the Lichfield diocese confronted their bishop outside the chamber (for a stunned Synod was still sitting) and accused him of betraying the Church. Afterwards, one of them said, 'I told him we considered we no longer had a bishop. I didn't go into prayers because it is very difficult to pray with people who have cast you out of the Church.'

For such as these, quite simply, there was no more Church of England; as the Vicar of All Saints, Notting Hill put it on the Sunday after the vote, in a sermon echoed that day in many parishes all over England, 'last Wednesday evening at five o'clock, the Church of England died'. Nothing less than that: 'The Church of England as we know it and love it and to which many of us hoped to dedicate our lives is no more. It died when the Synod took its vote on Wednesday.' Or, as another distinguished Anglo-Catholic priest more succinctly put it, 'The Church of England has taken itself to the vet.'

In Oxford, the reaction of Father Michael Brewin, Vicar of St Andrew's Headington, was similar: it was all over. 'When I heard about the vote', he told me at the time, 'the first thing I did was to take off my clerical collar, and put on lay clothes. A number of priests have told me they did the same thing, instinctively. Then I went to see my Rural Dean, and told him that with great regret I would not be attending any further meetings of the clergy chapter or the deanery synod. I shall stay in the Church of England; but I don't know anyone who thinks there's anything left.'

One priest who was not going to leave the Church of England, come Hell or high water, had, nevertheless, a very similar view about how utterly things had changed. It was as though a great oak had been struck by lightning, leaving a few branches with green leaves on its vast dead trunk. George Austin thought it was as bad as that: but he was not leaving because, as he put it later, 'I have nowhere to go: if I could go to Rome, I would have gone already'. His mature reflection did not move on from the assessment he made at the time:

> For us, whether you can understand it or not, on November 11, 1992, the Church of England we had known and loved, served, cared for, and suffered with, was taken from us and out of its ashes a new church was born.

To stay in it was to accept exile from the Universal Church: 'It seems now', he wrote two weeks after the Synod's decision, 'that for the remainder of my ministry, I must be outside the Church Catholic.' On the eve of the July Synod, the following year, his view was still that 'George Carey, the 103rd Archbishop of Canterbury, has become the first archbishop of a new Church'. George Austin was not going to leave; nor was he going to resign from the General Synod, not unless things became impossible.

THE LIMITS OF EMPATHY

One prominent member of the Synod who did resign – and who subsequently became a Catholic – had very similar feelings about how the decision of 11 November had changed the Church of England in the most fundamental way. John Gummer, the only defector from the Cabinet, said that the title of Archbishop of Canterbury was now no more than a courtesy title:

> whoever holds the post next cannot possibly claim that he is there as a successor of the apostles because that is no longer the claim of the Church of England. The Church [of England] has now claimed that its orders do not come from the apostles but are in fact open to change, the alteration and modification of the

General Synod and, therefore, the whole basis of the Church of England has been changed.

'One does have', he said, ' a very real feeling of the loss of something one loved.' These feelings were shared by many other lay people. Words like 'loss', 'bereavement', 'rejection' recurred frequently, as many faithful Anglicans tried to come to terms with their feelings. Mrs Elizabeth Mills, a leading member of the seven thousand strong organization Women Against the Ordination of Women (WAOW) told me that it was like being 'given the boot by someone you have loved for years, and who you suddenly realize never loved you at all'. Would she go to Rome? 'Well,' she said, 'you suddenly realize that the boy next door has always looked rather attractive; but it's not something you want to do on the rebound.' Others were not prepared to wait; a number of prominent lay Anglicans announced their imminent departure, including the junior minister, Ann Widdecombe.

The hope that those who had lost the vote were going to 'feel comforted by the great love for them in Christ felt by their fellow Anglicans with different views on this particular matter' was doomed to disappointment. Quite simply, there was little love left on either side; protestations to the contrary were just not believed. In a perceptive leading article published on 27 November, *The Church of England Newspaper* (itself in favour of women priests), offered a word of caution to those who had voted for the legislation:

> Be careful. Many, from Archbishop of Canterbury down, say they are aware of the pain dissenters feel. Many are trying to put themselves in their shoes. The plain fact is that however noble the intention they are not in a position to know what their feelings are, and there are limits to empathy ... no-one who voted in favour of the legislation is in a position to tell those opposed what to feel or what to do. That is up to the individuals and groups concerned, to their own consciences, and their personal discipleship. It is neither right nor possible to dictate how they should behave.

As George Austin put it in the same issue: 'If the vote had gone the other way, and I had offered to "share the pain" of a woman deacon refused ordination, I hope I should have understood if she had replied, "But you caused the pain!" – and then punched me on the nose.'

WHAT WOULD THEY HAVE DONE?

'If the vote had gone the other way' – that was no longer a live question; but as George Austin acknowledged, there had always been strong feelings on both sides. The opponents of women's ordination had been contemptuous of the way in which – so they claimed – the female supporters of MOW had paraded their 'pain and grief' at being excluded from the priesthood, as a tactical device. Now, their own pain and grief became a dominant element in the internal politics of the Church of England. This poses an interesting question, hypothetical but not without importance. What would have happened if the vote had gone the other way? Dr Carey and those bishops who voted with him were heavily criticized for failing to see how things would go if the legislation squeezed through, for not seeing how determined the dissidents were and how much trouble they would cause. But the dissidents were not the only ones who were determined, and Cost of Conscience was not alone in making alarming and realistically worked out threats of guerrilla warfare.

There were, by now, nearly one thousand women ordained to the diaconate in the Church of England, few of whom saw themselves as 'permanent deacons'. They had, for the most part, bided their time and awaited events. What would they have done if the legislation had failed on 11 November? A group of women deacons in the diocese of Ely had already published a kind of manifesto, which they distributed widely; nobody could say they had not been warned. Entitled 'After November', this spelled out the options. These were: to accept the new situation; to leave the ordained ministry; to leave the Church of England; to emigrate; or – last of all (and in many cases by far the most likely) – 'to initiate or participate in protest action'.

What might that have meant? One possibility would have been just as disruptive as anything Forward in Faith was later to achieve. A number (probably a rapidly growing number, as the tactic succeeded) of the most militant women deacons would have gone to America, where they would have been ordained as priests by sympathetic Episcopalian bishops (Bishop John Shelby Spong of Newark, New Jersey, would certainly have obliged; indeed he had already publicly made it clear that he would). They would then have returned to their parishes in England, and with the backing of their incumbents (there were plenty of those who would have defied authority) would have proceeded regularly to celebrate the Eucharist.

If the numbers doing this had been large enough (and with 1,000 women deacons, it would not have needed to be a majority to have had a very considerable effect) it is difficult to see what the bishops could have done to get the situation under control without the kind of coercion that Anglican bishops are extremely nervous about using, and which some would in any case have deliberately refrained from using as a matter of principle. In any diocese where the diocesan bishop failed or refused to control the situation, there would have been a traditionalist backlash. Forward in Faith might in any case have come into existence, and it might sooner or later have declared itself out of communion with 'tainted' bishops in much the same way as it did in 1994. The outcome could in the end have been similar to that in America, where unauthorized ordinations of women by maverick bishops led to a cave-in by the General Convention two years later. In England, however, the process would have been infinitely more destructive and long drawn out, either than it had been in America, or than it was to prove in reality

The simple fact was, that the unity of the Church of England was in peril from the moment the General Synod was given enough power to effect radical change of any kind. But from the moment it decided that there were 'no fundamental reasons' why women should not be ordained, it was doomed. One way or another, those defeated would have taken to the maquis. As it happened, it was the large 'traditionalist' minority. The only question, 'after November', was how far they would go, and in what direction. To some extent, it is a question whose answer has even now not yet fully emerged.

CHAPTER TWO

WHAT THEN ARE
WE TO DO?

And the options open to us? They are like the options open to everyone who suffers a bereavement. It is no option to pretend that it doesn't make any difference, that life will go on the same. We cannot sit in the room with the corpse propped up in the chair opposite the fire and pretend that it is not dead. We cannot live in our home, which is devastated and ruined, and pretend that it is the house we once inhabited. We cannot go on as if nothing had changed. We must, all of us, make a new life ...
Sunday sermon preached after the Synod vote by Prebendary John Brownsell, Vicar of All Saints, Notting Hill.

What then are we to do? What are the options?
The Rt Revd and Rt Hon Graham Leonard, *Catholic Herald*, Friday 20 November

ATTEMPTS BY THE bishops at a 'charm offensive' – to persuade the dissidents to settle down in the new order – were an almost complete failure. One priest in the Oxford diocese, when the bishop asked him what he could do to be helpful, replied, 'You can keep out of my parish for the next eighteen years, until I retire.' In another diocese, the same episcopal enquiry of a forthright priest from the Antipodes elicited an even blunter response: 'Piss off.' As Bishop Leonard commented when I telephoned him the following day, 'How can the victor console the victim without at the same time opening the wounds of controversy?' And he added, significantly, 'people feel trapped in a Church not of their making'.

STANDING FIRM

It was to their liberation from that entrapment that Bishop Leonard now turned his mind. It was an eventuality he had considered before; but now, what had been a matter of speculation about a theoretical contingency had become a present and urgent imperative. Now the moment had arrived, it was clear that there was no longer any future in resistance from within the Church of England. His *Daily Mail* article was the opening shot in a personal initiative which was to strike a chord, not only within his own constituency in the Church of England, but in the Catholic Church in England and in Rome itself.

But the moment itself had not been anticipated: the article had been commissioned after a courier on a motor bicycle had arrived at the bishop's home in Witney, with a message to phone Richard Addis, Deputy Editor of the *Mail* (Dr Leonard's ex-directory number was one of the best kept secrets as well as one of the hottest journalistic properties in London over the next few weeks). When he spoke to him, Addis remembers, he had attempted to edge Leonard towards publicly declaring something like a Roman Option – but this was further than he wanted to go at this stage.

Dr Leonard sat down immediately, wrote the piece, and faxed it in around 7 p.m. The last two paragraphs of the *Mail* article show that he had already realized that he had a role to play in the next stage of the drama:

> My job will now be to give all the help I can to those priests, deacons and lay people who want to be obedient to what God has revealed to us about himself and his purpose for us.
>
> My advice to the parish priest who is shocked by this decision is to stand firm and not to lose hope. There will be a delay now while the legislation is implemented which will give us time for considering the options. During this time we must talk to each other and make our plans as best we can.

His article appeared on Thursday 12 November, the day after the Synod's decision; but it does not seem to have been widely noticed. By Friday, the talk among the opponents was of resistance from within; but there was no common mind about how it should manifest itself. There was widely perceived to be a schism: 'They have legislated a schism

31

into being' was how one dissident put it. The main difference of opinion was between those who wanted the schism to be clear-cut and to mount a determined resistance, and those who thought it was still possible amicably to negotiate with the victors for a kind of officially recognized no-go area. Inside Faith House, Westminster, headquarters of the Anglo-Catholic Church Union, where resistance to women's ordination had been co-ordinated for twenty years, there was intense disillusion with those who had sought to work within the Establishment ('playing the Synodical game'), and an uneasy feeling that a spirit of compromise at this stage would serve only to complete the humiliation of the vanquished. 'We must make it plain to this lot', Father Geoffrey Kirk told me, 'that they have now lost authority.' 'This lot' meant, above all else, the Rt Revd Eric Kemp, president of the Church Union, at 78 the oldest bishop on the bench (he had escaped the rule of retirement at 70). There had been for some years doubts about Bishop Kemp's willingness to take on the Establishment; and his support for the cause of Anglican-Methodist reunion in the late sixties had not been forgotten.

RESISTANCE FROM WITHIN

The mood was determined. One veteran activist told me that 'there is a general feeling that we should say the Church is in schism, and that we should give a positive lead. There is a real determination that there should be no wetness in the future – we have played the Establishment game too much.'

But those who for twenty years had ruled the roost in Faith House – men like Bishop Kemp himself, Oswald Clarke (generally described as a 'veteran synodsman') and the vote-counter and political fixer, Maurice Chandler – were equally determined that they were not going to secede from the Establishment. Early moves to establish an effective resistance were dampened down. An advertisement had been mooted, to go into the church press, the wording of which would have been tantamount to a declaration of war. It would have said that those women who might be ordained as a result of any legislation would not be priests in the Church of God; it would have called on all of those priests and laity opposed to the legislation to act together in resisting any means used to put forward this new ministry; and it would have called for their complete withdrawal from the whole machinery of synodical government at all levels – from Deanery Synods, Diocesan Synods and from the General Synod itself. The effect would have been stunning; and by Friday morning it seemed to have been killed by an edict from Bishop Kemp.

Oswald Clarke and Maurice Chandler, too, were urging caution, saying that what was now needed was an accommodation with the victors. But they were widely seen as discredited. 'We've got to have nothing to do with any of it,' said one source inside Faith House. 'We've got to tell parishes not to sign these options (the declarations – envisaged by the legislation – that a parish could officially opt out of accepting a woman-priest) – if we do that, we will be agreeing that it's possible for women to be priests. We don't need to, we can stop it anyway, how would a bishop impose it if the people won't have it?'

There was intense anger at Bishop Kemp's spirit of compromise. 'It would be better, frankly,' said one disgruntled priest to me, 'if Eric went now.' 'There is a danger now', Father Geoffrey Kirk summed up the feeling on Friday morning, 'that there will be a split between those who want to carry on playing the old Establishment game and those who want to mount an effective defence.'

In fact, the possibilities for an effective guerrilla resistance were considerable. In the Church of England clergy are very hard to depose. They are in a position to carry out many sanctions, including the withholding of funds from the diocese. Father Kirk's organization Cost of Conscience (which had been founded partly to fill the vacuum left by Bishop Kemp's emasculation of the Church Union), was widely supposed to have detailed plans for such a guerrilla jurisdiction, including the names of a number of bishops prepared to cross diocesan boundaries to operate in 'hostile territory'. These were thought to include the name of Bishop Leonard.

PREPARING FOR SEPARATION

So, I telephoned Bishop Leonard to ask him whether he intended to become involved in such a resistance. He told me that he would be prepared to help ('I'm retired, there's nothing they can do to me now'). But he did not think there was any future for a 'dissident sect' within the Church of England. This led me to the real reason for my call. I asked him if he was thinking of reviving an earlier initiative, in which he had proposed to negotiate a way of taking those Anglicans opposed to women's ordination into communion with Rome (Rome had not in fact been explicitly mentioned, but everyone knew that was what he had in mind).

The circumstances are worth recalling. In 1987, the Church of England's House of Bishops produced guidelines for drafting the women's ordination legislation which Synod had now finally passed. Two passages in this report are interesting. One of them is a clear rejection of any kind of parallel jurisdiction. But another course was hinted at: the dissidents were encouraged to depart, apparently together. In the words of the Bishops' report, 'those who could not remain in communion with the See of Canterbury would need to find other ways of continuing their existence within the universal Church and would be entitled to explore such ways'. There were even hints that they might take with them some of the Church's resources. Dr Leonard promptly announced that 'we need ... to prepare for separation'. His announcement had created an immediate media sensation; but it had been followed by a long silence, particularly as the possibility grew that the legislation could actually be defeated.

The question I asked him was this: now that the legislation had actually passed, would he once more call for the dissidents to 'prepare for separation'? That was the question. There was a pause; then he told me that he was thinking of it, but was not sure that this was the right time. I told him that I was sure that this was the time for such an initiative, that to delay would be to miss the right psychological moment. There was an intense feeling of disorientation; to relaunch his Roman initiative now would be to seize the initiative from the compromisers on the one hand and the Establishment on the other. He asked how I thought it should be done. I said I thought it would be fatal to talk to anybody else; that would lead to endless discussions and the formation of committees. He should make it a personal initiative, and it should be not only a rallying cry but an actual approach to Rome. It could take the form of an article, preferably in the Catholic press. He replied that he had no contacts there. I suggested the *Catholic Herald*; at that time, I knew nobody on the largest Catholic paper, *The Universe*, and I suspected that *The Tablet* – a firm supporter of women's ordination with a substantial readership among Anglican liberals – would be unsympathetic, even hostile. Bishop Leonard asked when he would need to produce the article, and I said I thought the *Catholic Herald* would need it by Monday for the following week's edition. He said he was very busy that weekend; and he needed time to think. He told me to telephone him the following morning; in the meantime I was to contact the *Catholic Herald* to make sure they would actually want such an article.

CRISTINA TAKES A HAND

There was never any doubt about that: Cristina Odone, the vivacious and glamorous (Auberon Waugh's adjective was 'personable') new Editor of the *Catholic Herald* knew a major scoop when she saw one, and told me to tell Bishop Leonard he could write at whatever length he liked. On Saturday morning, Bishop Leonard told me that he had decided that now was indeed the time to get things moving, and that he would write the article.

By Monday afternoon, the *Catholic Herald* was beginning to get anxious; nothing had been faxed through. Then the article appeared on my own fax machine and Bishop Leonard telephoned to ask if I would read it through before he sent it off. The first half or two-thirds was a historical account of the origins of the present crisis of the Church of England; only in the second half did Dr Leonard mention his approach to Rome. I suggested that it would have been better if the two halves were reversed, since there was nothing new in the first half; or at least, that he might add an introductory paragraph, to emphasize what would be seen as the real point of the article. He replied that he thought the *Catholic Herald* would put something at the top to signal the article's purpose; and so we left it. Bishop Leonard faxed the article through.

The real news story began with Dr Leonard's scornful rejection (which as we have seen was instinctively shared by his whole constituency within the Church of England) of the idea that the dissidents could somehow be integrated into the new order. He described as 'extraordinary' Dr Carey's 'expressed hope that we will play a full part in the life of the Church when the legislation provides for us to be marginalized and finally extinguished'. He then put the question urgently being asked by all those who could not accept the outcome of the Synod debate: 'What then are we to do? What are the options?'

Before considering them, Dr Leonard pointed out that there was plenty of time before they had to decide. In fact, he realized that this was a double-edged element in the equation. It meant that there was no hurry, that they could work out their course of action in a considered and deliberate way; but he was privately concerned about the difficulty of maintaining the momentum of such a movement if the time-scale became too extended. His job was partly to sustain the resolution of the dissidents. Before considering the options, he said, two points had to be emphasized:

> First, the legislation will not become effective for at least twelve months. There is time to think and we must not make decisions precipitately. But during this time we must make it clear beyond any shadow of doubt that we cannot accept the change.

The second essential was that 'we should not become a sect'. That was what the Church of England had become by its unilateral action. The aim was in some way to stay together, not as an independent body but as part of the universal Church:

> We must seek to be admitted to the communion of the One, Holy, Catholic and Apostolic Church, and to do so not as individuals but as a body of those who are committed to orthodox belief and practice.

THE THIRD OPTION

'Not as individuals but as a body': what did that mean? Speculation as to what it might mean was to become a rich minefield of misunderstanding over the months to come. But it was less the form of the exodus with which Dr Leonard was most concerned at this point, than with the fundamental requirement that it should not be a source of further division. That was why he rejected the option of following the example of the 'continuing churches' formed by some of those who had broken away from Anglican Churches in the USA and in Canada, Australia and recently in England. 'While I admire them for having the courage of their convictions', commented Dr Leonard, 'it cannot be denied that, depending so much upon personalities, they seem to lead to further division.'

The Eastern Orthodox Churches were ruled out for a different reason: 'while they are sympathetic, they are so closely related in this country to the indigenous Churches of which they are part that it is difficult to see this as a realistic possibility.'

There was, in fact, only one realistic possibility; and Dr Leonard now launched it:

> The third option is to seek relationship with the Roman Catholic Church. This we should have to do as suppliants and without presumption, asking if a way could be found for us somehow to preserve our Anglican identity while being in communion with the See of Peter. I do not think that it is for us to suggest how this might be achieved. We can only hope and pray that the Vatican and the hierarchy here in England will give sympathetic consideration to any possibility of a way forward.

This, and this only – rather than any concrete proposal about what form a Roman Option might take – was Dr Leonard's initiative. It was not for him, he felt strongly, to make concrete proposals which might be seen as an attempt to establish a negotiating position. It was of the essence of his approach that he came as a 'suppliant'; it was a note echoed by those who were to join him in discussions with the Cardinal and his advisers later. This made a strong impression on many Catholic bishops; but it was to make none at all on the press, who wanted something concrete to report.

Dr Leonard made no suggestions; what he now did, however, was to speculate on his own account. He had always had a strong interest in canon law, the law of the Church. He now mused on what the Catholic authorities might come up with, what options were open to them. He first mentioned in passing the provisions whereby in the USA congregations of former Anglicans had been received into the Catholic Church and allowed to use a Catholicized version of an 'Anglican' Rite. These provisions might, he speculated, with some modifications, be adapted for use in England. Then he moved on to a more controversial possibility: the provision in the Code of Canon Law for what were known as Personal Prelatures. The controversy lay in the fact that the Canon had only been used once, to provide a legal framework for Opus Dei, an organization within the Catholic Church which had attracted furious opposition, not uniquely but particularly from the Catholic left. Dr Leonard, however, saw in the Canon (Canon 296) under which it had been set up the possibility of using it to establish a different and more widely based ecclesial entity; but he did not dwell on the possibility; as he put it later, 'I introduced the idea only to dismiss it.'

THE FIRST SIGHTING OF CANON 372

He dismissed it by making it clear that there was another possibility which seemed to him far more relevant to the present situation. Canon 296 was interesting. 'However,' he went on, 'the Canon which gives us most encouragement is Canon 372.' This was the enabling canon for the 'pastoral provision', the umbrella for the American 'Anglican-use' parishes. But the Canon seemed flexibly, even ambiguously worded; it certainly seemed to open up possibilities for the English situation:

> Having referred to the territorial nature of dioceses, paragraph two reads as follows: 'If, however, in the judgement of the supreme authority in the Church, after consultation with the episcopal conferences concerned it is thought helpful, there may be established in a given territory particular Churches distinguished by the rite of the faithful or by some other similar quality'.

What exactly does this mean? Does the phrase 'particular Churches' in this context refer to some form of parallel structure; or is it meant to refer to the local church, the parish? The American precedent seemed to indicate the latter: for although the 'pastoral provision' comes under the overall supervision of a 'director' (in this case Cardinal Bernard Law of Boston), individual parishes come under the authority of the local diocese. But there seems to be an ambiguity here. One authority speaks of 'the principle of qualified territoriality as a basic theme underlying the renewed diocesan and parish law': and he speaks of paragraph two, quoted here by Bishop Leonard, as reflecting 'the insight that exceptionally weighty pastoral factors, such as sensitivity to the spiritual needs of faithful of different rites may suggest establishing a particular church based principally though not exclusively on *non-territorial considerations*' [my italics]. Dr Leonard was not exactly sure what the Canon meant; but he brought it forward for general discussion. What these two Canons really established, so far as he was concerned, was that the Catholic Church had the capacity and the juridical structures to enable it to respond flexibly and creatively to the current situation.

He then spoke of the bleakness of the future for many Anglicans; the situation, he said, would bear particularly hard on the younger clergy who could not accept women-priests, 'and for whom there can be no future'. But it would also bear very hard on the orthodox laity, who might find that in their local church, sooner or later, they would not be able to continue to worship with a clear conscience: 'it would be of the greatest benefit to such people if, possibly as an interim measure, they could be permitted to make their communion in the local Catholic Church'.

This was a controversial request; suggestions that occasional inter-communion might be allowed had always been thought beyond the pale in England (though in France and Italy, local bishops often allowed Anglicans to receive communion if there was no local Anglican chaplaincy). Equally controversial – and more relevant to the discussions that lay ahead – were his comments on the vexed question of Anglican orders, a question

> ... which does present a problem for many Anglican clergy. Out of pastoral care for those to whom they have ministered, they would find it very difficult to accept that their ministrations are deemed utterly null and void.
>
> However, there are responsible people in the Roman Catholic Church who suggest that although the Bull *Apostolicae Curae* applied to the situation existing in 1896, subsequent developments – and particularly the participation of Old Catholic bishops in Anglican consecrations – could warrant a different response (at least for those ordained since then).

WAITING FOR THURSDAY

This was intriguing: who, exactly, were these 'responsible people'? Presumably they were senior enough for their opinion to make a difference. One thing was certain; that for the Catholic Church to find a way round the impasse represented by Pope Leo XIII's Bull *Apostolicae Curae* would be a major breakthrough. The Bull stated, uncompromisingly, that Anglican Orders were 'absolutely null and utterly void'. Partly, this judgement was based on the allegedly invalid episcopal consecration of the Elizabethan Archbishop Matthew Parker, from whose orders all subsequent Anglican orders were held to derive. This had been hotly contested at the time the Bull was promulgated; and scholars pointed out that Anglican orders could also be traced back to those of Archbishop Laud, among whose co-consecrators were bishops in the Irish and Italian successions. To counter this particular Roman objection, the practice grew up during the twentieth century of inviting bishops from the Old Catholic Churches (which had seceded from Rome after the first Vatican Council pronounced the dogma of Papal Infallibility) to participate in Anglican consecrations. From the Catholic point of view, their orders were irregular, but without any doubt valid. Thus – certainly in the Church of England itself (the Anglican diaspora was another matter) – Anglican orders could claim to have re-established a true succession, if ever it had been lost in the first place: at least, if a true succession had nothing to do with the faithful handing on of doctrine (a question to which it will be necessary to return).

But Bishop Leonard's request to reconsider *Apostolicae Curae* was not, he emphasized, an attempt at some kind of continuing Anglicanism under distant Roman protection. 'I would want to stress,' he concluded the article, 'that we are not asking for recognition to continue an Anglican ministry, but as those who have accepted the Magisterium and are in communion with the Holy See.'

The most crucial part of the article's intended audience was the Conference of Catholic bishops of England and Wales; by coincidence the Catholic bishops were meeting that week. Dr Leonard made sure that they would be well aware of his *démarche* before the *Catholic Herald* came out on Thursday; an advance copy was sent to Cardinal Hume. He was unsure whether there would be any immediate public reaction from the Catholic bishops; total silence might, at this stage, be the best that could be hoped for, since at least it would mean that his request had not been turned down. What he feared seemed at least possible on previous form. What might have happened would have seemed to many the most likely scenario: a reiteration of the traditional approach to prospective converts. This had always stressed that conversion was a matter for individuals; and it had seemed, to some outsiders at least, to stress the somewhat chilling idea of submission to an ecclesiastical authority rather than the more attractive notion of reconciliation with a living tradition of faith.

This pessimism was shared at the *Catholic Herald* office; when I phoned to make sure they had received the article, I was asked to make sure it was not leaked to any other paper. 'It will probably be dead in the water by teatime on Thursday,' was the way one reporter put it; 'but at least we will have had our scoop. '

'THIS ONE IS GOING TO FLY'

By Thursday lunchtime it was clear that, far from being dead in the water, the initiative had been successfully launched and was well on its way. Cristina Odone had made sure that Fleet Street would notice the article by faxing it, under strict embargo, to the religious affairs correspondent of the *Daily Telegraph*, Damian Thompson; the *Telegraph* scooped the other national dailies with a major front page article. The telephones started ringing early at the *Catholic Herald*, as the rest of Fleet Street tried to catch up with the story. *The Times* bought the original article for republication the following day. Dr Leonard's phone began ringing constantly (a state of affairs which he had to get used to); his ex-directory number had somehow leaked out. It was hardly the first time he had been the object of press attention; but now, in retirement, he had no entourage to protect him. His solution was to insulate himself by technology; he switched on his answerphone. Journalists, unless he knew and trusted them, would now get a response only by faxing him.

By late morning, it was clear, in the words of one reporter, that 'this one is going to fly'; the Catholic bishops, far from retreating into stony silence, issued a statement which made it clear they thought there was something to discuss: by normal standards an effusive welcome. It was a headline story on *The World at One*, the BBC's flagship radio news programme. Mike Wooldridge's report homed in on the idea (fostered by the *Catholic Herald*'s interpretation of Bishop Leonard's original article) that the proposal was specifically for a personal prelature, though Wooldridge described this loosely enough as 'a semi-autonomous structure under which Church of England priests and individual parishioners opposed to the ordination of women would be able to retain an Anglican identity, but would be under the jurisdiction of the Roman Catholic Church'.

The word 'prelature' turned out to be like a red rag to a bull to some Catholics. This emphasis in reporting the initiative was to lead to misunderstanding later – though, as we shall see, the notion of a prelature as a suitable vehicle for the Roman Option was not ruled out of court immediately by key players in both the English hierarchy and in Rome itself (and continued to be taken seriously in America as the situation there developed in the wake of the November decision in England). The broad idea of some kind of semi-autonomous structure was certainly taken much more seriously at the highest level than the short term outcome in England was later to indicate.

But such details were for the future; the extraordinary thing now was that a bishop of the Church of England was proposing to lead as many Anglicans as possible 'across the Tiber', out of a Church whose Establishment, as John Henry Newman had noted nearly 130 years before, 'have always testified an extreme aversion for what they term the power usurped by the Pope'. It was not the first time that Dr Leonard had floated the idea, certainly; nor was it the first time the press had given it a run for its money. Until now, however, such suggestions had been greeted by the Roman Catholic authorities with a deafening silence. Now, for the first time, the English Catholic bishops appeared to be responding; after years of caution, of doing and saying nothing to which the Established Church might take exception, there was a tiny sign of movement; and it was already on the one o'clock news.

THE SUN COMES OUT

Some vicarage telephones were jammed for hours. 'If it's on *The World at One*', said one excited Anglo-Catholic priest to a colleague, 'it must be happening.' 'The Roman Catholic bishops of England and Wales', Mike Wooldridge had reported, 'who have been in conference on other issues all week, discussed it this morning and significantly issued a diplomatically worded statement which, while not giving the idea the green light, didn't rule it out either.' It seemed, on the face of it, little enough: but to many Catholic-minded Anglicans, after so many years of coldness and rejection from that quarter, it was like the sun coming out from behind the clouds.

On Friday, the Cardinal made a statement, to the effect that Dr Leonard's proposals should be examined carefully – though there were, he said, 'serious practical difficulties' such as whether or not Anglican priestly orders were valid. That such difficulties were real was Dr Leonard's opinion, too (as the Cardinal was already well aware). But

Cardinal Hume's caution was very evidently the carefulness of a man who wanted something to come of all this, rather than the lack of enthusiasm of someone trying to kill it off. 'We ought to be able to find a way forward', he said, unambiguously enough, 'which would not wound the Church of England – that is very important – but would meet the real needs of people who cannot stay in the Church of England.' Cardinal Hume also spoke of his great respect for Dr Leonard; this was to prove a not insignificant factor in the way the Roman Option was to develop in its early stages. The two men had built up a close relationship during Dr Leonard's years in Westminster, less public than that of the high-profile ecumenical duo of Bishop Sheppard and Archbishop Worlock in Liverpool, but no less important for that.

The reaction of the Anglican Establishment was muted, though where it manifested itself there was clear alarm at this refusal to respond to the two Archbishops' attempt to play for time. The Bishop of Birmingham, Mark Santer, Anglican co-chairman of the Anglican-Roman Catholic International Communion (ARCIC), was glacial:

> Bishop Graham Leonard's latest *démarche* is exceedingly unhelpful. His article in the *Catholic Herald* breathes a spirit of hustle and alarm, when what is needed is time and space for discernment. My perception so far is that, among those who are dismayed and anxious, there are hardly two people who find themselves in exactly the same place. There is little enthusiasm for the schemes of alternative episcopal oversight which some have demanded, and still less for brigading traditionalists into the kind of 'personal prelature' which Bishop Leonard seems to envisage.
>
> My own hope is that the Roman Catholic Church will not give encouragement to groups of unhappy Anglicans, because such groups are in danger of being united in negativity.

The potential hostility of the Anglican Establishment became a less important factor over the next few months as the fundamental shift in the relationship of the two Churches became clearer. There could now be no return (for a generation or more, possibly ever again) to talk of the foreseeable reunion of the two Churches. The Synod's decision brought with it a falling of the scales from many Roman Catholic eyes. The repetition in so many speeches in the Synod debate (including Dr Carey's) that Rome's views were not a consideration of any overriding importance confirmed what the conservatives had said all along. Even the ecumenically minded *Tablet* concluded sadly that though 'the Church of England allows for high sacramental practice ... its doctrine of the Church stands revealed as Protestant'.

THE ESTABLISHED SECT

The consequence of this shift in perceptions was that the Catholic Church would increasingly find itself free to act in its own best interests and in those of the Anglicans now looking to it for protection. But at the time, one fear among Anglo-Catholics was still that a determined diplomatic offensive from Lambeth might bring pressure on the Cardinal to close the bridge across the Tiber to the Anglican refugees. Bishop Santer's hope, that 'the Roman Catholic Church will not give encouragement to groups of unhappy Anglicans', was certainly that of all the Anglican bishops; if enough of them had brought pressure to bear, it might well have caused a certain failure of nerve, which would quickly have dissipated the momentum which in its absence very quickly built up over the next four months.

Or perhaps not. Dr Leonard, certainly, was now convinced that it was precisely the fact that Rome could no longer have a relationship of potential union with what in his eyes had become an apostate Church, that liberated the English Catholic Church to act. Two days after the bombshell of his *Catholic Herald* article, he was being careful about what he said to the press: mostly he said nothing. But on this he was outspoken. In an interview published that Sunday in the *Telegraph*, I asked him two questions on the matter: first, whether a green light for Dr Leonard's initiative would mean the end of the discussions begun by Pope Paul and Archbishop Michael Ramsey in the sixties, which had resulted in the setting up of ARCIC; and second, whether, if Dr Carey were to declare – before Dr Leonard's initiative had had a chance to get under way – that the Church of England would take deep offence if he were encouraged, that would be the end of it.

Dr Leonard's response was, perhaps, predictable; but his assessment was more and more to be privately accepted within the Catholic Church. Any Anglican objections to his initiative, he felt, should be discounted, because of the significance of what the Church of England has actually done. One of the things I find distressing about the present situation is that those on the other side – if I can put it that way – do not seem to understand the consequences of their actions. What you've got in the Church of England is a new orthodoxy. You can be quite agnostic about the Resurrection or the Virgin Birth but not about women's ordination. The Church of England cannot claim any more to be anything more than a sect. It may be the Established Sect: but theologically it is now a sect. For the Archbishop of Canterbury to say that we can all carry on playing a full part in the life of the Church simply shows that he is not living in the real world. And I think you've got to start from the assumption that ARCIC is dead. Whatever the relations between the Church of England and the Roman Catholic Church are going to be from now on, they aren't going to be on that basis at all ... And I think this will remove a difficulty that I've always detected, that the English Catholic hierarchy didn't want to do anything that would jeopardize the possibilities for the future of ARCIC. Well, all that's gone now.

Whether it was gone or not, ARCIC was now an entirely different operation. Certainly, Bishop Santer, as co-chairman of ARCIC, was soon back in Rome, being kindly treated at the Vatican, and returned to England convinced that nothing had changed. But if his welcome was as warm as it had always been, that demonstrated nothing but the good manners and diplomatic skills of the monsignori: he would not be the first Englishman to return from Rome convinced that things had gone his way, only to find later that he might have spared himself the journey.

One thing, at any rate, was now clear enough to everyone, whether they liked the way things seemed to be going or not: that whether the Anglican members of ARCIC thought that Bishop Leonard's 'latest démarche' was 'exceedingly unhelpful' or not, it was being encouraged where it mattered; and though the Vatican's accustomed caution was to delay matters somewhat later, Rome did nothing to prevent the Roman Option from getting off the ground.

CHAPTER THREE

FIRST STEPS

EVENTS NOW GATHERED momentum. At the end of November, Cardinal Hume flew to Rome, to the considerable interest of the media. Nearly everybody assumed that it could be for only one reason: to discuss how to respond to Dr Leonard's initiative. Spokesmen for the Cardinal pointed out that Cardinal Edward Cassidy, the president of the Pontifical Council on Ecumenism, was not in Rome that weekend; also that the Cardinal's visit had been arranged for other reasons, long before the General Synod had decided to ordain women. One spokesman even described the idea that he might be talking about events in England as 'slightly peculiar'. But none of this convinced anybody, except those who did not want to believe that Dr Leonard was being taken seriously. If Cardinal Cassidy was away that weekend, it seemed inconceivable that the Cardinal would not discuss the matter with someone else. As we shall see, so he did, though the press never found out.

'WE DID NOT CREATE THIS PROBLEM'

But these discussions were not the first contact on the matter between the English hierarchy and Rome; and a consensus had already begun to emerge about Catholic policy towards the Church of England and its dissidents, now that the General Synod had finally decided to do what, in the interests of unity, Rome had repeatedly asked it not to do. Already, by the end of November, Cardinal Cassidy was pointing out that despite his responsibility for promoting Christian unity (and therefore doing everything possible not to encourage division in other

Churches), 'we must be clear on this point: we will seek contact with these people to help them to find possible forms of communion within the Catholic Church'.

The argument that to receive a substantial number of Anglicans might harm relations with Canterbury was not being seriously considered. And as if to confirm Bishop Leonard's analysis – that there would now be a marked change in the relationship between the two Churches after the Synod's decision – Cardinal Cassidy bluntly pointed out that 'we did not create this problem'. It was well known, he said, that many Anglican clergy were not going to accept women-priests 'before the Synod opened'. Now, it was for the Catholic Church to respond appropriately. Nothing was ruled out in advance. To the suggestion of a personal prelature, Cardinal Cassidy was not prepared to 'cite any counter-indication'. It was, he said, 'a question of considering all the hypotheses without excluding any of them. The prelature formula cannot be considered until we know the exact number of people it would concern.'

As we shall see, the 'prelature formula' had not been ruled out at this point either, in another milieu in which opinion was ultimately to come out firmly against it: Archbishop's House, Westminster. Bishop Leonard and Cardinal Hume had been in contact by telephone; and on 16 December they met at Archbishop's House for the first time since the Synod's decision, to assess the situation and to discuss future developments.

Bishop Leonard began by making three points: first, that the great majority of the many Anglicans who had written to him in support were not extreme Anglo-Catholics, but people who would describe themselves as 'just Church of England'; ordinary Anglicans, that is, who wished to stand by traditional doctrines. His second point was that women's ordination was not in itself the real issue: it was, rather the final straw, the end point in a process of liberalization and secularization. The Church of England now claimed the right to make unilateral decisions about both doctrine and the apostolic ministry. And Synod's decision was not merely an expression of opinion; it was 'both an act and a fact'. 'Once done', in Bishop Leonard's words, 'it affects the sacramental life of the Church of England. It does not simply involve an opinion beyond which appeal can be made to the formularies.'

The Cardinal made it clear at the outset that he accepted that the issue of women's ordination was not the only issue, or the most important issue, at stake: the real issues were to do with the doctrine of the Church and with the question of where authority lay. This perception of the Anglicans' motives was to become more generally accepted within the Catholic Church, though at this stage the Cardinal was probably in a minority; and by Low Week, when the Bishops' conference was again to consider the matter, there were still Catholic bishops who were taking a hard line against potential converts, precisely on the ground that they supposed that women's ordination was the only issue at stake.

The Cardinal told Bishop Leonard about his visit to Rome, where he had discussed Bishop Leonard's initiative, not with Cardinal Cassidy, but with his assistant Father Duprey at the Council for Ecumenism. The possibility of a visit by Cardinal Cassidy himself had been mooted; this was not yet thought to be appropriate.

In the meantime, matters were proceeding on the home front. The Cardinal would be discussing the next stage after Christmas, privately, at a preliminary meeting with what was to become the inner steering committee of the Roman Option: Bishop Cormac Murphy O'Connor of Arundel and Brighton; Bishop Alan C. Clarke of East Anglia, and the recently appointed Bishop Vincent Nicholls of North London. Bishop Murphy O'Connor was the Catholic co-chairman of ARCIC, Bishop Santer's opposite number. His membership of the steering group was important: for, though he continued publicly to stress the continuing importance of ARCIC, it was also clear that he was not a member of the group in order to undermine its work.

Bishop Nichols was the youngest of the three: personable, a skilful operator on the media, widely known for his boyish charm and deft footwork in his former powerful position as Secretary of the Conference of the Catholic Bishops of England and Wales, he was then thought to be on the fast track for very much higher things – archbishop, one day, of his native Liverpool perhaps; some speculation had it that he was destined for Westminster. Bishop Clarke, by contrast, was nearing retirement; a convert from Anglicanism himself (he was a cousin of the old Synod warhorse, Oswald Clarke), he was to become known as the Roman Option's warmest supporter among the English bishops. His pastoral manner and warmth of personality was to make a vital contribution to keeping the initiative afloat in some of the stormy seas it was later to encounter.

This group had yet to meet; first, Bishop Leonard and Cardinal Hume had to do the preliminary groundwork. The Cardinal told Dr

Leonard that three questions arose at this stage: the criteria for any arrangements that might be made; the expectations being entertained by the dissident Anglicans; and the kind of package which might emerge that would unite these criteria and expectations. He identified three criteria that Rome would expect to be fulfilled. The first was that though corporate arrangements might be arrived at, Rome would require every individual to make his own personal confession of faith. Bishop Leonard saw no difficulty in accepting this.

The second criterion was that the problem of Anglican orders would have to be solved. In 1896, Pope Leo XIII had promulgated the Bull *Apostolicae Curae*, which had in effect established a defining framework for Anglican-Roman Catholic relations ever since. Its conclusion was stark:

> We pronounce and declare that ordinations carried out according to the Anglican rite have been and are absolutely null and utterly void.

This, the Cardinal thought, would need to be looked at 'in its historical context'. This seemed to confirm what Dr Leonard had claimed in his *Catholic Herald* article, that 'there are responsible people in the Roman Catholic Church who suggest that although the Bull *Apostolicae Curae* applied to the situation existing in 1896, subsequent developments – and particularly the participation of Old Catholic bishops in Anglican consecrations – could warrant a different response (at least for those ordained since then)'.

The Cardinal suggested that conditional ordination might be the solution. Dr Leonard replied that this would be acceptable; though it met the need to resolve any doubts there might be, it did not require Anglicans to repudiate their orders. Conditional ordination was, in fact, later granted to Dr Leonard himself: this consists of the insertion in the ordination liturgy, immediately before the ordaining bishop lays hands on the head of the former Anglican priest being ordained, a statement including the words '*si non es iam ordinatus* ('if you are not already validly ordained'). Why conditional ordination was not thought to be a proper solution for all the Roman Option clergy (as the Cardinal himself had suggested) is an interesting question, to which it will be necessary to return.

STRUCTURES

Cardinal Hume now moved on to the question of how, in terms of structure, the Roman Option would manifest itself. At this early, exploratory stage, one possibility that had been bandied about was firmly ruled out: the establishment of a Uniate jurisdiction, along the lines of the Orthodox Rite jurisdictions of the East, whose Patriarchs accepted the supremacy of the Bishop of Rome, but which retained their own liturgies and spiritual traditions. Few seriously thought this model was a realistic possibility; the word 'Uniate' was generally used to designate some kind of corporate entity in communion with Rome but at one remove from it, one within which – as in the East – non-Roman liturgical traditions might be retained.

The 'counter-indications' (to use Cardinal Cassidy's expression) of any such scheme were, however, from the viewpoint of both Rome and Canterbury, both clear and overwhelming. Within the Roman Communion, the Uniate Churches were a constant source of difficulty. They were touchy and hypersensitive to imagined slights from the centre. They tended to regard themselves as being a more venerable and authentic manifestation of the Church. And they were a standing source of offence to the Orthodox themselves, who saw them not only as having sold out to Rome, but as presenting a challenge to their own position.

The establishment of what would inevitably be seen as a rival Church of England – one which could claim to be the authentic inheritor of the true tradition of Anglicanism, 'Catholic and Reformed' – would be tantamount to a declaration of war. And the potential dangers of such a body were not only to Canterbury but also to Westminster: for such an autonomous Catholic Church might also make claims to represent an authentically English Catholicism (as opposed to what one Catholic supporter of such an option was later to call the 'Anglo-Irish Church of the Latin Rite'). Such possibilities Cardinal Hume perceived from the outset; and he set his face against them.

Some separate Anglican entity more directly under the control of Rome, however, some compromise situated somewhere between total absorption and the problematical autonomy of Uniate status, was not, at this stage, being ruled out, either in Rome or at Westminster. In this first meeting with Dr Leonard, the Cardinal – having ruled out the Uniate Option – said that something more along the lines of a personal prelature would be more suitable: though the drawback here was that it did not provide a suitable place for the laity. This was, it might be thought, a curious objection, since the only personal prelature in the Church so far was Opus Dei, an overwhelmingly lay movement. However this might be, the Cardinal now concluded (as had Bishop Leonard in his *Catholic Herald* article) that something along the lines of Canon 372 might be more likely to open up the way ahead.

Once more, in other words, the American 'Pastoral Provision' was providing a starting point for discussion. Unlike the Uniate model, it had not yet established an autonomous structure (though its provisions could easily at some later stage be bolted on to such a structure). The parishes that had been received were under the direct jurisdiction of their local diocesan bishop; at the same time, they had a corporate identity, their own overall director, and their own distinctively 'Anglican' liturgy.

CRANMERIZING THE MASS

Some such condition of semi-absorption was, perhaps, particularly attractive for those whose spiritual lives had been nurtured by the language of Cranmer's prayer book, often recast into the forms of the old Roman Mass (as the 'interim Rite') by earlier generations of papalist Anglo-Catholics. Normally, though, the Book of Common Prayer did not undergo this exotic transformation, and in its original form (or in the slight recasting of it in the first of the modern reformed official liturgies known as 'Series One'), it was still important, particularly to older middle-of-the-road Anglicans, many of whom – slightly to his surprise – had written to Dr Leonard to tell him that his present *démarche* had their support.

The tradition of Anglicanizing Roman liturgical forms had continued into the new era of vernacular Catholic liturgy; the new Latin *Missa Normativa*, from which the new modern language masses were translated, became normative for many Anglo-Catholics, too – though in these circles there was some division over the language into which the new Mass should be translated for Anglican use. Many, particularly among the younger Anglo-Catholic clergy, simply installed the English-language translation of the new Mass.

Others knew they would never get that past their congregations, less because of any particular anti-Romanism than through resistance to liturgical change, especially to change in the language of worship. Just as, among conservative Roman Catholics, there was an often heartfelt resistance to the loss of Latin as the main liturgical language, so, among Anglicans, the often graceless language of 'Series Three' and then the Alternative Service Book (ASB) was bitterly resented, especially by the older parishioners.

But Anglican priests could not claim (as could their Roman counterparts) that they had no alternative but to begin using the new liturgy whether they liked it or not; in the Church of England, congregations retained a legal right to the old book, even against the will of their vicar. Many Anglican clergy who wanted to install the new rite – any new rite – had to move carefully. At St Mary Magdalen, Oxford, Father Charles Smith (later to become a Roman priest) installed what was, in effect, a Cranmerized Normativa: the *Missa Normativa*, translated into Cranmerian English (and using wherever possible Cranmer's own texts); Bible readings were taken from the Authorized Version. Many thought it more beautiful, more numinous, quite simply vastly superior to the translation into the flat and unpoetic mid-Atlantic English with which English-speaking Roman Catholics had been saddled. For such as these, an Anglican Rite would have had obvious attractions, and it was not ruled out at this stage: only later did it become a question whether or not such a solution would be a source of division in the English Catholic Church. Certainly, there had been no trouble in America; to establish such a liturgy, with the consent and authority of the Pope, had been the response of the Catholic Church in America to a similar crisis in the Episcopal Church some ten years previously; this had been their use of Canon 372.

Could the American 'Pastoral Provision', though, simply be brought into use here without any major adjustments? There were certain obvious differences between Anglicanism in England and in America or, for that matter, anywhere else in the Anglican communion. England was, to begin with, the only country in which Anglicans like Dr Leonard had believed themselves to be already members of the historic Catholic Church of the nation. When the Roman Catholic hierarchy had been reestablished, it had been condemned as a 'papal aggression' precisely because it was seen as an attempt to usurp the place of the Church of England: the differences between Rome and Canterbury had been, in the past, as much over jurisdiction as over doctrine.

EXPLORATIONS

All this was now more by way of being a kind of historical *après gout* than a matter of current moment: but it all formed part of the inherited sense of how Anglicans understood themselves. It was clearly necessary for the English Roman Catholic Church to understand what it was, exactly, that the Anglicans would bring with them. What, asked Cardinal Hume, would those who responded to such an arrangement wish to retain of Anglican tradition? Dr Leonard said that he would need to consider the question and consult with others; and he agreed to write a paper on the question by 9 January, when the small subcommittee of Roman bishops which the Cardinal had formed to consider the matter was to meet for the first time.

There were other matters to consider, too, matters of practical detail, to do with church buildings and, above all, finance: Bishop Leonard agreed to prepare a paper setting out the details of the Financial Provisions Measure which was enacted at the same time as the women-priests legislation; in the event, he delegated this task to Peter Geldard, who was to become one of his partners in the discussions with the Catholic bishops' steering committee. There was, in the early stages, a worry that the Catholic Church would quite simply not be able to take on the financial responsibility for a matter of hundreds, and possibly in the end over a thousand, clergy, many of whom would be married. Once the provisions for financial compensation – which the Synod had had to make in order to get the legislation through – had been clarified, there was considerably less anxiety on that score.

This, then, was the state of play by December, a bare month since the decision to ordain women had been taken by the General Synod. The Cardinal had been to Rome (on other business, it is true) and had discussed the matter with the Secretariat for Christian Unity. Cardinal Cassidy, the head of the Secretariat, had already gone on public record as saying that a way would have to be found to respond pastorally to the disaffected Anglicans, and had expressly not ruled out a personal prelature. Cardinal Hume (who had been in telephone contact with Dr Leonard) had had a meeting with him at which concrete details were discussed, in a way which makes it clear that at this early stage, the possibility of a separate Anglican entity of some kind was being considered: specifically, the possibility of a prelature was alluded to in passing; there had also been discussion of the canon under which the Anglican

Rite pastoral provision in America had been set up; and Dr Leonard had been asked to produce a paper for discussion, outlining how Canon 372 could be used in England, and what elements of the Anglican tradition he would like to see incorporated in the final package.

The assumption at this stage, then, was that what was in question was some arrangement whereby former Anglicans could corporately retain much of their identity, while nevertheless accepting the fullness of Catholic faith. This impression was strongly underlined at the end of this first discussion by Cardinal Hume, who reminded Dr Leonard of Pope Paul's phrase to describe the aims of the ARCIC discussions: that, in the end, the Anglican Communion, with its proper and legitimate patrimony of liturgy and devotion, should be 'united but not absorbed' with and into the Mother Church. As we shall see, this expression was to figure, more than once, in the discussions between the four Catholic bishops and certain Anglican representatives which were to take place in February and March: the Roman Option would be a way in which Anglicans might be reconciled with the See of Peter without abandoning all their heritage. Whatever might be said later, that was the aim then.

CHAPTER FOUR

THE NEW ORDER

IN THE MEANTIME, the state of the Church of England was becoming increasingly confused. This undoubtedly gave a certain urgency to the high hopes for the 'Roman Option' entertained by many (though by no means all) of the Anglican dissidents. As they perceived it, they had lived through a major cataclysm, in which everything they had known had been swept away. What they had begun to hope, hardly daring to believe it, but encouraged by every smallest kind word and auspicious sign emanating from the Cardinal's residence, was that the Catholic Church was going to respond with a package which would represent just as radical a shift in their present situation as they had just undergone, a kind of Dunkirk miracle. The Anglican Bishop of Oxford, Richard Harries, had once (offensively, some thought) compared the ordination of women to the destruction of the Berlin wall. He was right in one respect: that after it, nothing would ever be the same again. Now, the wall had finally fallen and the old order had passed away; how would the Catholic Church respond to the new era that had been ushered in? Everything – particularly the hitherto unthinkable – seemed possible in this suddenly devastated landscape.

But in the new year of 1993, it was on the condition of the Church of England itself that public attention now became focused. Observers began to offer analyses which saw its tribulations as part of an historical shift, not within English Christianity merely, but within society at large. It was noted that those two symbiotically linked institutions, the Church of England and the Monarchy, were simultaneously undergoing major tremors; and the thought began dimly to be entertained that perhaps both were now in a state, if not of terminal decline, at least of deeply uncomfortable metamorphosis. 'The Church of England', wrote William Rees-Mogg on 18 January, 'is experiencing a profound spiritual and ecclesiastical crisis'; what was involved, he thought, was 'a national institutional crisis, like those of the royal family or Parliament. In part it involves the unwinding of the original compromise which combined Protestant and Catholic elements in a single state church.'

For most of the Anglican bishops, the crisis was more immediate than any such broad historical perspective would imply. It had now become a matter of some urgency to find a *modus vivendi*, not only for as many as possible of the disaffected clergy and laity who were organizing themselves so impressively against their authority, but also for the small number of bishops who appeared to be supporting them – those bishops who had voted against women's ordination, and whose support for the dissidents would certainly lead to a major schism if it hardened. The problem, quite simply, was that those opposed to women's ordination now felt that they had no place in the Church of England, or, if they had, that they had been pushed to the margins.

NOTICE TO QUIT

This was not simply a matter of the paranoia of defeat. Unambiguous notice had already been served that no attempt to make any special internal arrangements for the dissidents was to be undertaken. There had, in fact, already been such an attempt: and it had been shot down in flames. In June 1986, the General Synod published the Maclean Report, a summary of the deliberations of an official Synod working group – generally a formula for mind-numbing predictability. The brief of the group had been to consider the consequences of ordaining women, and to suggest ways in which those opposed might be accommodated.

The report was the first sign of anything like an official recognition that ordaining women would indeed bring division and upheaval. Maclean's proposals to deal with this situation were radical. Parishes might petition to be 'exempt' from the 'spiritual jurisdiction' of their bishop. Alternatively, a 'non-geographical' diocese might be set up, to which all the dissenting congregations, clergy and bishops would be attached. Those clergy who could not accept any of the options available and would therefore resign might be offered generous financial compensation.

The report was greeted with jubilation by those opposed to women's ordination (who not unnaturally claimed that its conclusions supported their contention that ordaining women would indeed bring chaos) and with dismay by most of those in favour, who continued to maintain that the dissidents would soon come to accept the new dispensation without any such drastic measures. Some said that the report provided the only way in which some semblance of unity might be preserved; others that unless it was thrown out, it would be the beginning of the end of the Church of England.

The bishops – overwhelmingly in favour of women-priests – panicked. In the words of the Synod's general secretary, Derek Pattinson (himself privately sympathetic to the dissidents), they 'kicked for touch'. Further time, they said, was required for reflection; full consideration of the report would now be postponed until the following February.

After a time, the bishops produced their own report, which effectively superseded Maclean. The contrast with Maclean's attempt at accommodating all views within the same Church is striking. Whereas the earlier report had rejected the view that once women were ordained no one opposed to their ordination should be appointed bishop, the House of Bishops argued that 'it would be anomalous to appoint a bishop, who was actively opposed to the mind of the province'.

The message this sent out to the dissidents, despite much smooth talk of respecting their views, was perceived by them as unambiguously hostile. Any attempt to provide structures to provide for the continued membership in good conscience of traditionalist Anglicans had been excluded. Hence, Maclean's proposal for some form of parallel jurisdiction was flatly rejected as theologically incoherent. As one Anglican commentator pointed out at the time, theological incoherence had never unduly troubled the bishops of the Church of England before; it was distinctly suspicious that they should suddenly begin so warmly to deprecate it now.

And it was made very clear that any safeguards provided by the legislation to be drawn up on the basis of the report would be 'temporary'. As one dissident put it, 'we are being told to take ourselves off'. This was very widely seen in such circles as the message conveyed, not very subtly, by the words 'those who could not remain in communion with the See of Canterbury would need to find other ways of continuing their existence within the universal Church and would be entitled to explore such ways'. As we have seen, Dr Graham Leonard, the Bishop of London, then and later took this formulation as an invitation to 'prepare for separation': the House of Bishops could hardly grumble now if that was precisely what he was doing.

It is important to understand the profound and lasting psychological impact of the Bishops' Report on the dissident minority. When, the following February, it was endorsed by the General Synod, one of them, the high churchman Dr Gareth Bennett, wrote in his diary after the Synod debate that 'one could feel the atmosphere change to one of real hostility to the Catholic cause'. In the train back to Oxford, he wrote that he felt 'quite panic-stricken'; it seemed to him that it was 'all up with the Church of England' and that he was 'already in a lost minority in a church which has turned itself into a liberal Protestant sect'. These feelings were reflected in his famous Crockford's preface, published later that year, the Establishment backlash against which many thought contributed to his suicide. It is probably not too much to say that Bennett's death was seen by the large traditionalist minority as being almost symbolic of their own marginalized condition; certainly, the analysis of the Crockford's preface itself was wholly accepted by them as being both accurate and timely.

By the time the unthinkable happened and the General Synod passed the legislation enabling the ordination of women, the bitter mistrust of the dissidents for the liberal Establishment of the Church of England had been long recognized. Nor, despite the bishops' hasty charm offensive, had their underlying intentions changed. The talk emanating now from the victors was all of accommodation and magnanimity; but beneath the bland reassurances, there was already detectable in some dioceses a steely resolve that the victory should not be compromised by those who could not accept the new order.

One clergyman went to see his bishop, and asked how those, like him, who were still opposed to women's ordination would be treated if they stayed in the Church of England. 'Well,' the bishop replied, 'here is my forecast for the fifteen years that remain before your retirement. For the first five years, you will be treated with great patience and understanding. For the next five years, the patience and understanding will be wearing a little thin. For the last five years there will be no patience or understanding whatsoever.' The same bishop telephoned another of his clergy, a vicar in a parish, and took him for a drink to discuss his attitude of non-co-operation with the new dispensation. With him, the bishop was more direct. 'You are on the edge already,' the bishop told him: 'Now I want you out.'

This marginalization of the dissenters had been predicted during the November debate by the Bishop of London, Dr David Hope (who had been one of the voices reflected on the original Maclean Report and had drawn the inevitable inference from its suppression):

> Those who are opposed are now being given considerable reassurances that all will be well, that the Church of England will continue as ever it has and that there is a full and equal place for all, particularly those who are unable to accept the ordination of women as priests. I submit that the reality would be very different indeed, that if this legislation is passed the Church of England will without doubt be very different and that those who are unable to accept this new theological understanding with theological and ecclesiological integrity will inevitably and increasingly find themselves ignored and marginalized.

How could they be reassured that they did indeed have a real place in the new dispensation? That was the all but insuperable problem. For, as the Bishop of London had pointed out (as had Dr Leonard his predecessor), such safeguards as the legislation contained were merely temporary: it could scarcely have been otherwise, since they assumed the inevitability and – despite a great deal of quasi-theological prattle about 'a period of reception' – the irreversibility of the process now entered into. The legislation put it this way: the concessions were intended to 'give opponents an opportunity to plan their future'. As Dr Hope protested to the Synod, 'That does not sound very much like well-being and inclusion to me.' He recalled that a member of the legislation's drafting committee, four years previously (when the legislation was being first presented to the Synod), had explained that the various safeguards were 'exceptional provisions ... given by the majority to the minority ... so that that minority may have space to assess the reality of the ordination of women as it takes place in our provinces. However, because the provisions are exceptional they must in the end be seen as temporary.'

'Exceptional provisions', thus framed, had acted not as a reassurance, but as the very opposite: they were taken as a prolonged period of notice to quit. In the same way, exhortations to do nothing to exacerbate the situation had the opposite effect from that intended. It became clear almost immediately that opposition to the new order was going to be obdurate and persistent, and that 'crisis' was hardly too dramatic a word to describe the situation of the Church of England now.

FORWARD IN FAITH

At the beginning of December, all the major bodies which had separately campaigned against the legislation joined forces: Cost of Conscience, a body which had the support of over 3,000 priests; Women Against the Ordination of Women (WAOW), a formidable body, with a huge membership far outstripping that of the Movement for the Ordination of women (MOW); the Association for the Apostolic Ministry (AAM), itself a coalition of several Anglo-Catholic organizations, most notably the Church Union; and the Society of the Holy Cross (SSC), a priestly society which had always worked for reunion with Rome. Whatever the uncertainties about the future, it was announced, 'one thing is clear: we will not be operating the legislation ...'

Towards the end of the month, the new body made its first demand: for 'an assured succession of bishops who do not ordain women to the priesthood or recognize them as priests; liberty for clergy and parishes to associate themselves for all sacramental and pastoral purposes with those bishops; and places of theological education and training for the priesthood which respect the position of those whom such bishops recommend.' In other words, for a permanent, not a temporary, settlement which amounted, in effect, to a parallel Church of England free of women-priests and the bishops who recognized them.

These demands were presented as being supported by a third of the clergy and over twenty thousand laity. At a Forward in Faith rally, cheekily held in the Chamber of the Synod in Church House, Westminster (which any respectable body may hire if they have the fee), The Revd John Broadhurst, the new organization's chairman, made the grim resolution of the dissidents very clear. 'Until now', he said, 'we have been holding people back and telling them to act with restraint. It only needs us now to say "go for the throat" and the Church of England will break up.' At any other time in the last ten years, this would have been loftily dismissed, in the Bishop of Durham's sensitive phrase, as being mere 'huffing and puffing'. In the prevailing atmosphere, and with their concrete knowledge of the situation on the ground, the bishops were belatedly taking such pronouncements with deadly seriousness.

Their dilemma could be starkly summarized. The demand for an 'assured succession' of bishops – there was talk of wanting as many as ten of them – who would neither ordain nor even recognize the orders of women and who would have power to minister to all parishes requesting to be placed under their authority, if necessary without the permission of the local bishop, was politically impossible to grant. What it amounted to was a demand – explicitly defined in a letter to the bishops from Forward in Faith – that there should be 'a willingness on the part of some bishops to relinquish some power': a process which could only, most of them felt, lead to an acceleration of the present slide towards chaos.

'THE MESS WE HAVE GOT OURSELVES INTO'

Men like Archbishop John Habgood of York (who now, some thought, began to emerge as the real *de facto* leader of the Church of England) were not in the business of relinquishing power. But if nothing was done, there were two possibilities: either there would be an exodus much greater than was being predicted; or, even worse, Cost of Conscience would proceed with its threat to implement the long prepared and detailed contingency plans whose existence had been rumoured for some time, but which few had actually seen. These, if they existed, were thought to involve widespread and co-ordinated withdrawal of parishes from the structures and financial responsibilities of their dioceses. One – or even both – of these possibilities was beginning to look dangerously feasible. Some Evangelical parishes were already withholding payment of their 'quota' to the local diocese, on the ground that to do so would be to fund the prevailing apostasy: this was not simply on the issue of women-priests, but as part of a wider perception that the Church of the General Synod had capitulated to secularism and infidelity.

But it was not the Evangelicals who were causing the present crisis. One bishop, off the record, said simply that his diocese had become 'virtually unmanageable already'. Noel Jones, the traditionalist (but by no means Anglo-Catholic) Bishop of Sodor and Man, said that the Church of England had brought the crisis on itself by not recognizing the strength of feeling over women-priests. 'The time has come', he said, 'to make some very firm statements to enable clergy and laity to remain in the Church; I am horrified to see the mess we have got ourselves into and I am particularly surprised by the volume of dissent from middle-of-the-road Anglicans.'

But what kind of 'firm statements' would those have to be? They would have to amount to more than just more reassuring episcopal blandishments. There had been more than enough of those already, and they had changed nothing. The question now was this: what could be offered, that would look enough like a genuine concession to the dissidents' demands to take some of the heat out of the immediate situation? It would not be possible to satisfy all the leaders of Forward in Faith; but could enough be done to pacify some of them? If so, that would have the effect of dividing this already unstable coalition (not all of whose leading lights entirely trusted each other).

First, however, the dissident bishops had to be persuaded back into line. An emergency meeting of the House of Bishops (all the diocesan bishops, together with those suffragans elected to sit in the Synod) met in an hotel in Manchester. The twelve bishops on whom Forward in Faith were relying to put their case were heavily outnumbered. Stories emerged later of lone dissident bishops being backed into corners to be picked off by red-faced groups of their purple-shirted brethren; certainly, they were heavily subject to the emotional pressures of group dynamics, always an effective subconscious persuader where the majority see their corporate survival depending on the capitulation of a dissident minority. After four days, a scheme had been hammered out; the meeting ended with all the bishops, some in tears (of joy, it was said), spontaneously singing hymns together.

Among the members of Forward in Faith waiting for the bishops' decision, the scheme that emerged was greeted by some with qualified approval, by others with incredulity, even anger. Before the bishops withdrew into purdah, Archdeacon George Austin (who was determined to stay) said he thought that 'the very least we need to hear is that the principle of appointing provincial, or roving, bishops is acceptable'.

FLYING BISHOPS AND EPISCOPAL TAINT

The very least is what they got from the announcement, despite its length and complexity. The scheme was designed to cope with what the bishops thought was the real problem: that the dissidents wanted nothing to do with any bishop who ordained women. This had led to the invention (by whom, nobody is quite sure) of the notion of theological 'taint'. A bishop who ordained women – or had even voted for women to be ordained – was unacceptable to the dissidents; so much seemed clear. But what about a bishop who had not and would not? If such bishops were acceptable, would a reassurance that there would be a reasonable supply of them do the trick? A number of ways were devised, whereby bishops with 'clean hands' might be maintained for the pastoral care of parishes determined to reject the ministrations of 'tainted bishops'. Either a diocesan bishop might himself not ordain women, but would keep a suffragan bishop who did; or he might (as in most cases) ordain women but keep a suffragan bishop who did not; or, such bishops might borrow a non-ordaining bishop from a neighbouring diocese. But the key suggestion was for the appointment of

... not more than three bishops (two in the Province of Canterbury and one in York) to act as Provincial Visitors, with specific responsibility to assist the diocesan bishop in the provision of appropriate ministry. These might be the holders of existing suffragan sees but it might also be necessary to create new posts for this purpose and this might involve synodical action. Among the tasks of a Provincial Visitor would be ... to act as spokesman and adviser for those who remain opposed to the ordination of women to the priesthood and to assist the archbishops in monitoring the arrangements made for them.

The trouble was that it was not 'episcopal taint' that the awkward squad was worried about at all: it was the integrity of sacraments and the whole question of what was involved in being in communion with someone. Forward in Faith had sent the bishops a short paper on the subject, explaining their position, in time for it to be considered at the Manchester meeting; but it had been ignored. 'Impairment of communion between Christians results,' the paper argued,

when one group takes a step which others regard as unauthorized or unjustified: for example, one which raises doubt about the validity or authenticity of its sacramental life ... It is agreement about the authenticity, and so the mutuality, of the sacramental life of the community, based on orders received and continued 'from the Apostles' time', which has allowed

Anglicans to develop a wide variety of theological opinions within one ecclesial fellowship.

It was this entire question of the breakdown within Anglicanism of agreement over the 'authenticity of its sacramental life' and of mutual recognition of its orders which the bishops had fatally failed to address. A 'flying bishop' (for this became universally the mocking designation of the Provincial Visitors) would not solve for a priest or his laity the problem of the likely presence at any diocesan occasion outside the parish – deanery synods, diocesan synods, ordinations, retreats – of clergy whose orders they could not recognize, possibly administering sacraments whose validity they denied.

THE 'DOCTRINAL LEVITY' OF THE C OF E

As Forward in Faith protested about a month later, in an open letter to the eleven bishops, 'The view [expressed in the Manchester statement] "that in some way those bishops who participate in the ordination of women to the priesthood thereby invalidate their sacramental ministry" does not fairly represent our position. We see a necessity for sacramental dissociation, not because we think the bishop's ministry "invalid"… but because by his action he would have introduced into the college of priests over whom he presides those whose orders we and other bishops and priests cannot in conscience recognize.' By failing to recognize the real theological difficulty for the dissidents, and by knocking down an Aunt Sally of their own invention, the bishops had now introduced a further measure of ecclesiological confusion into an already incoherent situation. The dissidents did not expect most of the bishops to understand this; but they were astonished that the eleven they thought they could count on had become embroiled in the absurdities of 'episcopal taint'. As one priest protested in the *Church Times* after the Manchester statement (over the suggestion that a diocesan bishop unable in conscience to ordain women might arrange for a suffragan to do so in his place), 'If such a bishop regards these women as priests, why should he not have ordained them himself, and if he does not so regard them, how does he relate to them? It is a nonsense.' Dr Leonard described the Manchester statement succinctly as an example of the 'doctrinal levity' of the Church of England.

The Manchester statement was designed (as had been the 'safe-guards' enshrined in the legislation itself) to cope mainly with those Anglicans who were principally interested in their own parish life, and who would be content if the dreaded priestesses and all their works could be kept at arm's length. But for those who believed that the Church was a Divine Society; who saw the Church of England as part of the Church Universal; who understood the legitimacy of their own parish life as deriving from their communion with their bishop, and through him with the Apostles whose descendant they believed he was – for such Anglicans, the compromise was an alleviation at best, at worst a mockery.

George Austin was inclined to be easier on the proposals than some; he said they were 'good news, but a great deal less than we asked for'. But, for all that he was prepared to accept Provincial Visitors, his feelings vividly summed up how little confidence there now was in the bishops among the large minority opposed to women-priests, even among those inclined to accept the deal on the right terms. 'Unless these proposals are enshrined in law', he added, 'they will not be good enough'; traditionalists in the American Episcopal Church had found to their cost, he said, that bishops could not always be trusted in matters left to their discretion. Others were even more forthright. In a letter to the *Church Times*, the veteran synodsman Oswald Clarke – not a man given to ill-considered or intemperate outbursts – told the House of Bishops that they 'must recognize the brutal but undoubted fact that neither they corporately nor their Codes of Practice are trusted by us'.

NO LANDING RIGHTS

By some, then, the deal was accepted with resignation. By many others, it was greeted with anger and disbelief; many normally moderate Anglo-Catholics found themselves suddenly at one with the most exotic Anglo-Papalist extremes in their contempt for their bishops. Father Francis Bown, of the Anglican ultramontane society *Ecclesia*, was normally seen by many who thought of themselves as Vatican II Anglo-Catholics as a slightly embarrassing figure: as one of them put it, 'Frankie Bown is so OTT [over the top] he is practically in orbit'; though he added, 'but he is no fool'. Now, Father Bown spoke for many less accustomed to expressing themselves with his swashbuckling ferocity;

his reaction to the Manchester statement, in its analysis of the situation as well as in its angry tone, mirrored the feelings of many whose normal views were much nearer the Anglican mainstream. 'The bishops' plan', he wrote, in an *Ecclesia* newsletter characteristically entitled 'The House of Bishops and the Death of the Church of England',

> is that anti-priestess parishes can avail themselves of sympathetic bishops ... as long as such bishops are members of the House of Bishops of the Church of England with priestesses. So in the place of first-hand apostasy we are offered second-hand apostasy, as if indirect infection were somehow to be preferred to the direct.

> On what sort of ecclesiology these proposals are based, it is difficult to fathom. Certainly, it is an understanding of the nature of the Church which is unknown to Catholic Christians, for it must involve a concept of communion which would have appealed to the author of *Alice in Wonderland*.

> But, of course, the bishops are not fools. They must know that the only clergy who can accept their nonsense are the latter-day Vicars of Bray. Their proposals constitute a clear message to Anglican Catholics: 'Go – and good riddance.'

> So the decks have been cleared for action. The faithful must pursue more vigorously than ever before the real opportunity which now exists for reunion with the Holy See. The 450-year experiment – to attempt to maintain the Catholic Religion out of communion with the Holy Father – has finally failed. We must set our sights on our true destiny: an Anglican identity in communion with the Pope.

The 'traditionalist' bishops, who had supposed, in the enclosed atmosphere of the Manchester meeting, that they had pulled off a great coup, were shocked by the fierceness with which the settlement was now rejected by so many of those it had been designed to mollify. The Bishop of Sodor and Man had flown down to London the same day to explain the deal to the executive committee of Forward in Faith, which was meeting in Faith House, Westminster to receive him. 'He entered the board room beaming, like Neville Chamberlain with his piece of paper,' recalls Peter Geldard. He left the room two hours later, his face ashen, almost in tears.

Bishop Hope had an even rougher ride two days later at a Forward in Faith meeting in London. He was subjected to critical questioning. When one priest asked him if the traditionalist bishops 'were putting their collegiality before their concern for their people', he became, in the words of one WAOW member, 'beside himself with rage'. His reply was barely coherent. 'No, I don't believe that,' he protested; 'the traditionalist bishops are trying to do all they can to secure the kinds of arrangements that have so far been talked about. And you are running the risk, the way that it's going on, people ringing me up, calling me, you know – "you're apostate", all this and that, I mean, we're so busy putting each other out of communion, in and out of communion, I don't know who I'm in communion with at the moment. I assure you we are trying to do our best at this moment and you – the way we're going on, frankly I shall certainly not ... and there will be no other bishops either to be with you or to help you if this is the way it goes on ...' This outburst was greeted by the now largely hostile audience with outraged cries of 'Thank you very much, Father, that's very kind'; 'that's shocking'; 'yes it is' and 'disgusting'. Later, Dr Hope apologized, and the mood of the meeting, which had become for a time exceedingly ugly, calmed down; but it had not been a happy occasion.

What was the least that was needed to drain away support, on the Anglican side, for the Roman Option? The Anglo-Catholics wanted bishops they could trust to defend Catholic faith and order, bishops who could operate under their own authority, and not by grace and favour: that was, after all, precisely the attraction of Rome. What was the use of 'flying bishops', if they did not have automatic 'landing rights' (another expression that now joined the jargon of the times)? They would be safe men, collaborationists, the creatures of the diocesan bishops: the diocesans were now seen by many, every one of them, as being the enemy.

LIGHT ACROSS THE TIBER

The least that could have held those who had now begun to see light from the opposite bank of the Tiber was some kind of permanent ecclesial entity, at arm's length from the provinces of Canterbury and York. Peter Geldard told the *Daily Telegraph* that the only arrangement acceptable to his supporters was a full-blown parallel network for traditionalists, giving them their own diocese and bishops: '[The Manchester settlement] will hold on only to a few priests nearing retirement. There will still be a large section who can't accept this, and will go.' Geldard, in fact, had no interest in such a network: he was in contact with Bishop Leonard and with Cardinal Hume, and knew how much more attractive what was then being seriously discussed would prove to be – in Father Bown's words, 'an Anglican identity in communion with the Pope'.

Father Geldard – and a good number of his supporters – had decided to go anyway. Public speculation about the precise form of any Roman Option now began to mount. The day after Dr Hope's unhappy meeting with members of Forward in Faith, the *Sunday Telegraph* predicted – under the headline 'Rome ready for Anglicans' – that the Catholic bishops were 'expected to respond positively to the plight of traditional Anglicans who believe they have no future in the Church of England – despite the efforts of the House of Bishops last week to stem the tide of defections'.

The following day, the influential Catholic layman and *Times* columnist William Rees-Mogg speculated on the form such a positive response might take. He rejected any suggestion of a prelature or a uniate jurisdiction, but thought that those Anglicans who believed (correctly in his view) that the November decision further separated the Church of England from the majority of Christendom ought to be given special treatment: interestingly, he echoed the phrase adopted by Pope Paul, 'united not absorbed', which Cardinal Hume had already used in his conversations with Dr Leonard; and he picked up Dr Leonard's suggestion that Canon 372 might form the basis for such a non-absorbed entity:

> If they wish to rejoin the Catholic communion, then every provision should be made for them to do so, and to retain the particular spiritual characteristics which they have rightly valued in the Church of England ... in church law there is Canon 372, which allows groups to retain their particular character and be reunited with the Catholic Church but not absorbed.

The following day, the Cardinal issued a statement, making it clear that the Catholic Bishops had not yet had an opportunity to discuss the matter together, and that they would decide at their next bi-annual meeting in April 'at what stage they should refer the matter to the authorities in Rome'. In the meantime, he for his part had 'been listening carefully to the ideas and proposals being made to [him] by certain members of the Church of England'. This was taken by the *Tablet* as an attempt to dampen down speculation on the matter. If it was, it failed: 'Hume signals acceptance of C of E rebels' was the *Times* headline the following day over a piece by Ruth Gledhill, in which she wrote that 'Cardinal Basil Hume, Archbishop of Westminster, is prepared to consider how Anglicans unhappy about the ordination of women might be received as a group into the Roman Catholic Church'.

DID THE HACKS GET IT RIGHT?

How much of this was mere press speculation? Was the Cardinal in fact prepared to consider any such thing? Certainly, the Anglicans who had been talking to him were getting that impression. One important group of Anglican clergy, the Society of the Holy Cross (SSC) which had a membership of about 800, was being represented in talks with the Cardinal by its superior, Father Christopher Colven; he now said that a 'substantial number' would want to investigate the possibility of 'a corporate ecclesial grouping': this might involve the transfer of property, if a way could be worked out of doing this (Dr Hope was already signalling that he would be sympathetic to this possibility): 'it would make the whole package much more attractive', Father Colven thought.

Again, the question poses itself: was the press speculation during this period and later so very far from the mark as – with the hindsight of the Catholic bishops' declaration in Low Week – it now seems? On 15 February, for instance, Damian Thompson in the *Daily Telegraph* announced that Cardinal Hume 'and senior Anglican traditionalists, are close to agreement on setting up a national network of former Church of England parishes under the authority of Rome'. Many of the parishes, he reported, would keep their vicars; the network would be under the authority of a Catholic bishop; parishes would be 'allowed to retain aspects of the Anglican liturgy'; 'conditional ordination' would be allowed. Unknown to him, the first meeting of the steering group of Catholic bishops with a small group of Anglicans was taking place on the day his story appeared. How many of these speculations were in fact ruled out at that meeting? And how much of Thompson's agenda (almost all of which was excluded in Low Week as though it were impossible it could ever have been taken seriously) was in fact being actively discussed at this stage?

The fact is that although Damian Thompson was wrong about one thing (the appointment of a bishop to oversee a national network), none of his other suggestions were being ruled out at this point, and most were being taken seriously by those most closely concerned: he was much nearer to being right in broad outline than later became the case. The meeting took place at Archbishop's House, Westminster, on Monday 15 February. Those present were, on the Catholic side, the Cardinal himself, Bishops Clarke, Nicholls, and Murphy O'Connor, and the Church's senior bureaucrat, Monsignor Philip Carroll. The Anglicans were represented by Dr Leonard and by the Reverends Peter Geldard, John Broadhurst, Christopher Colven and David Skeoch (Dr Leonard's former chaplain, who took the minutes of the meeting).

The Cardinal opened the meeting with what he humorously called a 'speech from the throne'. He began by emphasizing that those on the Catholic side would have to report to the Catholic bishops' conference and then to Rome, either or both of whom might repudiate any suggestion made at the meeting; and said that as part of the process of consultation, he would be going to the North to report to the bishops there, and would then repeat the process with the Southern bishops. He said there were prejudices that would be difficult to overcome: this was a prediction which proved in the event to be well founded.

He went on to suggest to the meeting that there were four areas to be covered in their discussions; this would help him to clarify the situation for the Catholic bishops. What were they to expect in terms of numbers and geographical spread? What was the 'Anglican identity' it was hoped to bring into communion with Rome? What were the financial implications? Finally, the situation about buildings would have to be clarified if possible.

UNITED, NOT ABSORBED

The Cardinal then went on to tell the meeting what he intended to say to the Northern bishops, since he thought that might prove a good basis for their own discussions. He would emphasize that the Anglican suppliants were not making a request based simply on a refusal to accept

70

women's ordination, but on everything that the November decision implied. He would then present the request itself, after they had clarified precisely what this was: as he understood it, they were seeking a way in which they could be in communion with Peter, without necessarily, at this point, becoming 'ordinary Roman Catholics'. The request for 'corporate reunion while retaining an Anglican identity' would be based on Bishop Leonard's paper.

The Cardinal now made two crucial points. Firstly, that both Uniate status and a personal prelature were non-starters. This was not, in fact strictly speaking the case, since as we have seen, the idea of a prelature had been seen as an option to be explored, both in Rome by Cardinal Cassidy and in Westminster by Cardinal Hume, in the weeks following Dr Leonard's *Catholic Herald* article. So a prelature was not exactly a non-starter; but it had clearly fallen at the first fence.

Another of Dr Leonard's suggestions, however, was still in the race, and running strongly. Having dismissed a prelature and Uniate status, the Cardinal went on to say that the provisions of Canon 372, paragraph 2 should be thoroughly examined, and that they should discuss how the provisions of this Canon could be brought into effect: this was precisely the paragraph – which permits the 'erection' of 'particular churches which are distinct by reason of the rite of the faithful or some similar reason' – under which the 'pastoral provision' had been set up in America ten years before. This Canon had been at the heart of the Anglican hopes; at this stage it was also central to the Cardinal's thinking.

All this is vitally important in the interpretation of what now followed. Having said that he would present a request for 'corporate reunion while retaining an Anglican identity'; having made it clear that his idea of an Anglican identity would be based on Bishop Leonard's paper on the subject; and having then directed the attention of the meeting to Canon 372; the Cardinal now said he would remind the bishops what Pope Paul had said in 1970 and in 1977.

In 1970, at the beatification of the English and Welsh martyrs (which had offended some Anglicans, including Archbishop Ramsey) Pope Paul went out of his way to express himself warmly towards the Anglican tradition. 'There will', he said, 'be no seeking to lessen the legitimate prestige and usage proper to the Anglican Church when the Roman Catholic Church ... is able to embrace firmly her ever-beloved sister in the one authentic communion of the family of Christ ...' He made it clear that the 'worthy patrimony' of Anglicanism – its liturgical and spiritual tradition – would be preserved in a reunited Church. And in 1977, recalling the Malines conversations of the 1920s – a poignant example of premature ecumenism – Pope Paul had quoted the words of one of the Catholic participants, Dom Albert Beaudoin, that 'The pace of this movement has quickened marvellously in recent years, so that these words of hope "The Anglican Church united not absorbed" are no longer a mere dream.'

REUNION, POST-ARCIC

Why, at this stage, did the Cardinal refer to these two statements about Anglicanism by Pope Paul? How did he intend his hearers – not only the present meeting, but the Catholic bishops whom he also intended to remind of Pope Paul's words – to understand him?

There can surely be only one interpretation. In such a context, this has to be seen as perhaps the Cardinal's strongest commitment so far to the notion of a kind of faithful Anglican remnant – in the words of Canon 372 a 'particular church', representing the best of the Anglican spiritual tradition – as embodying the 'patrimony' of which Pope Paul had spoken so movingly. Now that the official Anglican Church had ruled itself out, it was this Anglican remnant that would become the object of the hopes for reunion that Rome had hitherto entertained towards Anglicanism as a whole.

This impression was strengthened later in the meeting, when a decision was made that the Cardinal should issue a statement convey-ing that the process in which they were involved was to be seen as a possible answer to prayers for unity; and as we shall see, it was clinched by the wording of the statement itself. The respect for the 'usage proper to the Anglican Church', and the vision that this would continue in an Anglican entity 'united but not absorbed' with and into Roman Catholicism, were now to be understood as referring not (as Pope Paul had meant) to the whole Church of England but to whatever Anglican entity in communion with Rome would emerge from the present ferment.

The Cardinal made it clear, however, that such an entity would not be expected to last for ever: it would be temporary, though possibly of some duration. It would come into being after a period of growing into full communion; here, the part of the laity would be important. For both individuals and groups, there would be a period of catechesis, followed by a profession of faith. The problem of orders would have to be resolved.

The Cardinal now wound up his remarks by saying that when talking to his bishops, he would try to stand back from 11 November, and leave them to discern what the Spirit was saying to the Churches. There was, he said, a definite feeling among all those involved in the present explorations that they were living in *kairos*, in God's time. On this high spiritual note he ended his 'speech from the throne'.

Ironically, as the meeting was taking place, Dr Carey was in, of all places, Malines in Belgium (where Lord Halifax had conducted the ill-fated discussions about unity between Canterbury and Rome with Cardinal Mercier and others, including Dom Albert Beaudoin). Dr Carey took the opportunity to bewail the current state of the relationship between Rome and Canterbury, which he blamed on the Vatican's inability to keep up with the pace-setting Anglicans. 'Roman Catholics', he claimed, 'are confused and disoriented by the movement throughout Anglicanism world-wide to ordain women to the priesthood.' Hopes for reunion between the two Churches, said Dr Carey, 'seem to have faded'.

NOW IS AN IMPORTANT MOMENT

The same day, Cardinal Hume issued his statement about the meeting over which he had just presided: it reads almost as though it might have been composed as a direct rebuttal of Dr Carey's remarks (though in fact the Cardinal was at this stage unaware of them). It is by any standards a remarkable pronouncement:

> In praying for Christian unity we have surely always recognized that visible unity will be a gift from God. Now is an important moment in that process. It has come upon us in an unexpected way.
>
> I have spoken with several members of the Church of England who want to explore the possibility of full communion with the Holy See. I have made it clear that the way forward, from the point of view of the Catholic Church, will be for the Holy Father to decide. He will doubtless listen to the recommendations of our Conference of Bishops. I believe the Holy See

will be sympathetic towards meeting the very real pastoral needs of those who wish to accept the authority of the Holy Father.

The way forward was to be strewn with pitfalls, more, certainly, than the Anglicans who had just left Archbishop's House were expecting; and in the end, it was not given to the Holy Father to decide it. The real question now was whether, supposing the Holy See was indeed minded to be sympathetic, any such sympathy would be allowed free rein on English soil.

CHAPTER FIVE

WORTHY
PATRIMONY

WHAT PRECISELY, FOR immediate practical purposes, would be regarded as the 'worthy patrimony', to be brought home to the rock whence it was hewn? It would have to be both distinctively Anglican, and at the same time susceptible of being 'united' with the Roman system, without being immediately 'absorbed' into it. It was not a new question; nor were these the first conversations between Anglicans and Roman Catholics in which the question of taking some elements of the Anglican tradition into the Catholic Church had arisen.

Nor was it the first time that women's ordination to the Anglican priesthood had been the catalyst for such discussions. In 1976, at the biennial General Convention of the Protestant Episcopal Church of the United States (PECUSA) in Minneapolis, the necessary legislation had been narrowly passed by a simple majority. Over the next two years about a third of the Episcopal Church's members departed, over this and other issues. The most important of these had been the suppression of the 1928 American prayer book (a version of Cranmer's liturgy deriving from the Scottish Prayer Book of 1637) and its replacement by a liturgical compendium whose orthodoxy was in considerable doubt. These developments, taken together, were seen by many as representing a calculated abandonment of 'Classical Anglicanism', and a takeover by the new theology and the new morality.

THE O'HARE HILTON PROPOSAL

Some went, individually, to Rome; others, 'to the golf course'; yet others to newly invented 'Continuing Churches'. Among those who remained, a small group of Episcopalian priests and bishops began a series of discussions with members of the Catholic Church. As one of them wrote in May 1977, to one of the Catholic bishops who later became deeply involved in the talks,

> It has become increasingly clear to me that it is not possible to hold, teach, and practise Catholic faith and order ... in accordance with the Anglican experiment of the last 400-plus years. Anglicanism did produce many graceful and beautiful attitudes and modes, all of which I would never wish to abandon, but the outward and visible must reflect the interior life if there is to be integrity and honesty. Whatever faults there may be within Roman Catholicism, its adherence to authority, and therefore the truth from which it springs, has preserved it alone, as the only visible expression of the true Church in the universal sense. The only way I viewed my priesthood, as an Anglican, is in relationship to the whole Catholic Church, which I used to believe could be fully practised within our communion. My doubts are heavy and serious now as I view the disassembly of our 'branch'...
>
> A realignment of those of us who believe in Catholic Christianity now seems in order, and the great Church of the West is the only possible home ... While a Uniate model might have seemed offensive to some on both sides in the past it doesn't have to be if properly undertaken. Perhaps the agreements produced by ARCIC would make such an establishment rather easy, and could be viewed as the natural conclusion or development of all those years of conversations.

By March the following year, a joint Catholic/Anglican working party had produced a detailed proposal, 'for the reconciliation of certain members of the Anglican communion to the See of Peter'.

The proposal, which emerged from a meeting at the O'Hare Hilton Hotel in Chicago, contained suggestions which were, as we shall see, very much more ambitious than those contained in the paper written some fifteen years later by Dr Leonard, and accepted by Cardinal Hume

as the basis for discussions with the English bishops. The overall aim
was that:

> There be recognized or established by the Holy See a separate
> ecclesiastical jurisdiction in which [Anglican] traditions and
> customary usages, where not inconsistent with Catholic doc-
> trine, can be preserved and in which the allegiance of its mem-
> bers to the See of Peter and the acceptance of the Holy Father's
> jurisdictional and magisterial authority can be expressed.

> The jurisdiction would have its own bishop; it would prepare
> its own internal laws; the Holy See would commit itself to recog-
> nizing the traditions to be enshrined in this law; furthermore, 'the
> permanent retention of this valid tradition is anticipated'. There
> would be no law of celibacy, for either priests or bishops. Clergy
> and laity would nominate bishops, 'for selection by the Holy See'.
> Finally, 'the liturgical traditions of the Anglican Community
> would be retained where consistent with Catholic doctrine'.

THE PASTORAL PROVISION EMERGES

Of this ambitious set of proposals, only the final one survived, to be
incorporated in the 'Pastoral Provision' for Anglicans set up in the early
eighties. There was to be no separate jurisdiction, though there would
be an overall director; congregations could be received with their pastor, who would be ordained as a Catholic priest and continue to serve
them, but they would come under the direct jurisdiction of the local
bishop. There would be an 'Anglican' liturgy: this was similar to the
new (1979) Episcopalian prayer book, which had both modern and traditional language alternatives; Catholic Eucharistic Prayers would be
used; either those of the new Roman Mass (for the modern language
Eucharist) or, for the Mass in Cranmerian English, a glorious Tudor
translation of the Roman canon. Significantly, this translation was
attributed to – of all people – the Augustinian Friar who was later to
become the reformer Coverdale (whose translation of the psalms later
became the Prayer Book Psalter). Coverdale's translation (reprinted
here as Appendix C, p. 252) had little hope of Papal approval when he
made it as a reforming Catholic; but after nearly five centuries it was

approved by Pope John Paul II for use within a Catholic Church which had in the end embraced a vernacular liturgy. The ease with which it slots into a Cranmerian Eucharistic liturgy is easily explained: first because Cranmer's own liturgy has largely medieval Catholic sources; second because Coverdale's translation may well have influenced (linguistically if not theologically) the composition of Cranmer's own Eucharistic Prayer.

The rejection by the Holy See of most of the Chicago proposals came as a terrible blow to some of the Episcopalians involved in these discussions. The Pastoral Provision, though it would have been welcomed with enthusiasm by English dissident Anglicans fifteen years later, was not enough to overcome the difficulties of most of the dissident Episcopalians. As one of them wrote to one of the Catholic bishops involved in the talks, 'a crisp, clear and clean Anglican jurisdiction is obviously ruled out *which signals the virtual impossibility of attracting any significant number of the laity* (my emphasis) ... To program the disappearance of an Anglican identity only heightens the perception that our experience, a satisfying experience in large measure due to our Catholic heritage, has no value in the long run and nothing of an enriching nature to offer. It is being viewed as a put down by many who have expressed themselves to me.' If, he asked, an Anglican jurisdiction was not a possibility, then 'what validity could ARCIC possibly have? The whole aim of these discussions was Catholic reunion without uniformity at every level of Church life.'

Nevertheless, out of the ruin of this ambitious scheme had emerged the Pastoral Provision. It was a small step towards the dream of an Anglicanism 'united but not absorbed'; but it was real enough to those who became involved in it. By the time of the Westminster conversations of 1993, there were in all only six parishes (mostly in Texas) who had been received with their clergy under the scheme, though others were 'in process'. It did not occur to anyone involved in the talks with Cardinal Hume, however – on either side of the table – to suggest that the small scale of the experiment thus far had invalidated it as a model for possible use in England. There was, indeed, some discussion at the first Westminster meeting in February 1993 as to why the Pastoral Provision had not been more popular in America; the suggestion was made, probably correctly, that there had been very little effort to make its existence known throughout the huge American Catholic Church. There was also the possibility, it was thought, that it had to do with a higher level of anti-Roman feeling among American Anglicans, even among those of a Catholic theological persuasion. What nobody suggested was that the small scale of the experience so far had any relevance to the question of whether or not something like the Pastoral Provision might be used in England. Here, too, a public position inconsonant with the spirit and substance of these discussions was to emerge later.

WORKING PROPOSALS

Meanwhile, however, Canon 372, under which the Provision had been (in the correct canonical language) 'erected', was the name of the game in England. The paper which Cardinal Hume had asked Dr Leonard to write (and which was now to form the basis of his own approach to the Northern and Southern bishops) was entitled 'Pastoral Provision for Anglicans wishing to be reconciled to the Catholic Church'; and its preamble explains that 'The details and procedure which follow are in response to a request from the Cardinal to set out how Pastoral Provision might be effected under Canon 372 for Anglicans wishing to be reconciled to the Holy See while retaining from Anglican tradition that which is compatible with Catholic Faith and Order.'

Only the document's opening sentence – that 'The Holy See would appoint an archbishop or bishop as Director' (a proposal obviously modelled on the American provision) – was ruled out without further discussion, even though Cardinal Hume had in the early stages suggested to Bishop Leonard that a 'prelature' might be appropriate; he had even, to another Anglican dissident, suggested that he himself might take on the responsibility of being the relevant prelate, in order to ensure there would be no tensions between the mainstream Catholic Church and the newly created body: thus, there would be no 'multiplication of entities' (the possibility of which was later given as one of the reasons for not proceeding with a separate formal arrangement for Anglicans). By this stage, however, things had moved on, probably because the Cardinal had been made well aware (shades of the Anglican bishops' Manchester meeting) of the difficulty of persuading the bishop of a diocese to relinquish authority within his own territory. The directors of Pastoral Provision parishes would therefore be appointed by the bishops for their own dioceses.

The rest of the paper, at this stage, remained intact as a working proposal. Dr Leonard envisaged that as events progressed, from the point at which the scheme would be made public and individuals and groups (as appropriate) were instructed and received, 'Congregations of the Anglican Rite would be established as appropriate'. There would have to be a gap between the coming into effect of the Measures authorizing women's ordination and the establishment of the congregations. Clergy dependent on the Church of England's provisions for financial compensation would not be able to resign until then; in the interim, congregations would have to continue to worship as Anglicans in Anglican churches 'while making it clear that they do not regard themselves as in communion with the Anglican bishop'.

What, precisely, was meant by 'Congregations of the Anglican Rite'? What Rite, precisely, would that be? Dr Leonard's thoughts on this had developed in some respects since November, when I interviewed him for the *Sunday Telegraph*. Some, he thought, in the immediate aftermath of his *Catholic Herald* article, would want a traditional rite, of the kind now being used in America under the Pastoral Provision (alongside a modern Catholic Rite based on the 1979 Episcopalian Prayer Book). Others

> would want a modern Rite but not at all like the Alternative Service Book. I think you would find that an Anglican Rite could be put together which would use traditional language or modern language which did represent a kind of Anglican ethos of worship in the way that adaptations of authorized rites have already developed. We wouldn't want to take over, I think, the whole Roman Missal, because the Anglican ethos would then simply disappear; the thing, for example that one would miss terribly as Anglicans would be the Prayer Book collects – which are magnificent, and are so rich, compared with the poverty of many of the collects in the modern Missal, which are really pitiful in their language – there's something we would want to retain. We'd obviously use the same lectionary and so on.

WHAT RITE?

By the time he came to write his working paper, the notion of a modern Anglican Rite had disappeared. There was one obvious reason for this, quite apart from any resistance from the Catholic side: that in many of the parishes which might be expected to take the Roman Option, it was the modern Roman Rite, rather than anything even vaguely identifiable as Anglican, that was already in use, and in some cases had been the basis of liturgical life ever since it had first been published. This raises an important question: in what way were such parishes identifiable as representing Anglican tradition, apart from the fact that they were in communion with the Archbishop of Canterbury rather than the Pope? Dr Leonard's initial reluctance to use the Roman Missal had been on the grounds that 'the Anglican ethos would then simply disappear'. But there were already many Anglican parishes using it: and there were innumerable ways in which such parishes could be seen as essentially Anglican rather than Roman; nobody except a newly arrived foreigner would ever mistake one for the other.

It was not easy to put your finger on the very real difference, but it was there; and it was there tangibly enough to justify the provision of special pastoral measures for those who might be lost for the lack of them. It might be something you would need an anthropologist rather than a theologian to define: but was not an essential ingredient in post-Conciliar Catholicism that it recognized and respected human culture as something to be fulfilled rather than crudely uprooted?

And had not the Catholic Church always, when it was being true to itself, tried to speak through local cultures, so that the Gospel might be heard more clearly by those whose native element they were? The difficulty with the cultural argument is that there were, in particular parishes, differences which were difficult to present as valid reasons for any special provision: class differences, for example, or cultural distinctions of another sort entirely, exemplified by one Roman-Rite Anglican parish priest with a predominantly West Indian congregation who, when I asked how his own parishioners, if they went on the Roman Option, would fit in as members of the nearby Catholic parish, replied simply, 'They wouldn't: my blacks can't stand the Irish.'

There were, nevertheless, some features in the anthropology of the average Anglo-Catholic parish which were of more universal application and were distinctive enough to justify the use of Canon 372, which specifies that a 'particular church' may be erected, 'distinguished by the rite of the faithful *or by some other quality*'. [my italics] What might that quality consist of? It would have to be strong enough to form a barrier which itself had no doctrinal component to communion with the

Holy See: the whole point of the pastoral provision was that it was pastoral, it had to do with obviating unnecessary obstacles.

The most obvious sociological distinction between Anglican parishes and Catholic parishes is a consequence of their difference of size. Some Catholic parishes (whose boundaries will typically include six or seven or even more Anglican parishes) have anything up to 1,000 people at Mass; and there will need to be several Masses on a Sunday. This means that the parish itself cannot be a tightly knit community in the same way that Anglican parishes – which will vary from around 50 to 150 – often are. Anglo-Catholic parishes tend to be especially tightly knit, for a very particular reason, a reason with which cradle Catholics might be expected to sympathize. It is that their history is often one of persecution and marginalization by the Anglican Establishment. This often led to a very powerful bond between congregation and clergy, part of which was explicable by a sense of insecurity about the future: what would happen when their vicar retired? Would his successor de-Catholicize the parish? Anglo-Catholic clergy often spent their whole ministry in one parish for such reasons; in the words of one of them, 'what every priest fears most is his successor'.

These were the negative reasons for the powerful comradeship of many Anglo-Catholic parishes. But the positive fruits were tangibly there, too, in a community-based spirituality (including a good deal of lay involvement) which was often very close to the reality that the Vatican Council aimed at recapturing. It is against this background that the great care given to the liturgy, the high musical standards, and all the other characteristically 'Anglican' features of such parishes must be understood. The loss of the personal immediacy of these communities is sometimes cited by converts as one of the things they miss most, particularly at first. It is true that this loss is balanced by gains which are overwhelmingly greater than anything that has been sacrificed: above all the powerfully felt perception of moving for the first time in a much wider community, of being in communion with all Catholics everywhere, both living and dead. But these transcendent gains are often only dimly suspected from the other bank of the Tiber. The beauty of the American Pastoral Provision was that the heart-stopping cultural wrench was avoided, while the new sense of wider community had time to grow and become predominant.

THE IDEA OF A UNIVERSAL CHURCH

In more traditional Anglican parishes, the question of what made them Anglican was more easily discerned. For them, Dr Leonard's paper envisaged 'an approved rite, recognizably derived from the Book of Common Prayer, in Prayer Book language, suitably modified where necessary to ensure that it expresses Catholic doctrine'. At this stage, Dr Leonard regarded this as essential (though he was later to change his mind about it). He had received many letters from unhappy traditionalists who were middle-of-the-road Anglicans rather than Anglo-Catholics, but who were, nevertheless, supportive of Dr Leonard's initiative.

The main issue for them (as for all the dissidents) was the question of authority, and the nature of Anglicanism itself, which they had always profoundly believed to be not an independent system of belief but a particular expression of mainstream Catholic faith, of – to use the words of Vincent of Lérins, in his famous threefold test of Catholicity (a favourite Anglican text) – 'what has been believed everywhere, always and by all, (*quod ubique, quod semper, quod ab omnibus creditum est*)'. For such Anglicans, the Prayer Book had always been the embodiment, not of a rebellious independence from the universal Church, but of a kind of unrecognized autonomy within it. Its full title was 'THE BOOK OF COMMON PRAYER and administration of the sacraments and ceremonies of the Church according to the use of THE CHURCH OF ENGLAND': The Church of England, in other words, was part of something wider called simply 'The Church', *tout court*. As Charles Moore – still uncertain about whether or not to become a Catholic – put it,

> Nobody needs to move very fast. Like many confused Anglicans, I do not know exactly what I shall do. But the point is this. Do you think that the idea of a universal Church is essential to Christianity, or do you think that Christianity is a matter of personal opinion? That is now the key division among Christians, certainly in England, and perhaps throughout the world. I believe that once one works out which side one is on, one's right course of action will gradually become plain.

Dr Leonard was anxious that the Roman Option should embrace as wide an Anglican constituency as possible. Thus, he made a point of insisting in his paper that 'The provision of a rite in Prayer Book language is very important as many of those who are likely to respond are committed to it, while being orthodox in doctrine.'

But it was not only middle-stumpers who had an emotional attachment to the Prayer Book. One school of thought within Anglo-Catholicism had always insisted that the Anglican tradition (as they understood Anglicanism) was not merely consistent with Catholicism, but that it was itself the authentic English expression of it. They had in the past sometimes referred to the Roman Catholic Church in England as the 'Italian mission', though this hoary witticism fell into rapid disuse after 11 November. Their view of Anglicanism could be supported amply by a selective use of the Book of Common Prayer, whose origins were largely Catholic despite the Zwinglian and Lutheran elements to be found at key points in it. Many of its prayers (including most of the sumptuously translated collects) were drawn from medieval liturgical sources. Mattins and Evensong were heavily influenced by the work of the Spanish liturgical reformer Cardinal Francisco de Quinones, who had been commissioned by Clement VII to compile a new breviary; among other features taken over by Cranmer was the recitation of nearly the whole Bible during the course of the year (the Quinones breviary was eventually proscribed by Paul IV in 1558). In his Eucharistic liturgy Cranmer's own aims had, in some ways, anticipated those of the liturgical reforms which followed the Second Vatican Council: to encourage greater involvement of the people and more frequent reception of Holy Communion. Cranmer's devotional prayers and exhortations intended to encourage worthy reception of the sacrament might have come from any Catholic manual. '... It is our duty', reads one of the 'exhortations' appointed to be read out by the celebrant,

> to render most humble and hearty thanks to Almighty God our heavenly Father, for that he hath given his Son our Saviour Jesus Christ, not only to die for us, but also to be our spiritual food and sustenance in that holy Sacrament; Which being so divine and comfortable a thing to them who receive it worthily, and so dangerous to those who will presume to receive it unworthily; my duty is to exhort you in the mean season to consider the dignity of that holy mystery, and the great peril of the unworthy receiving thereof ...

Within the liturgy itself, the people said together the prayer of humble access, in which they prayed that they might be granted

... so to eat the flesh of thy dear Son Jesus Christ, and to drink his blood, that our sinful bodies may be made clean by his body, and our souls washed through his most precious blood, and that we may evermore dwell in him and he in us.

THREE CHURCHES OR ONE?

The sacramental understanding underlying all this was spelled out in the Prayer Book's catechism:

Question. What meanest thou by this word Sacrament?
Answer. I mean an outward and visible sign of an inward and spiritual grace given unto us; ordained by Christ himself, as a means whereby we receive the same, and a pledge to assure us thereof ...
Question. What is the outward part or sign of the Lord's Supper?
Answer. Bread and Wine, which the Lord hath commanded to be received.
Question. What is the inward part or thing signified?
Answer. The Body and Blood of Christ, which are verily and indeed received and taken by the faithful ...

All of this was not merely consistent with a Catholic understanding of the nature of sacraments; it was in its formulation clearly derived from such an understanding. The fact that it was designed to be consistent also, though only just, with a Zwinglian, or receptionist, understanding (note the words 'received and taken') fully explains Roman Catholic doubts about its orthodoxy; but for Anglo-Catholics, since Zwingli was wrong, any Zwinglian component simply did not form part of its necessary subtext. What such texts demonstrate is the essential function of deliberate ambiguities of this kind in maintaining the tenuous stability of the Elizabethan settlement of religion and of the Anglican tradition which derived from it. The Roman Church has always demanded clear and unambiguous definition; the Anglican Church has not only preferred but has needed for its very existence the cloudy and the ambivalent, has always done business in language which has relied less on clarity and consistency than on resonance and rhetorical force.

It was not so much that Anglicanism represented a new synthesis of, or a 'dialectical tension' between, different traditions; rather, it was designed to hold together traditions which were mutually exclusive, by enforcing a dispensation in which it was possible for them uneasily to coexist: not so much in mutual tolerance as by means of steadfast non-communication. The Church of England, as John Henry Newman explained in 1866, in the preface (reprinted in the author's Everyman Paperback edition) to the first French edition of his *Apologia pro Vita Sua*, 'contains three powerful parties in which are embodied the three principles of religion which appear constantly and from the beginning of history in one form or another; the Catholic principle, the Protestant principle and the sceptical principle. Each of these, it is hardly necessary to say, is violently opposed to the other two.' As the Dominican Father Aidan Nichols puts it, 'The notion that the three schools somehow complement one another in a richly "comprehensive" Church requires a lot of swallowing.' Father Nichols goes on to quote the great Anglican Catholic theologian, Eric Mascall:

> The fundamental incoherence of the three school theory can be seen from the obvious fact that the existence of each one of the schools can be justified only on the assumption that its characteristic theological assertions are true. But in that case all the three schools must be mutually compatible. And in that case there is no reason why we should not accept them all ... But what then will have happened to the three schools? It is quite ridiculous to envisage the Church as a tricorporate society, each of whose parts is committed to upholding one third of the truth. Regrettable as this no doubt is, it is because each school has not been convinced that everything the others were holding was part of the truth that the schools have remained recognizably distinct.

WHO DEFINES ANGLICANISM?

This was always the difficulty in mutual understanding between Canterbury and Rome, and it was a difficulty which persisted into the new era of ecumenical dialogue: with whom, precisely, was the Catholic Church doing business in, for instance, the ARCIC conversations? Who or what did the Anglican members of the commission represent, apart from their own opinions? Who would determine what the Anglican view was? The General Synod? Some thought it did not have the power to determine doctrine, others that it did claim such an authority. But even if the General Synod could indeed claim the authority to determine the beliefs of the Church of England, it had no such powers over the rest of the Anglican Communion, in which already, under the new policy of 'provincial autonomy' in such matters, new doctrinal inconsistencies were already opening up. The English ASB's Rite of Baptism, for instance, embodied the traditional Anglican (and Catholic) doctrine of Baptismal Regeneration; but this fundamental doctrine was entirely excluded from PECUSA's 1979 'Baptism' service. It was not an insubstantial divergence: and there was no way of knowing when, where and in what way equally central doctrines might be modified, unilaterally and without notice.

Where was Anglican doctrine located? Who determined it? Who could even say what it was? To these unavoidable questions, there were shifting answers. As the Anglican revolution of the seventies and eighties ran its course, the ARCIC discussions were based, more and more, on a mutual misapprehension. The Anglicans on the Commission hoped that the Catholic representatives (because of their own *aggiornamento*) would be less and less dogmatic in doctrinal matters, more and more prepared to move away from old formulations: and up to a point so they were, but not quite in the way the Anglicans – who thought the new openness meant that Catholics were now more Anglican – assumed. Anglicans looked into the ARCIC documents and, as they always had with their own formularies, saw in them what they wanted to see. The Catholic representatives, for their part, looked at the distinguished and civilized Anglicans around the table and assumed that they represented a coherent intellectual and spiritual tradition: where they did discern the different traditions within Anglicanism (the Canadian Dominican Jean Tillard, for instance, specialized in the Evangelicals), it was in the supposition that these represented different aspects of an Anglican 'comprehensiveness' with which they could do business.

But 'comprehensiveness' had always been (just as 'theological pluralism' was to become at the 1988 Lambeth Conference) an illusion. It is tempting to say that it was a kind of ecclesiological spin-doctoring, designed to mask the incoherence that had always lain beneath the surface, rather as political spin-doctors try to present the press with the image of a united party, particularly during periods of internal conflict. But spin-doctoring is a conscious, even a cynical, process. There was nothing cynical here; the idea of 'comprehensiveness' was an illusion which, as many illusions are, had been gratefully received into the Anglican subconscious as a protection from the stark realities of Anglicanism's fundamental doctrinal instability.

UNITY WITH AN ANGLICANISM SELECTIVELY DEFINED

'Comprehensiveness' was finally shattered forever on 11 November 1992; but its shortcomings for ecumenical purposes were already beginning to be perceived by some Roman Catholics. In *The Panther and the Hind* (published after the November decision, but written before it) Aidan Nichols put the case for an Anglican-Roman Catholic unity scheme selectively defined. 'Supposing', he asked,

> that Anglicanism is so very much three churches within one that no satisfactory ecumenical relations can ultimately be carried out with it (not, at any rate, to the point of organic reunion), what is to be done? An Anglican Church united with Rome but not absorbed ... is perfectly feasible, but it can only be constructed on the basis of a selection from among the elements I have mentioned. It might be a church with a religious metaphysic drawn from the Cambridge Platonists, supplying as this would a doctrine of creation ... a doctrinal and sacramental ethos taken from the Restoration divines, with their stress on the inseparable interconnection of Incarnation, Church and liturgy; and a missionary spirit drawn from the evangelical movement ...

Father Nichols' particular selection of Anglican elements capable of 'repatriation in the Western Patriarchate, in peace and communion with that see with which the origins of English Christianity are for ever connected', was, in the end, overtaken by events. As things turned out, the selection virtually made itself. There were no identifiable Cambridge Platonists involved in the Westminster conversations (though the recovery of a viable theology of creation had been one of the priorities of the movement for Catholic Renewal in the Church of England, in which all the Anglican participants had been involved since the seventies). But they had no stomach for a distinct theological approach to Catholicism; Dr Leonard proposed that the new Catechism of the Catholic Church would be the basis for all catechetics, and there were no dissenters.

But the sacramental ethos and evangelical missionary spirit of which Father Nichols writes here were fundamental priorities for the Anglican suppliants. And the perception that unity was now to be with an Anglicanism selectively defined had become one of the implicit assumptions of the discussions. In his statement of 15 February (see p. 73 above), Cardinal Hume went far to make this explicit: he made it clear that 'Now is an important moment' in the 'process' towards 'visible unity'; that unity, he seemed to be implying, would not come as a result of the ARCIC discussions with official Anglicanism; on the contrary, '*it has come upon us in an unexpected way*' (my emphasis). The sentence which follows appears to clarify what that way was, and how that visible unity which could only be 'a gift from God' was now to be pursued: 'I have spoken with several members of the Church of England,' the Cardinal continued, 'who want to explore the possibility of full communion with the Holy See.' It was with Anglicans such as these, it seemed, now that Anglican comprehensiveness had definitively broken down, that unity was to be pursued.

THE CONVERSION OF ENGLAND

The meeting after which this statement was issued took place on Monday, 15 February. On 19 February, the following Friday, John Wilkins, editor of *The Tablet*, saw Cardinal Hume to record a seventieth birthday interview (which appeared the following week in the issue of 27 February). The Cardinal made a point of emphasizing the theme of authority in the Church in a way particularly relevant to the experience of the Anglicans he had been seeing. He warned against

> the danger that the Catholic community is now losing sight of how the Magisterium, the teaching authority, operates. I had a letter from a woman this morning accusing the Catholic Church

of denying her the right to be a priest. The culture was going that way, she wrote, and she herself felt a strong vocation. But that is not how we operate. You can have your views and express them. But what matters to me profoundly is the existence of the Magisterium.

It was, thought the Cardinal, ironic that just when Catholics seemed to be irked by the Church's teaching authority, high-church Anglicans were feeling the need of it. He may well have been thinking of his discussions the previous Monday (though the need for authority, and the expressed willingness of the Anglican suppliants to accept the Magisterium, had surfaced in all the talks he had had so far). At any rate, Dr Leonard had said that many Anglicans, having felt shattered on 11 November, had since been overtaken by the conviction that they were no longer trying to salvage something from the wreckage, but rather that God was calling them to move forward into unity and communion with the Holy See.

He insisted, too, that they did not wish to set up yet another source of authority; and he added, interestingly, that many middle-of-the-road Anglicans who had no connection with the Anglo-Catholic wing of their church were coming to the same conclusion: that they needed to have a central teaching authority under which they could live and grow as Christians. Cardinal Hume told John Wilkins that he had been struck by the humility of those who had been discussing with him the possibility of a path from the Church of England to Rome.

The Cardinal then made a statement he may later have come to regret; certainly, he felt it necessary to apologize for his wording the following week. Nevertheless, his words were entirely consistent with what we know he had been saying elsewhere: there is no reason at all to suppose that his remarks did not represent his true feelings. They represented a vision of the future of Christianity in England which was so radical that it encouraged many Anglican Catholics to believe that a 'package' would soon be on offer which would itself be radical enough to make the vision a reality. There was only one indication in the Cardinal's statement (though it was vividly enough expressed) that in the end all might not, from their point of view, be well:

This could be a big moment of grace, it could be the conversion of England for which we have prayed all these years. *I am terrified now we are going to turn round and say we do not want these newcomers* [my italics]. We have prayed for Christian unity and now it could be happening: a realignment of English Christianity so as to bring us closer together, in two blocs, instead of lots of blocs.

THE EDGE OF A MELTING POT

For the second time in four days, Cardinal Hume was setting forth a new vision of Christian unity, in which (as he had put it in his 'speech from the throne' that Monday) they were living in a *kairos*, in God's time; it was a 'big moment of grace', in which God, as he always did, was answering prayers in his own way and not in theirs.

The Cardinal's vision was one he shared with all the Anglicans with whom he had spent so many hours talking, not only in groups with other bishops present, but also with individual clergy and laity, alone. Their experience had all been identical: what had begun as a shattering blow had become for them a moment of truth. Accusations from some Catholic quarters that they were merely using the Catholic Church as a bargaining counter for a better deal within their own Church were particularly wide of the mark. In January, Christopher Colven had written to the members of the Society of the Holy Cross – the 800-strong clerical society pledged to the ultimate reunion of Canterbury with Rome – of which he was the Superior. 'I do not know what is going to emerge,' he had written,

> but I do believe that something better and fuller awaits us, if we discern God's will rightly, and have the courage to try to fulfil it. If we had lived at the end of the fifteenth century, we would have been aware of an impending upheaval within Christendom, but unable to discern the patterns which Reformation and Counter-Reformation would create. Terms like 'Roman Catholic' and 'Anglican' were unknown in the way that we have come to use them. I believe that we stand on the edge of a melting pot for English Christianity the like of which has not been seen since the end of the seventeenth century. We will need to find a new language to express fresh concepts (new wine bursts old wine skins, the Lord tells us!). To change the image, the kaleidoscope

is turning, and entirely uncharted and unexpected territory will be coming into view. We have grown up against the background of an ecclesial view where we know our place as Catholic Anglicans, and how we fitted, or hoped to fit, into the wider pattern of the Church militant. Now, it seems, the inadequacy of that view is being revealed, and we have to allow God to reveal something more to us. We all feel confused and disquieted and none of us likes to feel the rock we have stood on, with such surety, is shifting (and even proving to have certain sandy properties we have never wanted to admit), but Jesus's prayer on the Cross is of surrender to the Father's will, and that is where we must base our hope. In human terms, yes, so much we have worked for seems to have collapsed, for ourselves and for our brothers and sisters. But, perhaps this is God's moment, and through the breakdown of what we have known and valued, something infinitely grander and closer to his Heart, is beginning to emerge.

How would it come into being, this 'melting pot for English Christianity'? Cardinal Hume, the following month, was to call it a 'realignment of English Christianity': he envisaged that it would 'bring us closer together, in two blocs, instead of lots of blocs'. What, precisely, did he have in mind?

What would happen in the aftermath of a decision to ordain women had exercised Anglican Catholics for years: the 'two bloc' scenario had, in fact, been around for some time. It was partly based on a particular analysis – which events were now authenticating – of the internal political dynamics of the modern Church of England. This envisaged that there would be – as there clearly now had been – a rapid and fundamental shift of power on the floor of the General Synod, once the fateful vote had taken place. The Catholic group's 'blocking third' – which it had hitherto been able to put together (often by involving such unlikely allies as the conservative Evangelicals) – had already been eroded, little by little, during the protracted politicking which had preceded the final synodical debate over women-priests. They had lost that vote by a whisker. But now that so many of the group's most committed members had already resigned or were about to, what remained of its potential to frustrate change collapsed overnight and what remained of the group was reduced to impotence. It was not merely over the single issue of women-priests that the liberals had finally triumphed: on 11 November they became undisputed masters (and mistresses) of the Church of England for any foreseeable future.

THE END OF THE BLOCKING THIRD

This meant that revolutionary possibilities hitherto foreclosed were opened up again. In the past, major schemes involving reunion with the Methodists and later 'Covenanting' – which envisaged joint confirmations and ordinations – with the mainline liberal Protestant Churches (the Methodists and the United Reformed Church) had run into enough opposition to defeat them. These defeats had been encompassed by determined Anglo-Catholic political activity – in which Dr Leonard had been the most prominent opponent – to defeat the requisite Synodical Measures. The rationale of these successful guerrilla operations had been, at root, precisely the same as that of the more prolonged resistance to women-priests: that the success of the proposed Measures would involve an abandonment of the Catholic claims of the Church of England and a loss of sacramental integrity: they would therefore mean the end of hopes for reunion with Rome.

With the destruction of the synodical balance of power, these schemes (though probably not yet for some time openly) would be on the agenda again – so ran the 'two bloc' scenario. Nothing any longer stood in the way of the ultimate reunion of the Church of England, now indisputably and irreversibly in the hands of a liberal Protestant ascendancy, with most other English liberal Protestants. Dr Carey had even seemed to hint in his speech to the General Synod that if there had to be an ecumenical choice, this was the one he would make. There were those who were troubled, he had said, 'by the ecumenical implications of a yes vote today'. He recognized this, he said; 'but this consideration is not completely overriding':

> … Significant parts of Christendom do not ordain women to the priesthood, but there are many traditions in which the experience of women in ministry is not a burden but a joy, not a handicap to mission but a strength. We must not look in one direction only.

It was clear to Anglican Catholics, however, that on this issue you could not look in more than one direction. If you voted for women-priests, you were voting, for all practical purposes, against reunion with Rome; the only direction you could look then would be towards pan-Protestant unity. Dr Carey insisted that 'constructive, loving relation-ships can and will continue whatever the outcome of our vote today'. Perhaps so: but the possibilities for growth of these relationships would not remain the same.

A vote against women-priests would have continued the interdic-tion against unity with the Free Churches. Similarly, a vote for them would constitute, in the Pope's words, 'a grave obstacle' to unity with Rome; and as one wit said, 'when this Pope says "grave obstacle" he means "over my dead body"'. The ARCIC conversations would, no doubt, continue to be 'constructive': but since what they had been con-structing until the November vote was about to be demolished, they could hardly continue as before. Did Dr Carey really not understand this? Some found it difficult to credit: but it did not go unnoticed that his argument in the Synod debate seemed to assume that ministry and priesthood were the same thing, that his theological understanding of the matter was precisely what you might expect from someone whose evangelical background had been supplemented by the modernist influ-ence of the House of Bishops.

'CATHOLIC ANGLICANISM IS NOW FINISHED'

For the Anglo-Catholics, Dr Carey was a disaster. He was, however, from another perspective, precisely the right man in the right job at the right time. For, as things had turned out, it was in many respects to his particular theological outlook that the Church of England now seemed, willy nilly, to have committed itself. For the first time since the Refor-mation, the Church of England had the potential to become what some within it had always wanted it to be, an unambiguously Protestant denomination. This would mean that the Catholic tendency within Anglicanism now had ultimately only one place to go: to Rome. As Father Broadhurst said to the author, a few days after he had attended the first of the Westminster conversations, 'Catholic Anglicanism is now finished; those who talk about recolonizing the Church of England are living in a fantasy world.'

The 'two bloc' scenario now had the potential to unfold: and the Cardinal saw such a possibility not as a threat to unity but as a blessing, not merely for those of Catholic instinct on both sides of the Tiber (who in his vision would now be reunited in what Newman had called 'the one fold of the Redeemer'), but also for an emerging united Protestant Church of England. We would all be 'closer together, in two blocs, instead of lots of blocs'.

How convincing was the thesis that there might now be a major realignment in English Christianity? One senior Catholic bishop (though one who was later to be welcoming to refugee clergy) pooh-poohed the idea that anything fundamental had changed, in very much the same way that Anglican bishops had done before 11 November – comparing the 'huffing and puffing' that had preceded the vote to that at the time of the Gorham judgement or the South India scheme. But few Anglican bishops were making such comparisons now that the huffing and puffing appeared to be strong enough, if not quite to blow the house down, at least to inflict severe structural damage.

What had happened was more than a simple adjustment in the Church's ministry, to which the dissidents might, with a little good will, adjust themselves. As the smoke cleared, it was perceived by more and more dispassionate observers (though not yet, necessarily, by those involved in mopping up operations) that the Church of England had now undergone a revolutionary and irreversible transformation. It was not simply that there was no long-term future in it now for Anglo-Catholics, that the Oxford Movement seemed definitively to have run its course. The Bishop of Durham later admitted (having safely retired) that 'the traditionalists are quite right to be scared stiff by the ordination of women to the priesthood, which in the Catholic tradition is really the centre of authority. It means there has been a pretty cataclysmic change in the location of authority ...' As for future problems arising from the issue, he thought that 'we are only just at the beginning of them, and that may well add to (though of course we are all planning, working and praying that it shouldn't) more fissiparous tendencies.'

THE ART OF CREATIVE REDEFINITION

But none of this meant, by itself, that there would be a major realignment outside the Church of England as well as inside it, if it meant large-scale departures. A realignment of that kind was not what the Anglican bishops wanted at all, and they were prepared to go a long way (perhaps far enough, perhaps not) to prevent one. The watchword now was 'business as usual'. The *Church Times* greeted the final 'Act of Synod', which in the autumn was to enshrine the 'Flying Bishops' scheme, as yet one more example of the Church of England's genius for accommodating differences, a compromise which reflected enormous credit on its maturity and its underlying unity. The angry divisions of the preceding twelve months now became transformed, by the centuries-old Anglican craft of creative redefinition: Anglican disunity became a shining example of the honesty with which such issues should be treated, the furnace out of which a future unity would be forged. The absurdities of the flying bishops scheme became lovable English muddling through. It was an example of precisely the kind of bland self-congratulation that Anglo-Catholics had always found most detestable about the Establishment mind. With such large issues at play, the *Church Times* happily opined,

> the wonder is that the debate has not been more quarrelsome than it has, and that the instinct for cohesion has been so dominant. Some intensity in the argument was necessary, in order that – the real achievement of the past few years – both sides in it should perceive that the other had a powerful case strongly held, and was not to be bought off or discouraged ... Episcopal visitors and the Act of Synod can readily be dismissed as institutionalized division, subverted episcopacy, illogical ecclesiology. Any amount of polysyllabic denunciation can be wheeled up. In fact the settlement simply shows that both sides still belong together, and as such it is a grown-up way of ending a dispute, and an example to the world at large. All institutions, even the most august, have their absurdities, their points where theory and practice have to part. Institutions can nevertheless be of huge value as repositories of loyalty and vehicles of continuity. *To keep them cohesive is a good in itself* (my italics).

Whatever the sea-change in the fundamental character of the Church of England, however revolutionary the effect of 11 November, the C of E's liberal ascendancy was not going to acknowledge anything more than a little local difficulty: to accept the fact of the final break-up of Anglican 'comprehensiveness' could only, so the bishops supposed, lead to further disintegration. Reality was irrelevant: the overriding priority now was institutional survival. 'Institutions', as the *Church Times* inimitably put it, could be 'of huge value ... To keep them cohesive is a good in itself.' The Elizabethan settlement of religion might now have begun to unravel; but running repairs and a cheerful face on things might keep the fabric looking good for some time.

A CASE FOR TREATMENT

The bishops of the Church of England had done what they could to preserve the unity – such as it was – of their own 'bloc'; but they would have to be careful about future synodical adventures in the direction of pan-Protestant unity. Any more attempts at creative breakthroughs to a unity with English Protestants, forming in effect one of the Cardinal's 'blocs', would have to wait if one of the main priorities now was to discourage the departure of too many Anglo-Catholics. It would be only the departure (or the growing torpor) of the Anglo-Catholics and their fellow travellers that would open up that particular development, though the two Archbishops were already in preliminary talks with the Methodists by the end of 1994. The assumption was that, in the end, the traditionalists would cease to matter, that their present effectiveness might wane through disunity or attrition. Concrete moves towards unity with the Free Churches could then safely begin. Before that, there were other possible pan-Protestant initiatives. One of them looked, on the face of it, less inflammatory to Anglo-Catholic susceptibilities: the possibilities being opened out by talks at Porvoo in Finland, for a kind of federation of northern European Protestant Churches which had bishops. In fact, the Porvoo scheme had its pitfalls, too: but at this juncture, they were only the size of a man's hand, far away on the horizon.

All that would take time. In the end, the best and cleanest way for Anglo-Catholic obstacles to Protestant unity to be removed was not one the bishops of the Church of England wanted to contemplate: a large-scale and co-ordinated defection of Anglo-Catholics to Rome. That in turn depended on what the alternatives to staying would be. The Anglican bishops had offered Provincial Visitors as a palliative; but would it be strong enough? What would be the response of the Catholic bishops? That was the real question now.

CHAPTER SIX

SOWING THE
SEEDS OF MISTRUST

THE FEBRUARY SESSIONS of the General Synod, by coincidence, took place during the same week as the first of what I have called the Westminster conversations, in which Cardinal Hume, with three other Catholic bishops, met four Anglicans generally accepted as representative of those Anglican clergy and laity now looking to Rome. In fact, there had been many other conversations with individual Anglicans, both clergy and laity, in Westminster since 11 November. They tended to come away from Archbishop's House saying that they had been given by Cardinal Hume what few of their own bishops had ever given: the feeling, not only of having been taken seriously but of having been pastorally cared for.

But there were only three major meetings of the eight, two before the pivotal Low Week meeting of the Catholic bishops, and one (the proceedings of which were very different in tone and substance) afterwards. The Cardinal had already met the Anglicans who attended the first Westminster conversation individually: they were Bishop Leonard; Christopher Colven, Master of the SSC; Peter Geldard, leader of the Catholic Group in the General Synod; and John Broadhurst, chairman of Forward in Faith.

THE QUANDARY OF FATHER BROADHURST

Of these four, it was generally assumed that Bishop Leonard and Fathers Geldard and Colven would eventually be received into the Catholic Church whatever happened. Father Broadhurst's position was more difficult to work out. His first priority appeared to be co-ordinating the Anglican resistance to the November decision. This was, on the face of it, a very different intention from that of those who now thought they could do no more for the Church of England, and wanted to find the best way of leaving it together. Father Broadhurst was, nevertheless, known to be in touch with Cardinal Hume: on one occasion, the Cardinal phoned him at Faith House while he was chairing a meeting of the Forward in Faith executive. 'It's the Cardinal for Father Broadhurst,' said an excited secretary, poking her head round the door of the board room, as the other members of the executive exchanged significant glances. Forward in Faith was a coalition held together by common opposition to women's ordination; between half and two-thirds of its members had no intention of taking the road to Rome.

Broadhurst's position was difficult. He was, and remained, long after others had set out to cross the Tiber, chairman of an umbrella organization whose members needed to remain united in their tactics if they were to continue to have influence over events within the Church of England. He was, in other words, one of probably hundreds of clergy who realized, each in his own way, that their particular pastoral responsibilities precluded their making a personal decision at a time of their own choosing. Two days after he had attended the meeting at Archbishop's House, he gave the keynote speech at a 'synodical consultation' (generally described by the press as a 'walk-out') in the Central Hall Westminster. Most of the 180-strong Catholic Group had left the Synod chamber towards the end of a debate on education (though not in a co-ordinated exodus), and crossed the road from Church House. A few Evangelicals turned up; the suffragan Bishop of Dover was also spotted, keeping an eye on the proceedings, though he made it clear that he was not there on behalf of his diocesan, the Archbishop of Canterbury.

John Broadhurst's speech was greeted by a standing ovation. But what was he asking for? At one point, it seemed clear that he wanted some kind of *Ecclesiola in Ecclesia*, or Church within a Church. 'It is difficult', he said,

> to see any way in which the traditionalists can continue without seriously undermining their own relationship with God unless the present structures are modified ...
>
> Our vision is of an ecclesial community in which our children and grandchildren can grow in the faith, a community which will

continue the orders of bishop and priest as the Church has received them and can guarantee a true sacramental life ...

We are not seeking a temporary refuge but rather legally safeguarded means to be Catholic Christians in accord with the faith and order that we have received from the past – and which we have neither changed nor wished to change.

THE SIGNALS BECOME CONFUSED

How did this tally with the aspirations of those who had had enough of the Church of England, and who wanted, if a way could be devised of doing it, to take their Anglicanism with them into communion with the Holy See? On the face of it, not at all, unless what Broadhurst had in mind was a consolidation of the 'traditionalist' constituency as a prelude to some such outcome. This seemed to be hinted at later in the speech, when he suggested that an ambition for reunion was necessary for doctrinal integrity. Both the Eastern Orthodox and the Roman Catholic Churches were referred to; but it was a reunion with the Latin Church of the West which clearly had priority. 'To protect ourselves from any further errors,' he insisted,

and to secure the faithful proclamation of the Gospel we state quite clearly and unequivocally that we are committed to pursuing corporate reunion with the great churches of West and East as soon as possible. We need to bring alive the ARCIC process which has been wilfully wounded by our church's decision. It appals me that there is no expression of penitence in the C of E's recognition of the setback to ARCIC. When we have an established ecclesial structure we will want to continue where ARCIC left off.

What could that mean? Did it mean that, once they had established a Church within the Church of England, they would begin separate negotiations with Rome towards reunion? Was this a rival version of the Roman Option currently being discussed with Cardinal Hume and his colleagues? If not, what was it? Perhaps at that stage it was an attempt by Father Broadhurst to say what had to be said to unite a disparate constituency. Those who wished to stay would see in it a commitment to establishing a faithful remnant with a distant ecumenical goal; those who wished to leave would see it as a message that they were being held together in the short term so that when Rome came to a mind about what it was prepared to offer, they would be a visible entity rather than an indeterminate number of disgruntled individuals.

Some genuinely did not know what they would do, and were pursuing a twin track policy until the possibilities for the future became clearer. Dr Habgood had made it clear that no further concessions would be offered by the Establishment, that 'there is a line beyond which the House of Bishops will not go'. But what would the Catholic bishops offer? As Geoffrey Kirk put it, responding to Habgood's *ne plus ultra*, 'it looks as if the bottom line is extremely rigid and if that is the case, we will have to push ahead with our own form of episcopal oversight, while always keeping an eye open for the main chance, which is a reunion of some kind with Rome'.

The signal sent to some Roman Catholics by speeches like Broadhurst's, and by quotations in the press from others known to be talking to the Cardinal, was very different from anything they could have intended. To some Catholics, it seemed as though the Anglican dissidents were using the discussions with the Catholic Church as a bargaining counter for better terms from the Anglican hierarchy than they had been offered in the Manchester statement. As the distinguished columnist Clifford Longley put it, 'the Roman Catholic Church is being drawn into the Anglican game whether it wants to play or not. It is being used for the time being to try to extract further concessions from the Synod majority, so that traditionalists can remain Anglican.'

INFALLIBLE?

It was light years from the truth of what was actually taking place; but such an analysis could be defended all too easily by pointing at the apparent evidence. Here were Anglicans, apparently thinking of going to Rome, and simultaneously, or so it seemed, making arrangements to stay. In fact, given the actual outcome, it can certainly be argued that they were wise to have made alternative arrangements, in case things went wrong. But it was confusing for Catholic observers, and it played into the hands of those who wanted to undermine the Westminster conversations. What did these Anglicans actually want? How inclined towards the Catholic religion, in fact, were they? What did they believe?

Would they really accept Roman doctrines? After the synodical consultation, Father Broadhurst appeared on BBC2's *Newsnight* programme with John Taylor, the Bishop of St Alban's, who tried to convince him that the Manchester terms were adequate. The programme's presenter, the thrusting Jeremy Paxman, asked Broadhurst, suddenly: 'Do you believe in papal infallibility?'

The real answer to this question, as Broadhurst told the *Catholic Herald* a few days later, was that he had no problems with the doctrine 'as defined by Vatican II in terms of collegiality': that is, in the general context of the doctrinal authority of the Church as a whole. In other words, Broadhurst had no difficulty with the authentic Roman Catholic teaching. He did not believe in the doctrine as normally misunderstood by such as Jeremy Paxman (and Bishop Taylor for that matter), to convey a crude personal authority unilaterally exercised; furthermore, he had his very mixed Forward in Faith constituency to consider. What was he to say? He would be misunderstood whatever he said; and he had a split second to decide. What he said was 'no'.

This led to precisely the kind of misapprehension on the Catholic side that had dogged the Roman Option from the beginning. If Father Broadhurst could deny papal infallibility and at the same time suppose that there was any future in his discussions with the Cardinal – so ran the inference – then the Anglican suppliants must be imagining that they could be received into communion with the Holy See without fully accepting the whole of Catholic teaching. In fact, Father Broadhurst supposed no such thing; neither did anybody else who counted. But it was difficult to draw any other inference than that he did at the time. Understandably perhaps, Clifford Longley now pounced: 'A straight denial of infallibility', he wrote in the *Daily Telegraph* two days later, 'notwithstanding the sweet nuances that progressive theologians may spread over it to make it more palatable to themselves and each other is, in Roman Catholic terms, a sure disqualification.' This, Longley went on, 'is at the heart of the Anglo-Catholic dilemma':

> What Father Broadhurst hopes for, apparently, is Anglican comprehensiveness under Roman auspices. Sadly for a painless solution he will not get it. Rome has always seen Anglo-Catholicism as a chimera, not as a church ... Some traditionalist Anglicans will have greeted this week's news of conversations between their representatives and Cardinal Basil Hume of Westminster as

a sign only of further darkness at the end of the tunnel. Relatively few will have been unconditionally delighted ... As time passes the mood of the rest may change, but at present they view the prospect of transferring to Rome with anxiety or even distaste.

TABLE D'HÔTE OR À LA CARTE

It was a fantasy based on a chimera: the chimera was that those working for a Roman Option envisaged an operation infinitely larger in scale than anyone involved in the discussions had for one moment imagined was remotely possible. 'The prospect here is a dramatic one,' Longley had written. 'The transfer of allegiance to Rome of a third of the Church of England's clergy and laity could enhance the size and standing of the Roman Catholic Church in England to the point where the Church of England would be eclipsed.' But nobody in the Church of England (certainly none of the Anglican dissidents) had ever entertained so grandiose a vision. That there might take place such very large-scale transfers of personnel, who would be allowed to change their allegiance without any doctrinal questions asked, was a fantasy believed by nobody in the Church of England. But it was believed on the Catholic side, at any rate by enough people to make a real difference to the outcome, that that was what the Anglican suppliants were asking for. The Cardinal knew that it was untrue. But the notion that the Roman Option was about the autonomy of an unreconstructed Anglo-Catholicism under the protection of Rome now began to take hold. It was a balloon which some on the Anglican side (justly or not) believed had been deliberately inflated for the purpose of being burst. Clifford Longley now burst it. The traditionalists, he wrote, were

> misleading themselves if they think Rome finds that prospect so attractive that they will deal with them by Anglican rules. (In fact most Roman Catholic bishops seem to find the idea unattractive in any circumstances.)

The Anglicans talking to Cardinal Hume and the other bishops were thus, in this and other accounts, not only over-ambitious to the point of fantasy, but intent on achieving contradictory goals. They wanted to use Rome as a bargaining counter so as to be able to stay in the Church of England; simultaneously they wanted to take a third of the Anglican clergy and laity to Rome without accepting the whole of Catholic doctrine.

In fact, as we have seen, that third of the Church of England which remained opposed to women-priests was a diverse constituency. Some wanted to go, others to stay. But they all respected each other, and were prepared to form a temporary alliance against the common enemy until the possibilities for the future seemed clearer.

Those who wanted to go had no notion of 'playing by Anglican rules': Anglican rules, particularly when it came to 'comprehensiveness', were precisely what they wanted to get away from. There was and never had been for them any question of anything but a total acceptance of what Cardinal Hume was later to call (addressing his own constituency more than the Anglicans) the whole *table d'hôte* menu of Catholic doctrine. The new Catechism of the Catholic Church, it had been suggested from the Anglican side during that Monday's discussions at Archbishop's House, might be the basis for the instruction of those who would be received under the Roman Option. The suggestion was unanimously accepted without discussion: there had never been any question of wanting less than the full menu.

'WE'RE ALL AGAINST YOU'

Such overheated speculations as Clifford Longley's, nevertheless, were now running rife among both bishops and faithful in the Catholic Church. Some Anglicans, unjustly no doubt, saw such notions as having been dreamed up precisely with the purpose of undermining what the Cardinal was trying to achieve. Suspicions of this kind were common at the time in dissident Anglican circles: it had become clear that those within the English Catholic Church who were bitterly opposed to any form of special pastoral provision for Anglicans had been mustering from the beginning. These enemies inside the Catholic Church tended, in Anglo-Catholic demonology (and in some cases almost certainly in reality) to be mainly, though not exclusively, radical Catholics whose ecumenical links were with precisely those liberal Anglicans who had made the running over women's ordination.

Not only were such Catholics in favour of women's ordination themselves; they wanted to do nothing to harm relations with the

Church of England any further. Apart from anything else, they were enthusiasts for ecumenism on principle: if the C of E ('our sister Church', Pope Paul had called it in happier days, though what he would say now nobody speculated) was no longer available as a realistic ecumenical partner, with whom could they now be ecumenical? They tended to get over the difficulty by assuming that the papal interdiction against women-priests was a temporary matter, that once the present Pope had died, he would be replaced by one who would obligingly put women's ordination back on the agenda. Peter Hebblethwaite, the eminent Vaticanologist, former Jesuit and enthusiast for ecumenical relations with the Church of England, was pushing the candidature of the Jesuit Cardinal Martini, Archbishop of Milan, who had enigmatically stated that there would be no women-priests in the Roman Catholic Church 'in this millennium'.

Supporters of women-priests in the Catholic Church were by no means discouraged by the Pope's reaction to the General Synod's decision. On 24 March, four Catholic women and two representatives of the Anglican Movement for the Ordination of Women (MOW) launched a new organization, Catholic Women's Ordination (CWO). 'We are doing this', said one of the Catholic women involved, 'because we love the Church.' That evening, CWO had its first public demonstration; over 100 supporters walked in a silent circle in front of Westminster Cathedral, wearing Lenten purple. Their gesture, according to The Tablet's report, 'was intended to be evocative of the women of Argentina who protested against the disappearance of their children, but the commemoration this time was for women's lost gifts and abilities within the Church.' Catholics who wanted women's ordination in their own Church were correspondingly inclined to be hostile to those Anglicans who refused to accept it for themselves. Shortly after he had launched his initiative, Dr Leonard had bumped into Lord Longford, a member of The Tablet's editorial board; 'We're all against you at The Tablet,' he told Dr Leonard: 'we're all in favour of women priests.'

THE RESISTANCE GROWS

The Tablet, too, had become heavily dependent on its Anglican readership, which it had built up during the ecumenical seventies and eighties in the heyday of ARCIC, and which now made an appreciable contribution to its circulation. It had appealed increasingly, not to orthodox Catholic-minded Anglicans (to those, in other words, who were now looking to the Roman Option) but precisely to those responsible for the present dilemma of such Anglicans. By publishing articles and book reviews by such Anglican liberals as David L. Edwards and Alan Webster, the former Dean of St Paul's (a dogmatic radical and leading supporter of the women-priests lobby), it had tended to alienate a potentially much more substantial readership of papally-minded Anglo-Catholics.

Now, what might be described as Catholics of the *Tablet* school of thought began to take fright at the idea of an influx of a substantial number of Anglicans of a traditionalist kind, Anglicans who might be expected to sit much more easily under papal authority than they were inclined to do themselves. As the Cardinal noted in his *Tablet* interview, it was precisely of the necessity for the Magisterium that the dissidents' experience had convinced them. A number of distinctly jaundiced analyses of what was going on now began to be propagated by Catholics who were far from sharing the Cardinal's warm feelings about the Magisterium: the word 'misogynist' was not infrequently bandied about. Resistance to any special arrangements for the Anglican dissidents was muted at first: but it was picking up momentum, and it was to become more vocal and more open as the Catholic bishops' Low Week meeting approached.

CHAPTER SEVEN

COUNT-DOWN TO LOW WEEK

THE WESTMINSTER CONVERSATIONS remained on course: or so it seemed to those involved in them. The second meeting took place on 27 March. Though there was still no hint of the reversal of Anglican expectations that Low Week was to bring, there appears now to have been a growing sense that there would be no clear-cut or dramatic breakthrough at this stage.

The Cardinal opened by saying that he would have to cope with the growing press interest in the Low Week meeting by playing it down, though he realized this would present problems. He had, however, good hopes of Low Week, especially after his meetings with the Northern and Southern bishops. He had also been keeping in touch with the Vatican, from which he was getting 'good vibes'. He believed that keeping in touch with the English bishops and with Rome was important; he had also been keeping in touch with the Catholic clergy.

'THESE NECESSARY THINGS'

Both Anglicans and Catholics involved in the discussions were faced, he thought, by a 'central dilemma'. Simply put, this was that everyone needed to know what was on offer: at the same time, they were in a necessarily provisional situation. There were major decisions which would have to remain in the future; that would not make for an easy situation, in view of Anglican anxieties. But he told them of two things from Rome which could only encourage them. One was yet another confirmation that Pope Paul's quotation from Dom Lambert Beaudoin, 'united not absorbed', was still a guiding principle of their common enterprise: Rome kept this, he said, constantly in mind.

'The Holy Father has also asked us to remember,' he went on, looking at the back of an envelope (on which, it seemed, he had just taken it down from the telephone), 'Acts 15, verse 28.' Nobody could remember what that was; a Bible was produced, and the verse found: 'For it has seemed good to the Holy Spirit and to us to lay upon you no greater burden than these necessary things.' What did the Pope mean? Scripture does not help here, since it goes on to specify that 'these necessary things' are 'that you abstain from what has been sacrificed to idols and from blood and from what is strangled and from unchastity'.

Presumably this was not what the Pope had in mind. What, in this context, were 'these necessary things'? It clearly meant at the least an acceptance of Catholic teaching; but the purpose of the quotation can only have been to reassure the suppliant Anglicans that their approaches were being dealt with in no spirit of unbending rigorism. The Church would concentrate on the essentials of the faith rather than erecting unnecessary obstacles, that seemed to be the message: and since the Roman Option itself was an essentially pastoral operation, the purpose of which was precisely to remove unnecessary obstacles of a psychological and cultural nature, the Pope's message seemed to be one of encouragement for their aspirations.

'BY NO MEANS DEPRIVED'

This intention was clearly evident in one major breakthrough announced to the meeting, also apparently on the authority of the telephone call from Rome. The question of the validity of Anglican orders had always been a major stumbling block for many Anglicans. One theoretical solution was to ordain former Anglican clergy 'conditionally', and this procedure had been followed in the past in a small number of cases; it was to be used, as an exceptional concession, in the ordination of Bishop Leonard as a Catholic priest (though not without interminable agonizings at the Vatican). But it was, for a number of reasons, not a procedure that Rome felt able to authorize as normal practice (though there was a rumour that Cardinal Hume himself had no such reservations).

What Rome was prepared to do instead, however, was in one sense much better. To make an ordination conditional was to contemplate the possible nullity of a man's orders, and to supply a technical remedy for it. What Rome now proposed was to concentrate less on the assumed inadequacies of his orders, and more on the reality of his ministry up to that point: its approach would be positive rather than negative. Ordination as a Catholic priest would be no longer (as it had always seemed in the past) an unambiguous denial of orders previously received: it would be the bringing into communion with Peter a ministry previously exercised, which would now reach its fulfilment. This was an approach which Rome was now justifying by a specific reference to chapter 3 of the Conciliar document *Unitatis Redintegratio*, the Council's Decree on Ecumenism. After a paragraph on the unity of all the baptized, this chapter continues:

> Moreover, some, even very many, of the most significant elements and endowments which together go to build up and give life to the Church itself, can exist outside the visible boundaries of the Catholic Church: the written Word of God; the life of grace; faith, hope and charity, with the other interior gifts of the Holy Spirit, as well as visible elements. All of these, which come from Christ and lead back to him, belong by right to the one Church of Christ.
>
> The brethren divided from us carry out also many liturgical actions of the Christian religion. In ways that vary according to the condition of each Church or community, these liturgical actions most certainly can truly engender a life of grace, and, one must say, can aptly give access to the communion of salvation.
>
> It follows that the separated Churches and communities as such ... have by no means been deprived of significance and importance in the mystery of salvation. For the spirit of Christ has not refrained from using them as means of salvation which derive their efficacy from the very fullness of grace and truth entrusted to the Catholic Church.

Cardinal Hume did not quote from this standard English translation, but directly from the Latin, translating as he went; this, he felt, brought out the appositeness of this passage more accurately.

BYPASSING THE IMPASSABLE

This Conciliar teaching, it had now been decided in Rome, was to be given liturgical expression in the ordination of former Anglican clergy to the Catholic priesthood. The ordination itself was to be absolute; this could, it was felt, only be the case in view of the very different understanding of the two Churches, at the official level at any rate, of the nature of priesthood. But the change in Rome's attitude to Anglican orders was revolutionary. *Apostolicae Curae* was to stand, together with that thunderous judgement on the validity of Anglican orders, that they were 'absolutely null and utterly void'. It was to remain because there was no alternative; it was a can of worms that would cause nothing but trouble if it was opened.

But it was now possible to regard it, not as a kind of anathema, but as a technical statement. It had been an impassable obstacle on one of the rockier and more circuitous roads to Rome; now, another and broader road was to be built which arrived at its destination by a sunnier and more direct route. The new understanding was to be expressed in the form of a prayer to be used in ordination Masses of former Anglican clergy, the first draft of which Cardinal Hume now read out from the back of the same envelope on which he had taken down the Pope's reference to the Acts of the Apostles:

> Almighty Father, we give you thanks for the X years of faithful ministry of your servant N ... in the Anglican communion [or; in the Church of England] whose fruitfulness for salvation has been derived from the very fullness of grace and truth entrusted to the Catholic Church.

A few months later, a preamble was added before this paragraph, and a concluding paragraph after it. The preamble was as follows:

> N [candidate's name], the Holy Catholic Church recognizes that not a few of the sacred actions of the Christian religion as carried out in communities separated from her can truly engender a life of grace and can rightly be described as providing access to the community of salvation. And so we now pray. (A period for silent prayer follows.)

And the prayer concluded in this way:

> As your servant has been received into full communion and now
> seeks to be ordained to the presbyterate in the Catholic Church
> we beseech you to bring to fruition that for which we now pray
> through Jesus Christ our Lord, Amen.

The prayer was to be followed by the formula of ordination itself. In this
way, said Cardinal Hume, it would be made clear that the ordination
was the 'culmination' of a ministry already exercised in the Anglican
Church.

From this moment, it is probably true to say, for most Anglican clergy, *Apostolicae Curae* ceased to be the rock of offence it had been ever
since it had been promulgated in 1896. Rome's difficulties, and even
more Cardinal Hume's, were well understood. It was not in his power to
remove or modify a Papal Bull; but everything that Christian charity
could do to remove its hurtfulness had been done, in a gesture which
united imagination with evident good will. Some Anglo-Catholics continued to worry at *Apostolicae Curae*, obsessively; but for most it
became part of history for all practical purposes. Those present remember this as a deeply moving moment; Bishop Leonard, it was noticed,
was close to tears. There can be little doubt that for most of those
Anglican clergy who had previously refused to entertain the notion of a
second ordination, on the grounds that they were not about to have the
ministry of a lifetime set at nought, it was the beginning of a new chapter.

CATHOLIC BUT NOT ROMAN?

This breakthrough, though it was announced at a meeting which was
supposedly secret, did not – could not in the nature of things – remain
secret for long. On the grapevine of the dissident Anglican clergy it
spread like wildfire. But it was not only the Anglicans who were leaking
the proceedings of the Westminster conversations. On 3 April appeared
a leading article in *The Tablet*, which seemed to mark a distinct change
of attitude, a real attempt to meet the criticisms of its editorial stance
which had been general among the Anglican dissidents. To those who
were informed about what had been happening at Archbishop's House,
it was clearly the result of an off-the-record briefing. It suggested that a

way through the problem of Anglican orders might be found in chapter three of Vatican II's Decree on Ecumenism, and quoted the same passage that Cardinal Hume had quoted in Archbishop's House; it referred, too, to Dom Lambert Beaudoin's now famous *unie, non absorbée*. 'There has,' said *The Tablet*,

> been much publicity in the press for those Anglican clergy who have been exploring with Roman Catholic bishops a way that would realize, though temporarily, the Malines vision of Anglicanism 'united not absorbed'. The question here is whether a circle can be squared. For these clergy will say that while they wish to come into full communion with the Holy See, they do not wish to be Roman Catholics.

The idea of being in communion with the Pope without being necessarily 'Roman Catholic' in the early stages was, interestingly enough, the way the Cardinal himself had put it to the February meeting in his 'speech from the throne'. Most of the clergy involved, in fact, had no difficulty at all with becoming Roman as well as Catholic. But they were aware, as the Cardinal said at the March conversation, that there was a large body of lay Anglicans who felt that they could not stay in the Church of England but who did not quite know what Rome was, and might well be afraid of her; it was, after all, so as lay upon them 'no greater burden than these necessary things' that the whole enterprise had been undertaken in the first place.

But was it a viable operation? *The Tablet* saw the aim of being 'united not absorbed' as being inconsistent with that of being Catholic but not necessarily Roman: but the two locutions were simply different ways of saying the same thing. It was not, in fact, *Romanita* that was the difficulty; to a far greater extent, it was the self-absorption (and the consequent sense of remoteness conveyed to outsiders) of the Catholic Church in England: Anglicans tended to identify much more easily with the Church in France or Italy. *The Tablet* summarized the hopes of the Anglicans concerned as being 'to bring into the Roman Catholic Church their widely based evangelistic expertise, their English liturgical style (rather than an "English rite" which hardly exists in reality), and their tradition of lay involvement.' This was not wholly to the point; most Anglicans looking to Rome, lay or clerical, saw the comparative lack of lay involvement (at any rate as practised in the Church of

England, with its endless layers of bureaucracy and synodical government) as being wholly to be desired. Many of them, too, hoped for some kind of Catholicized Anglican rite.

LIFE ON THE MARGINS

What they did hope to bring with them (and this was also the way some Catholic bishops saw it) was their sense of vocation to the nation as a whole. The greatest psychological barrier, perhaps, for English Anglicans attracted to Rome but simultaneously wary of her, was their fear of a kind of withdrawal from the mainstream of English life and history into what, it seemed to many of them, was something like a self-contained and deliberately self-perpetuating ghetto. This was the way Catholicism in England had all too often presented itself to outsiders: not as being too Catholic, but as being, in one sense, nothing like Catholic enough. Anglican clergy had a deep sense that it was to the entire population who lived within their parish boundaries that they were to minister. This understanding was only partly to do with their consciousness of operating within an Established Church. Much more fundamentally, it was a pastoral imperative inherited from the Catholic Middle Ages: and it was this, if anything, that many Anglican clergy now hoped to 'repatriate' into the modern English Catholic tradition. Roman Catholicism in England had been marginalized by history, and had settled down to life on the margins. English Catholics behaved, it could too easily seem to outsiders, not like members of the universal Church, with a message that was valid for society as a whole, but all too often as though they were offering a kind of chaplaincy for recusants or for immigrants and their descendants.

So far as the Roman Option was concerned, this was not just a problem for some Anglicans. After centuries of exclusion, English Catholics had become defensive of their own identity. Now, many of them were beginning to scrutinize the signs emerging from Archbishop's House with growing nervousness. The reactions picked up by the Cardinal must have made him more and more aware, as Low Week approached, that he was being called on to fulfil two contradictory aims: to go as far as possible towards a pastoral provision for Anglicans that really would address their problems; and at the same time, to allay the growing anxieties of his own people. More and more, it was this second preoccupation that now came to the forefront.

For the most part, the dissident Anglicans were still either too over-whelmed by their own predicament or too excited by the prospect they believed they saw opening out before them, to give very much thought to the difficulties of those to whom they were now turning. Quite simply, they did not take sufficiently seriously the importance of under-standing the very different perspective of English Roman Catholics. There was, here, a real problem of mutual incomprehension.

To take one important example: for the Anglicans, *Apostolicae Curae* had always been a source of deep offence. To the English Catholic clergy they now hoped to join, however, it had been for generations a formative element in their perception of how their own priesthood fitted into the whole context of English life and history. Only a generation before, the Catholic Truth Society tract cases at the back of their churches had displayed pamphlets with titles like 'Through Anglicanism to the Church' and 'When is a priest not a priest?' (Answer: when he is an Anglican). Such titles were no longer in print in these more ecumenical days, but the sentiments they contained had gone underground as much out of courtesy as from any deep conviction that what they conveyed was actually mistaken.

THE OTHER SIDE OF THE COIN

The conviction of the English Catholic clergy that theirs was an authentic priesthood always had an implicit corollary attached: that the priesthood of the Anglican Church – which had usurped the place and even the title of the ancient Church of the nation, the *Ecclesia Anglicana* – was quite simply bogus. So Leo XIII's words 'absolutely null and utterly void' were not merely a resonant denial of the sacramental integrity of Anglican orders: they were an assertion of the uniqueness and irreplaceability of their own.

Thus, Cardinal Hume had to address two wholly different constituencies: he had to be all things to all men in a particularly demanding way. On 1 April, for instance, he spoke to a meeting of his own clergy at which, for about an hour, he briefed them on current developments. This meeting took place less than a week after the March meeting just described; the notes made by one of those present vividly convey, not only the very different anxieties of this group of Catholic priests, but the very different tone the Cardinal had to adopt in order to meet them. 'There is no question whatsoever', the notes summed up the Cardinal as saying, 'of reversing *Apostolicae Curae*. Rome will not consider anything like "conditional" ordination for convert clergymen. Their ordination to the Catholic priesthood will be "absolute". They could perhaps be shown that their eventual Catholic ordination will be the "culmination" of their vocation to serve God, by their being "'inserted into the Apostolic Succession".' He went on to insist that

> no new structures will be established; that any concessions made to possible groups of Anglicans will be temporary – the Cardinal stressed this. No new permanent rites will be granted. Limited permission for some aspects of Anglican worship might be possible, such as the Office. He does not personally favour their being allowed to continue with Anglican Eucharistic rites.

There are two ways in which this account contrasts dramatically with the record of the March meeting with the Anglicans. First, there is a striking difference of tone: this, in itself probably derives partly from the divergent preoccupations of those recording the proceedings, but it also very evidently reflects the Cardinal's own sensitivity to his two audiences. On 27 March, the Cardinal was seen sustaining a vision; on 1 April, he was reassuring wary Catholic clergy that he was not about to abandon all the defences of the Catholic Church. Thus, on 1 April, the Cardinal was pressed by one priest – a Jesuit – to say what happens 'when an Anglican minister says the words of institution over bread and wine'. Cardinal Hume replied 'nothing happens' – but stressed nevertheless that God does not deny grace to those receiving such sacraments, the teaching of *Unitatis redintegratio* he had expounded at much greater length for the Anglicans.

THE PRESSURES MOUNT

To such an audience, at such a time, *Apostolicae Curae* was not to be sidestepped; thus, there was 'no question whatsoever' of reversing it. To the Anglicans he had said simply that Rome did not want to reopen the question. Similarly, to his own priests, the new liturgical prayer to be used in ordinations of former Anglican clergy was not mentioned at this stage; the new emphasis was presented as a possible future concession rather than as an achieved major breakthrough. Numbers of possible converts were played down: 'it is very unlikely', it was noted, 'that there will be large or numerous groups'. The realignment of English Christianity would be a very gradual process. 'We are not going to rush into anything.'

Similarly, to his own clergy, the Cardinal stressed only the temporary character of any 'concessions'; to the four representative Anglicans at the 27 March meeting, it was recorded that he had said that though any 'accommodation' (a word with very different overtones) would be temporary, nevertheless

> 'Gradualness' was very important – people would move towards
> Rome at different speeds and this must be allowed for.

The assumption of the Anglicans was that this was consistent with some kind of continuing Anglican entity that might last – on the basis of a kind of planned obsolescence – for a generation, perhaps even more. How else could these 'different speeds' be catered for in a way which genuinely moved on from the old model of individual submissions? This interpretation was strongly encouraged by the fact that Rome itself was still encouraging them to think that they would be 'united not absorbed' – a phrase which had been repeatedly introduced into their discussions from the Roman Catholic side and not by the Anglicans involved.

The real question now was how much forward movement the English Catholic Church was capable of tolerating. The Cardinal saw that he had to be careful: but it is clear, too, that he was concerned when talking to his clergy to encourage them 'to welcome anyone whose conscience leads them to the Church'. In his own words, 'we have lovely treasures to offer them'. His advice was to be pastorally 'sensitive' about using the authorized scheme for receiving converts, the Rite for the Christian Initiation of Adults (RCIA). Clergy preparing converts for reception should not force well-informed converts through a programme designed for those preparing for baptism. They should 'be flexible, and adapt as necessary'.

But could exhortations such as these, by themselves, measure up to the magnitude of the challenge now facing English Catholicism? This question brings us to the second way in which the two meetings differ. For, there seems to have been a distinct shift in Cardinal Hume's thinking, of which the Anglicans were at this stage unaware, and which can only be seen as representing a retreat from the high hopes for the Roman Option that so many – including the Cardinal himself – had entertained. This change of view seems to have taken place quite rapidly, possibly under the growing pressures that now bore down on him as the bishops' meeting approached.

NO FLAGS OF CONVENIENCE

There had been no specific mention of Canon 372 at the March meeting; but there had been no rejection of it, either: it was assumed that it was still being actively considered, but that there was nothing further to be said about it at this stage. Now, however, the Cardinal was indicating, first, that he himself was coming out against the idea of an Anglican Eucharistic Rite, and second, that 'no new structures would be established'. Both of these things – an Anglican rite and a loose but definitely existent structure for Anglican Catholic congregations – had been at the heart of Bishop Leonard's proposals (requested by the Cardinal) for the implementation in England of Canon 372 and discussed in February, and they were still on the table in late March. Now, at the beginning of April, there appears to have been a shift: the summary of the Cardinal's remarks on 1 April which I have given above goes virtually the whole way towards the reduced version of the Roman Option that emerged after Low Week. The question is, what had happened in the meantime?

It is a fascinating question; and one to which, at this historical juncture, it is not possible to give a satisfactory answer. Writing about what is going on in the Church of England is a comparatively easy matter: sooner or later, someone in the know will spill the beans. Most English Catholic bishops, by contrast, are awesomely discreet. But persistent enquiry, combined on this occasion with a surprising level of indiscretion on the part of one particular Catholic bishop, does justify certain conclusions.

By the beginning of April 1993 it had become very clear to the Cardinal that there were all too many Catholics, including some particularly obdurate Catholic bishops, who were in no mood to 'be flexible, and adapt' to the new situation. As Low Week drew nearer, opposition from within the English Church gathered momentum. On Saturday, 10 April, the Cardinal flew to Rome to discuss the crucial Low Week meeting, now less than two weeks away. The same week, the Rt Revd Crispian Hollis, Bishop of Portsmouth, had openly criticized the motives of the prospective converts in a way which could only be interpreted as a suggestion that those who had spent so much time actually talking to them (above all the Cardinal himself) had been guilty of considerable naivety.

'The Catholic Church', said Bishop Hollis, 'is not a flag of convenience. It is not something you can change to just because its suits you. To make that change requires a profession of faith and that includes accepting the wholeness and the authority of the Catholic Church.' It was hardly an original perception or, by now, one that needed to be spelled out to anybody; but what Bishop Hollis went on to say revealed an ignorance of their real motivation for which, by this stage in the proceedings, there was little excuse.

'THE CARDINAL HAS GONE MAD'

It was an ignorance all the more difficult to understand in view of the Cardinal's conscientious efforts to explain the issues to the bishops. 'I think what is worrying many of my colleagues,' said Bishop Hollis, 'is the question of the single-issue convert. There are far more serious issues to Catholicism than simply the issue of women-priests.' But Cardinal Hume had been telling the bishops for months now that it was not a single-issue question, that it was fundamentally to do with the Church's authority; for Bishop Hollis to claim he really believed that 'many of [his] colleagues' were worried about 'single-issue converts' was simply not credited by those who knew what was actually going on, though it may well have had the effect of stirring up the anxieties of ordinary Catholics.

The general feeling among the would-be converts themselves was that Bishop Hollis's reaction was to be expected. He already had a reputation for being less than effusive towards prospective Anglican converts. This was despite his own markedly Anglican episcopal manner. He tended to stand at church doors after Mass, wearing a casual jacket, grinning and shaking hands with members of the congregation as they departed. Towards Anglicans who had no tendencies in a Romeward direction, he was affability itself: but an Anglican who was showing signs of disloyalty to the Established Church he seemed to regard with the deepest suspicion.

His determined opposition to any sizeable influx of Anglicans like these was something Bishop Hollis made very obvious. He made his views known publicly more than once, even appearing in a television interview during the course of the Low Week conference itself, a very unusual thing for a Catholic bishop to do. It does not require an over-active imagination to infer that he also made his views clear to Cardinal Hume personally, in advance of the Low Week meeting. His views, in brief, were that the Cardinal had become dangerously over-enthusiastic about the Roman Option, and that he needed to be energetically restrained. Privately, his language was colourful in the extreme: 'But don't you see that the Cardinal has gone mad?' was how he discouraged one Catholic enthusiast for the Roman Option. Or as he put it to a group of his clergy about two months after the bishops' meeting, 'Basil tends to go over the top rather: we had to claw him back from the edge of the precipice.' How many bishops that 'we' included is one of the tantalizing historical questions that cannot yet be answered. It would not need to be very many to have a considerable effect: what Cardinal Hume needed at the Low Week meeting was unanimity. But Bishop Hollis was clearly not alone, except in one respect: his tactics.

Ironically, his campaign had a distinctly Anglican feel about it. Catholic bishops were normally reluctant to break ranks. Anglican bishops, in contrast, had fewer inhibitions about taking their own line or using the media to launch their own personal views. Peter Hebblethwaite (whose own hostility to the dissident Anglicans was clear enough) wrote that 'Bishop Crispian Hollis ... has emerged as the tough policeman to Cardinal Hume's nice cop.' As Hebblethwaite also explained, 'Cardinal Hume is ahead in wanting to make it "easy" for them to move as a group.' He continued, enigmatically, 'He is a man of prayer. Some bishops trust his intuition.' In other words, perhaps, he has his head in the clouds and some other bishops do **not** trust his intuition. 'Bishop Hollis,' wrote Hebblethwaite, 'grandson of an Anglican bishop – he wears his ring – knows that the Anglo-Catholic party has acted as a political faction, using bluff and pressure to get its own way. It cannot be allowed to do that in a Catholic context. Back to the individual solution.'

SISTERS AND BROTHERS

What was behind all this? Why was Bishop Hollis so very hostile to 'the Anglo-Catholic party', which had not in fact been using bluff and pressure 'in a Catholic context' at all; on the contrary, Cardinal Hume had made a point of saying in his *Tablet* interview that he had been 'struck by the humility of those who had been discussing with him the possibility of a path from the Church of England to Rome'.

Did Bishop Hollis have a particular reason for his intense opposition to the conversion of a sizeable body of Anglicans? Might it be, some asked, that he had a particular sympathy with one 'party' within his own Church, with those who wanted the ordination of Catholic women too? It was difficult to know; it was not a subject over which Catholic bishops were encouraged to be forthcoming if their private beliefs differed from the official view. But it did not go unnoticed that his objection to a group migration of supposed 'one-issue converts' was precisely that currently being hotly argued by a particular Catholic constituency: it was, in fact, the characteristic objection of a small but disproportionately influential group of radical Catholic feminists and of those who were their natural supporters. As the bishops' Low Week meeting began, *The Times* reported Sister Myra Poole, founder of Catholic Women's Ordination (CWO) as saying that it would be quite unacceptable to allow hundreds of 'Anglican ministers' to join the Catholic Church together:

> We are concerned because opposition to women priests is a negative reason for joining. If 500 or so come into our Church, what effect will that have on our traditions? Individual conversions would be all right provided they were sincere, but we should not allow en bloc conversion just on this one issue.
>
> These people probably have no idea how radical the Catholic Church is and just do not realize how strong we are on things like liberation and feminist theology. We are concerned that their outdated ideas could put back the progress we have been making by 100 years. I can assure you that there will be quite an outcry if they come across *en masse*.

Did Bishop Hollis have sympathy with views such as these? Some of his clergy remembered a letter he had sent after the General Synod's decision to ordain women. It had sounded to some of them almost as though Bishop Hollis wished he could ordain women himself. The letter stated that he regretted the decision: but this was the official line, and he could have done little else. He did not give reasons of his own for regretting it, but quoted a statement from Cardinal Hume. His own comments were a study in ambiguity. At the time, he wrote, he had felt very conscious of how many Anglican 'sisters and brothers' must have been feeling as the result was declared. For some, he observed, it was a moment of great joy and rejoicing; for others it must have felt as if their whole world was being destroyed.

Catholics, he continued, had been able to stand back from such reactions, though he himself still felt able to share and understand them. Ecumenical relations, he claimed, would not be damaged. Though, at the level of the official dialogue between the Churches, there now existed a new and major challenge which had to be faced and overcome, he felt confident that 'the working together and the growing together' would not suddenly wither away 'simply because the local Anglican vicar happens to be a woman.'

The search for unity, he concluded, must continue; and he asked his clergy both to join him in that commitment and to continue to demonstrate it 'to all our sisters and brothers in the Church of England'.

THE SEARCH FOR THE LOST GODDESS

What was one to make of that? 'You could read it either way,' thought one parish priest. It might, if you wanted to make something of it, be interpreted as the letter of someone privately in favour of women's ordination; at the very least it had to be seen as reflecting a mind conscious of feminist pressures and willing to respond by using politically correct language: that smooth and twice repeated 'sisters and brothers' did not go unnoticed by those long accustomed to spotting the encroachments of feminist influence over susceptible bishops. The letter could also be read as strangely congregationalist coming from a Catholic bishop, implying that real Christian life was at the local level, and that the universal dimension of the Church was just 'the level of ... official dialogue'. But none of this, by itself, made Bishop Hollis a closet feminist, though his letter certainly reflected the fact that he was not exactly on the conservative wing of the Church.

It also reflected his strong ecumenical instincts. These had led him, in the past, to stray over the boundaries of what his Church authorized: 'the working together and the growing together', when he had been a chaplain at Oxford, had included giving communion regularly to non-Catholics, a practice he had by no means wholly discontinued – to the outrage of some of his clergy – as Bishop of Portsmouth. But he had never been given to excessive deference to the rules laid down by the Magisterium in Rome, or for that matter to those who represented that authority: this was, indeed, another subject over which he had been on at least one occasion surprisingly indiscreet, and in his most colourful manner: 'I've just had another letter from that bloody Delegate,' he said to one startled group of laity, brandishing a letter from the Papal Nuncio, Monsignor Luigi Barbarito.

More directly relevant to his attitude to the Roman Option, however, was the Mary Grey affair. Mary Grey was 'Professor of Feminism and Christianity' at the highly radicalized Dutch Catholic University of Nijmegen, and about as hostile to papal authority as they came. She was also hostile, in the most radical way, to much of what the Magisterium of the Church actually taught. Her position was that of those radical feminists who – in the words of Catharina Halkes, her colleague at Nijmegen – 'find the image of a Father-God a challenge and a direct confrontation'.

Her views were well known. In 1991, for instance, she had given a public lecture later published in *Signum*, a newsletter for religious, published by the Catholic Media Trust (of which, as it happened, Bishop Hollis was one of three trustees). She believed, she said, that Christianity should 'creatively engage in resources outside the Christian tradition': most notably, this meant the neo-pagan 'goddess movement', including 'the movement of witches recalling the memory of witches in the past'. This movement, she asserted 'is reclaiming the wit and wisdom of the wise woman, recalling their rituals'. The other manifestation of the goddess movement with which, she felt, the Church should 'creatively engage' was the 'search for the lost goddess from before the rise of patriarchy, dated from the twelfth century BC'. It was, she claimed 'only from this level that we get the whole sense of what it means to have the divine imaged as female'. In all this, her teachings reflected the influence of the American feminist guru Rosemary Radford Ruether, who in 1984 had helped a group of radical feminist activists (including Grey herself) to set up in England a ginger group called the Catholic Women's Network (CWN).

THE MARY GREY AFFAIR

When a new chair of Catholic theology was established (on the merger of the Catholic La Sainte Union college with Southampton University), and Mary Grey was appointed to it, alarm bells began to ring. With all the wealth of theological talent available in the English Church, this not particularly distinguished candidate had been chosen to fill the country's only specifically Catholic chair; it looked to many like an ideologically motivated appointment. How did it get through?

The new professor had been chosen by a joint committee of Southampton University and La Sainte Union: the most influential committee member on the Catholic side had been Bishop Hollis, who had an effective veto as chairman of the governors. When outraged representations were made by one priest to Bishop Hollis afterwards, his response was not to defend the appointment but to insist that the University had wanted it and that he had not had the power to prevent it. But the then Vice Chancellor of the University had made it clear when the chair had been established that he would never insist on a candidate unacceptable to the Church. The minutes show that the choice of the committee was unanimous, and that this was, therefore, an appointment that Bishop Hollis had sanctioned: 'It marks,' he said at the time, 'an exciting moment in the history of theological teaching in Southampton and in the diocese.'

All that was in the past now; but when, in Low Week 1993, Mary Grey joined the campaign against the Roman Option with an article in *The Times*, connections were made. Perhaps the conspiracy theorists, here at least, saw a little too much; and perhaps this reflected the general paranoia of the times. But certainly, like other feminists (and like Bishop Hollis himself) Professor Grey did assume that the Anglican dissidents were looking for 'safe havens' where 'women's ordination is hardly likely to become a troubling issue'. On the other hand, she did not deny that authority rather than women was the central issue for these Anglicans; what she did instead was to mount a strong attack on the very idea of authority as it prevailed within the Catholic Church. What she disliked about the would-be converts, it seemed, was not that they might not be obedient to the Magisterium, but that they all too obviously would be. They would, in other words, swell the numbers of those within the Church who wished to defend a Patriarchal notion of authority which according to Mary Grey totally ignores those of us within the Catholic Church inspired by a very different notion of authority, a dynamic notion which respects the experience and wisdom of baptized and committed lay women and men, the dignity and fullness of the local and regional church, the discernment of the grassroots experience of those living out Christian witness in the street, under the bridges, in the despair of the ravaged cities.

The obvious rejoinder to this, that down the ages, obedience to Catholic teaching had been a 'dynamic notion' which had inspired a great deal of 'Christian witness in the street' (Mother Teresa being the obvious modern example), was not to the point. What was precisely to the point in Low Week, 1993, was that it had become very clear to everyone that the Roman Option had struck an exposed nerve in the body of the Catholic Church. In his seventieth-birthday interviews, Cardinal Hume had pointed out

> that the Catholic community is losing sight of how the Magisterium, the teaching authority, operates ... You can have your views and express them, but what matters to me profoundly is the existence of the Magisterium. I rejoice that the Holy Spirit is given to the Holy Father in a way that it is not given to me, except in so far as I am part of the college of the bishops. He has a guidance which I don't have. If I did not believe that, I would cease to be a Catholic.

SNIPER ATTACKS FROM THE HILLS

Those who thought as Mary Grey thought, very emphatically did not believe that: they equally emphatically insisted that they were not going to cease to be Catholics. Catholic feminists believed in the classic revolutionary tactic of entryism, or 'working within the structures', to bring about radical change. The movement's leading ideologue, Rosemary Radford Ruether – who was on record as saying that her devotion to the Blessed Virgin was 'somewhat less than my devotion to some more powerful females that I knew: Isis, Athena, Artemis' – told members of the Catholic Women's Network (of which Mary Grey was a founder member) that feminists 'should use the institutional resources that have disempowered women to re-empower women': thus, Mary Grey's own appointment to the Southampton chair had been a triumph for classical Catholic-feminist operational tactics, and it had been brought about with the active support of a sympathetic Catholic bishop.

But this was just one skirmish in a much more broadly based guerrilla conflict within the Roman Catholic Church, in which feminist demands contributed only one *casus belli*; it was a war into which the Anglican refugees had innocently stumbled, only to find themselves the targets of sniper attacks from the hills. Refugees they might be: but they were not perceived as neutral. The Cardinal himself had unwittingly affixed targets to their backs. 'He finds a certain irony', *The Tablet* had recorded, 'in that just at the time when Catholics seem to be irked by the teaching authority, high-church Anglicans are finding a need of it.' So it was not just that Catholic feminists and their allies were unlikely wholeheartedly to welcome Anglicans whose conversion had been precipitated by women's ordination (even if they could be convinced that women's ordination was the occasion rather than the real cause of their defection). There was a more fundamental reason why the would-be converts were unwelcome to them: it was that at a time when so many liberal Catholics (whether feminists or not) were 'irked' by the Magisterium, for Anglican dissidents to say they had come to see the need for it was hardly a defence calculated to soothe their doubts.

As Low Week approached, the Anglican dissidents were thus caught up in more than one treacherous cross-current of history. Some Catholics mistrusted them because they seemed to threaten the defences the English Catholic Church had had to erect over the centuries to protect its own integrity: others, because they were seen as potential recruits on the side of the blackest of Tridentine reactionaries. This second perception in particular was almost always either oversimplified or wholly misjudged; of those Anglican priests involved in the Westminster conversations, for example, all three saw themselves as 'Vatican II Catholics': they had all pulled out their altars from the walls, and installed just the same package of 'liturgical renewal' as their Roman Catholic counterparts.

By Low Week, however, the realities of the situation had become submerged. Two powerful mythologies of conflict were in play. One mythology had its roots deep in the history of four hundred years, and it drew on ancient fears and resentments on both sides of the divide between Anglicans and Catholics. The other mythology was more recent, but the fears and resentments were no less active. They were, however, infinitely less powerful in their emotional effect on the Anglican dissidents than they were on Roman Catholics, especially on those who had lived through the upheavals within the Church since the sixties. For the Anglicans, they were as yet, for the most part, unrealized perils: they were like a dangerous undertow beneath a calm and hopeful sea.

PART TWO

CHAPTER EIGHT

ANGLICAN DISSIDENTS AND THE SPIRIT OF VATICAN II

Once meat on Friday was possible, I argued even in those days, the whole ball of wax melted. Add a commission to investigate a possible change on birth control and you created a heady environment in which not only could anything change, but it was firmly expected (by the clergy and religious and many laity) that everything would change.
Martin Greeley, *Confessions of a Parish Priest*

I rejoice that the Holy Spirit is given to the Holy Father in a way that it is not given to me, except in so far as I am part of the college of the bishops. He has a guidance which I don't have. If I did not believe that, I would cease to be a Catholic.
Basil, Cardinal Hume, February 1993

'WE SHALL ONLY know what the Council means,' commented one sage observer on the day it ended, 'ten years from now.' But a decade later, there was still no real consensus on the matter; and even today, 'What does the Council mean?' is a question which tends to invoke, among Roman Catholics above a certain age at least, either partisan clichés or hesitant and rambling answers. For Anglican Catholics, Vatican II was always a very different, and much less difficult, phenomenon. Its effects were certainly felt among Catholic-minded Anglicans, but they were virtually painless. The Council's most dramatic after-effects – the suppression of the Old Mass, the uprooting or undermining of many traditional pious practices, the installation of a vernacular liturgy – had all been painfully, even brutally, accomplished within Anglicanism four centuries earlier. For Catholic-minded Anglicans whose forebears had done the suffering on their behalf, it was all gain and no pain.

THE END OF THE AFFAIR

For Anglo-Catholics, there were two major positive results of the Council. First, it seemed to bring closer a recognition they had always longed for but never supposed would come their way, at least in their own lifetime: the recognition that in some ways at least, Anglicanism had paved the way for the renewal of the Catholic tradition that now seemed to be happening. Centuries before, the Church of England had installed some of the liturgical reforms that had been in the air in the Catholic Church on the eve of the Protestant Reformation. Now these reforms, and much else besides, were being installed in the Mother Church herself. The Anglican emphasis on the Bible as the necessary accompaniment to the Sacraments was now being asserted by the Catholic Church. Exposition of the Scriptures was being rediscovered as a necessary part of the ministry of the Word. In these as in so many ways, Anglo-Catholicism (or so Anglo-Catholics felt) was now being vindicated as a legitimate expression of Catholic faith and practice.

Their second reason for welcoming the Council was a corollary of the first: that it seemed to legitimize their own position within Anglicanism. In many ways, the Vatican Council, precisely because it removed so much of the alien exoticism of the Roman Catholic Church, gave their own position a legitimacy and credibility which it had never had. With Archbishop Ramsey's visit to Pope Paul, and the setting up of the ARCIC conversations, the new ecumenism for Anglicans seemed, almost inevitably, destined to lead to reunion with the Holy See. All this was to lead to a final flowering of the Anglo-Catholic tradition which proved in the end to be cruelly deceptive.

It was all blown out of the water by a new issue whose very existence they had scarcely suspected: the growing campaign for the ordination of women to the priesthood. This led the majority of Anglo-Catholics – thoroughly impassioned by the new Romeward-bound ecumenism – to identify Anglican feminism as an essentially liberal

Protestant movement, whose success within the Anglican tradition could only lead to the end of their hopes for reunion with the Holy See. Ironically, whereas the 'Catholic Renewal' movement within Roman Catholicism came to be synonymous with radical adventures (including women's ordination), the catalyst for the short-lived but at the time apparently successful Anglican Catholic Renewal Movement was precisely the battle to the death against the ordination of women to the priesthood.

A CASE OF MISTAKEN IDENTITY

This was not an inconsistent position. Catholic Anglicanism's basic criticism of women's ordination was not that it was too radical, but that it was radical in the wrong way. As the Anglo-Catholic Sarah Maitland (already well-known in the secular feminist world) put it in a speech to the 1978 Catholic Renewal Conference at Loughborough, 'the problem of what to do about women in the Church is not going to be solved by shoving them into men's orders'.

But women's ordination really was not the issue in itself. Roman Catholic feminists were astonished that the November vote to ordain women should provide the occasion (a 'moment of liberation', she called it) for Sarah Maitland's own conversion to Catholicism; just like all the supposed Anglican 'misogynists', she defected on the fundamental issue of authority in the Church at exactly the time when Catholic feminists were so furiously suspicious of the Anglican dissidents who were claiming the same motivation. But it was not a lame excuse, thought up at the last minute: as Maitland pointed out, many Anglican Catholics had been saying it patiently for years. 'Authority', she explained in *The Tablet*, 'has become such a dirty word that popular opinion was unable to grasp that anyone could actually mean this: it must be just a rationalization for psychological defects like misogyny and fascism. But oddly, authority – submitting one's individual desires to the needs and desires of the community – has always been a mark of the radical left, not the reactionary right, who have preferred the language of personal rights and liberties.'

For many Anglican Catholics, therefore, the enthusiastic acceptance of the Council and its aftermath (including 'left-wing' social encyclicals like *Populorum Progressio*), on the one hand, and the defence of Catholic tradition against modernist encroachments, on the other, were not only not contradictory: it was necessary to say more than that: that they were inseparable. It was no wonder that Catholic liberals did not know what to make of them.

The Anglican dissidents, for their part, found themselves, after November 1992, considering conversion to a Church of which, though in some ways they knew it very well indeed, they were wholly ignorant in others. They had steeped themselves for years in its theology and devotional practices; they had taken to themselves and illegally celebrated a version of one or other of its liturgies, ancient or modern; they had emotionally identified with it as much as and in many cases more than they did with the Church of England. But the dark and swirling waters of the internal politics of post-Conciliar Catholicism, these the refugees understood as little as cradle Catholics understood the refugees. Partly, the Anglican dissidents misunderstood why they were mistrusted; wholly they were misunderstood by many of the Catholics who sought to stand in their way. Essentially, the problem was this: that Catholics had their own problems and their own internal divisions; and the only way they could make sense of these strange Anglicans was to translate them into Roman Catholic terms. Thus, the Anglican dissidents became, for Catholic liberals, part of Catholic problems and divisions.

A personal anecdote makes the point clearly enough. When I was on the verge of being received into the Catholic Church I received letters from three main sources. There was the Protestant hate mail (mostly from Northern Ireland and Scotland); there were a good number of letters from both Anglicans and Catholics wishing me well on my pilgrimage; finally, there were letters from a number of Catholics who, having perceived that I was described in press reports as an Anglican 'traditionalist', kindly sent details of where I could find the 'Old Mass' celebrated, and how I might become involved in the campaign to restore its regular use and much else besides. But I had never attended the Tridentine Mass; it was nothing to me. The Mass I wanted to attend was the Mass everyone else attended: not because it was self-evidently the most perfect liturgy ever produced, but because it was what the Church did: it was what would make me one with all other Catholics.

GOING HOME

For the Anglican dissidents, 'swimming the Tiber' was never seen as a matter of going from one embattled subculture to another: it was seen as a return to the rock whence they were hewn, or, to mix metaphors yet again, a rejoining of the mainstream. That was not necessarily how they were perceived from the Catholic side of the divide. As we have seen, Catholic liberals like Bishop Hollis saw them very differently indeed, as 'a political faction, using bluff and pressure to get its own way'. And he was determined that they 'cannot be allowed to do that in a Catholic context'. In fact, there had never been the remotest risk of that: one of the great attractions of Rome for Anglo-Catholics had always been the ultimate prospect of peace after the storm, of final release from the perpetual struggle of maintaining a Catholic position within a Church which, however hard they tried to believe otherwise, had always been intrinsically hostile to them and everything they stood for. 'The heaviest burden you will have to bear', said Canon Donald Nicholson in 1977, at a retreat for ordinands from the Anglo-Catholic seminary, St Stephen's House, 'will be the burden of being faithful priests in an apostate Church.' The last thing any of them wanted now was to carry on the endless battle: before them at last was the reality that Newman had described in a famous passage from the *Apologia pro Vita Sua* that had been a beacon in the night to so many Anglican converts down the years:

> From the time that I became a Catholic, of course I have no further history of my religious opinions to narrate. In saying this, I do not mean to say that my mind has been idle, or that I have given up thinking on theological subjects; but that I have had no variations to record, and have had no anxiety of heart whatever. I have been in perfect peace and contentment; I never have had one doubt. I was not conscious to myself, on my conversion, of any change, intellectual or moral, wrought in my mind. I was not conscious of firmer faith in the fundamental truths of Revelation, or of more self-command; I had not more fervour; but it was like coming into port after a rough sea; and my happiness on that score remains to this day without interruption.

Roman Catholics, however (whether 'conservative' or 'liberal') did not tend to perceive their own Church – the Church of the post-Conciliar period – as a tranquil 'port after a rough sea', and did not believe that the would-be converts possibly could either. The truth was, however, that, no less than Newman himself, Anglican converts always had and always would so perceive it. The divisions of the post-Conciliar Church were and remain irrelevant, next to the almost universal experience of former Anglicans that at long last they have come home. If Catholics had difficulty in empathizing with this perception, Anglicans for their part could not quite understand Catholics who spoke to them in admonitory tones of the divisions they would find within the Catholic Church itself as though they were in any way commensurate with what they had experienced all their lives.

This particular Anglican attitude was wholly justified by the reality of the situation, for the divisions within Catholicism, such as they were, were of a wholly different degree of seriousness to those now bringing about what was – so far as the dissidents could see – if not Anglicanism's final disintegration, certainly its radical transformation into something else. But Catholic perceptions of the chaos and disunity of their own Church were no less distressing for that. They formed an important element in the modern Catholic psyche; and the modern Catholic psyche was a vital part of what the Anglican converts now had to comprehend. Just as immigrants to the United States learn the Gettysburg address by heart, so the great battlefield sagas of the Council and the post-Conciliar period would have to become part of their own acquired historical memory: for, to become a Catholic is not merely to be convinced by a particular theology, it is to be absorbed into a culture, and therefore into the mythology that forms that culture. The only difficulty was that the history was still being written, and there were several mythologies to choose from.

'WHAT DOES THE COUNCIL MEAN?'

What the Council had meant to them as Anglicans would never be lost. But if it was to mean anything now, it would have to become part of something wider. They now had to be integrated, not so much into an already achieved understanding of what the Council meant to the Western Church as a whole, but into the as yet incomplete process whereby the meaning of the Council was still emerging. The questions they would have to begin asking were exactly the same questions that cradle

Catholics were still asking after thirty years: not only 'What does the Council mean?' but 'What, exactly, is it that has been happening, in the Catholic Church and to the Catholic Church, for the last three decades?'

Many certainties, indeed, the converts would be granted on being received into the Catholic Church: but the answer to that question would not be one of them. There is still no consensus on the matter: when you ask a random sample of thinking Catholics, who actually lived through the changes, how they see the years that followed the Council, the result can still be reminiscent of nothing so much as the opening paragraph of Charles Dickens's novel about the French Revolution, *A Tale of Two Cities*: 'It was the best of times, it was the worst of times, it was the age of wisdom, it was the age of foolishness, it was the epoch of belief, it was the epoch of incredulity, it was the season of Light, it was the season of Darkness, it was the spring of hope, it was the winter of despair ...'

The confusion and unrest were thought obviously undesirable by many Catholics, whether lay or ordained. But for some, the crisis was desirable in itself. 'In the past,' wrote Peter Hebblethwaite,

> every hint and rumour of conflict tended to be suppressed. The front remained solid. The bland led the bland. But what was suppressed did not disappear: it simply went underground and poisoned the Church's life, causing bitterness and frustration. The openness of conflicts in the post-Conciliar Church represents a victory for honesty, and it transforms our idea of the Church: no longer a vast monolith marching inexorably forwards and brushing aside the accidents of history, it becomes a people, with all the diversity, turbulence, pressure groups, public opinion and tough argument that characterizes a real people.

What most came under threat was one of the claims of the Catholic Church that many Anglicans – who had had quite enough of diversity, turbulence, pressure groups, public opinion and tough argument – found most appealing: the belief that the Church had authority to define and if necessary impose doctrine. The weakening of the unquestioned authority of the Magisterium was for many the principal gain of the chaos of the post-Conciliar period. 'At its best,' wrote Hebblethwaite in *The Runaway Church*, 'the transition from pre-Conciliar to post-Conciliar was one from arrogance to humility, from unjustifiable certainty to legitimate doubt, from security to hesitation, from swagger to stammer, from triumphalism to sharing in "the joys and the hopes, the griefs and the anxieties of the men of this age" (On the Church in the Modern World, I) .'

But the question for many was this: do we best help our fellow man in his anxieties by becoming anxious ourselves? One man's 'legitimate doubt' is another man's refusal to accept that the truth may indeed be known by the Church with certainty, and defined and taught by her. According to some observers, the results of this transition from 'unjustifiable certainty to legitimate doubt' – in some parts of the Church at least – have been catastrophic. 'In doctrine now,' according to James Hitchcock, a former editor of *Communio*, 'a Catholic (including a Catholic priest) may be anything from a Tridentine rigorist to a Unitarian. The spirit of liberation from old rigidities is so pervasive that many of those in a position to shape the present spirit which governs the Church seem determined to avoid at all costs anything specific, distinctive, or unique, anything which could delineate a Catholicism as a way of life.'

But how true is this? The question is of obvious relevance to potential Anglican converts, since one of the obstacles every one of them has to surmount at some point is to be told that of course, Anglicanism is divided and uncertain, but there is no longer any certainty to be had anywhere: that if they go to Rome, they will be going from the frying pan into the fire. Hitchcock's assertion that 'a Catholic (including a Catholic priest) may be anything from a Tridentine rigorist to a Unitarian' sounds uncomfortably like a confirmation that that is precisely what they will be doing.

The reality could hardly be more different, however. In the Anglican Church, in which every vicar or rector is his own Pope and there is no appeal to the beliefs of the Church at large (because nobody knows how to ascertain what they are), it matters desperately if your own vicar is a heretic. Catholics, on the other hand, liberals included, really do believe in the universality of the Church, that they really are part of a genuinely (though not always smoothly) functioning *sensus fidelium*: if their parish priest is a heterodox quasi-Marxist progressive, or for that matter, a heterodox Lefebvrist reactionary, it is a local irritation rather than something much worse. There is such a thing, Catholics believe, as the truth; it is the same truth for everyone, and in one way or another the Catholic Church will receive it and declare it: there may be periods of confusion, and the process may be prolonged: but in the end the Spirit will lead the Church into all truth.

It is worthwhile to emphasize this distinction, for it is at the root of the growing appeal of Catholicism to members of what Americans call the 'mainline' liberal Protestant churches. However similar the conflicts within Anglicanism and Catholicism may seem to an outsider, for an Anglican to become a Catholic is by no means a matter of moving from one uncertainty to another: it is to leave behind what they perceive as a fundamental and ineradicable incoherence to become part of the bone and tissue of an ecclesial organism, *in which an indestructible unity is part of its essential nature.* It has, of course, immediately to be added that this unity is sometimes – at this point in history as so often in the past – partly obscured to the naked eye. But the difference between the two Churches is that, however depressed by the present state of the Church some Catholics may be (and I suspect that they are, in any case, fewer than is sometimes supposed), they have a real faith that in the end the Church is built on solid rock, and that against it the gates of hell will not prevail. Few Anglicans (even those who remain staunchly loyal) have any such faith in the long-term future of their Church; and modern Anglicanism, by contrast, is expressly built, not on a body of revealed, more or less clearly delineated and objectively understood truth, but on the sands of relativism and doubt – so much is this the case that relativism and doubt are almost regarded as signs of intellectual integrity.

The distinction between modern Anglican and Roman Catholic divisions, that is to say, is one of kind and not of degree. It has to do with the contrast between, on the one hand, the inbuilt Catholic instinct that the Church's perception of truth emerges in the end from the community's encounter with God and, on the other, Anglicanism's growing dependence on achieving an ever shifting balance, continuously negotiated between innumerable private subjectivities. It is a distinction which establishes modern Anglicanism (in sharp contrast with previous Anglicanisms) as a fundamentally – and probably irreversibly – liberal Protestant phenomenon, within which the Catholic mind no longer has any tolerable resting place.

THE END OF THE TRUCE

None of this is to imply that Catholics have nothing to learn from Protestants (though it is one of the achievements of the Council that they have considerably less to learn now than they did). It is to say, however, that Catholics and Protestants have fundamentally irreconcilable theologies of the Church, with all that flows from that for scholarship, spirituality and the day to day exercise of faith. Edward Norman points to the essential difference between a Catholic assembly such as the Vatican Council and such Protestant-dominated gatherings as the World Council of Churches (and, he might have added, Anglicanism's Synods and Conventions, including the Lambeth Conference itself). 'In place of the Council Fathers,' comments Norman,

> with their sense of internal authority and organic responsibility, these Protestant gatherings are occasions of individual judgement by the collected assemblage of diverse moralists. The results are resolutions of majorities, not the discovery of the mind of an organic unity. There may, of course, be all kinds of good reasons why this is the case, and if Christ did not, after all, commit the knowledge of himself to an infallible institution then a periodic demonstration of scarcely controlled ecclesiastical shambles might be an unavoidable accompaniment of the diversity of truth as perceived by fallible men. Or it could be too great an absorption into the world's own priorities.

Norman's preference for 'internal authority and organic responsibility' over 'scarcely controlled ecclesiastical shambles' is clear enough, and it is worthwhile to point out in passing that Norman represents a classical Anglican view of the Church rather than a specifically Tractarian or Anglo-Catholic one. His view could indeed, only a generation ago, have been cited as representing mainstream Anglicanism; this in itself demonstrates modern Anglicanism's growing instability. Norman's analysis also exemplifies something else: it is an excellent example of the kind of polemical writing that until the sixties would have been produced not by a member of one of the 'separated Churches' about his own side, but by a Catholic apologist establishing the superiority of his own position. It is an example, that is to say, of how polemics have come to be produced within more than between ecclesial communities.

The old style of anti-Catholic polemic, however, saw something of a revival in the period following Low Week 1993. Some of it – especially that coming from certain Anglican laymen – was, as we shall see, of a fairly uninhibited kind. Just as interesting (though much less invigorating) was an example of polemic masquerading as reasoned argument produced by that archetype and model of the Anglican liberal intelligentsia, the former Provost of Southwark, the Very Revd David L. Edwards.

His book *What is Catholicism: An Anglican responds to the official teaching of the Roman Catholic Church* (1994) has the initials 'RC' – the habitual patronizing designation of Catholics in England – in huge shocking pink letters taking up most of its front cover. For the most part, however, the book's anti-Papist offensiveness subsists in its bland and studiously 'charitable' tone – Pecksniff rather than Paisley; David L. Edwards is a smooth man, not a hairy man.

The book provides a perfect demonstration of what it is that distinguishes the Catholic and the liberal Protestant views, not only of the Church but of Truth itself: it also epitomizes what it is about the liberal ascendancy within Anglicanism that so many Anglicans (not necessarily Anglo-Catholic by any means) have come to find quite literally intolerable. At the very root of the distinction is the way in which this kind of Anglicanism has come to see its relevance to our times as being wholly dependent on its own absorption into the *Zeitgeist*.

The logical process goes something like this:

1. We live in a sceptical age, in which people do not believe what falls outside the boundaries of human reason.
2. Therefore we need a new kind of religion, which is designed to fit within these new limitations.
3. Since the Catholic Church continues to assert a faith which is not subordinated to the human mind's capacity to demonstrate it, it is to that extent irrelevant to the modern age.

The first of these general propositions is at the heart of Edwards's attack on Catholicism. 'In the industrial or post industrial nations which are becoming increasingly science-based in their cultures as well as their economies,' he asserts, 'the spiritual and moral vacuum left by the decline or disappearance of definite religious belief also grows. No answer to this crisis will seem convincing if it depends on mythology

[sic] or metaphysics. This modern or post-modern world of thought wants things it can see and touch, the rest being thought of as "imagination" or "emotion" or "guesswork" or "personal preference". And so if it wants a religion, it wants one which stands within the limits of experience alone although it may reach out to a mystery beyond.'

But there is a fundamental question here. It is whether or not any kind of viable and commonly held faith – that is, any faith which has both objective content and spiritual potency – can actually exist if we stand 'within the limits of experience alone': for everyone's experience is different and everyone's experience too, from a religious point of view, is by definition inadequate: for if it were not inadequate, we would not need a religion in the first place. If we demand a religion 'within the limits of experience alone', what we will end up with is a religion which has neither a universal identity nor any power to change us, since it is a human construct designed to respond to our propensities and perceptions as they are already formed. We will end up with a kind of ecclesiastical Disneyland, offering us the choice of a whole series of spiritual rides, on any one of which we can stay for as long it continues to excite us, but which by its nature makes no demands on our commitment or our obedience to anything beyond ourselves. In short, we will end up (if we are English) with something very like the Church of England or, if we are American, like the Episcopal Church, each of which has not only its own multiform liturgies, but its own particular set of theological choices, designed for the English and the American markets.

THE NEW INFALLIBILITY

The inadequacy of 'experience' as a source of religious authority is not only that it canonizes subjectively based opinion: it is also that it reduces God to the point at which we can not only understand him but control him too – it is precisely the sin of the children of Israel, who melted down their personal knick-knacks to make a golden calf of their own specification, which they then proceeded to put in the place of God. The effect of this remodelling of Christianity for a sceptical market has been (as it was intended to be) revolutionary, particularly in the way it has virtually eliminated the authority of Holy Scripture.

This demotion of Scripture has been carefully planned. Liberal Protestantism over the last 150 years has constructed a purpose-built biblical scholarship, one of whose working principles has been method-ically to exclude the possibility of any manifestation of the miraculous or the supernatural. To take a simple example: the dating of the biblical texts. Jesus is shown, for instance, (in Luke 21:6) prophesying the fall of the Temple, which actually happened in AD 70. Since Jesus could not – if we exclude supernatural foreknowledge – have known this, the con-clusion of modernist scholarship is not only that he did not say it, but that the date of the text itself must be later than AD 70. But suppose the modernists are wrong? Suppose he actually did have the power to fore-tell the future, as Christians have always supposed? It then becomes perfectly possible, not only that the story is true, but that the gospel account has an earlier date than AD 70.

By the application of modernist textual criticism of this kind (criti-cism which essentially assumes what it proceeds to conclude), liberal reductionists like David L. Edwards are enabled to dismiss the Catholic Church's understanding of fundamental doctrines such as the Virgin Birth and the bodily Resurrection of Christ as 'mythology'. This kind of intellectual sleight of hand is still little understood, and this is not the place to give it the detailed attention it needs:[1] it is enough here to say that modern biblical criticism has its own hidden agenda, based on its own set of essentially secular intellectual presuppositions. These amount to a kind of antique mechanistic scientism which is itself look-ing increasingly outdated, particularly among scientists. And in the words of the eminent biblical scholar Henning Graf von Reventlow, 'Now ... when we can see the intrinsic fragility of these presupposi-tions ... it is desirable that we should dig deeper and uncover the ideo-logical and social roots to which more recent biblical criticism owes its origin ...'

David L. Edwards's attack on the authority of the biblical record is precisely the same as his attack on the authority of the Catholic Magis-terium itself: essentially, it stems from a refusal to accept that God acts directly in human affairs, that the supernatural can irrupt into the nat-ural world. The Church, for him, is a man-made human experiment;

---

[1] For the best analysis of the intellectual processes of modernist biblical criti-cism see Hankey, Wayne, 'The Bible in a post-critical age', in ed. Oddie, William, *After the Deluge: Essays towards the Desecularisation of the Church* (London, 1987), pp. 41–93. See also pp. 23–4.

for Catholics by contrast it is a divinely instituted organism which is directly under the authority of God, whose power flows through its sacraments directly into the lives of the faithful. The Bible, for Edwards, is a series of texts which have no authority which is not established by human scholarship. For example, 'we cannot,' he says, 'rely on the words in John's gospel where Jesus speaks of the glory which he had with the Father before the world began, for it is generally agreed by the scholars that those were not the words of the historical Jesus'. Even if this were so, this would not, by itself, rob the words of authority if we still believe that in some other way they were divinely inspired. But there is another point to be made here: it is that nowhere does Edwards ask to what extent we can 'rely on the words' of the scholars themselves: he simply assumes that the biblical texts are factually unreliable but that the liberal scholars he agrees with are for all practical purposes infallible.

ONLY AN HYPOTHESIS

The fact is, however, that 'modern scholarship' has proved nothing whatsoever: it is all simply a matter of opinion. We know little more about the texts themselves than we knew in the Middle Ages: in the words of one unusually frank liberal Anglican biblical critic, Canon Anthony Harvey (in his 1980 Bampton Lectures), 'Nothing new has been discovered. The evidence is exactly the same as it always was: the bare text of the Gospels ... *There is no discovery, only an hypothesis* [my italics].'

On the basis of an unprovable hypothesis, in other words, liberal Protestants like Edwards assail not only the authority of Scripture but that of any Church which still holds to belief in Scripture's divine inspiration. Biblically based documents like the Catechism of the Catholic Church are thus presented as obscurantist and out of touch with 'the assured results of modern scholarship'; most obscurantist of all is the Pope who authorizes its teachings with such simple-minded faith (Edwards's patronizing attitude to Pope John Paul – who is hardly an intellectual lightweight – is particularly unattractive).

It is worthwhile remaining with the distinction between the Catholic mind and that of Dr Edwards for just a little longer: for, though Edwards's views have certainly not been uncontested within Anglicanism, he was for two decades and more the most prominent spokesman and ideologue in England for the ecclesiastical party which embodies what Newman called the 'sceptical' principle within Anglicanism – the party, that is, which is presently in the ascendant, and whose greatest political triumph has been women's ordination.

Where does the real difference lie? We can see it most strongly, perhaps, in the distinct ways in which the two Churches see their relationship with the *saeculum*, the passing age. The Catholic Church thinks in centuries, not in decades; the old cliché sums up the difference as well as any. Liberal Anglicanism carries within itself little notion that the provisional intellectual orthodoxies of the particular historical period to which it is currently responding are anything but set in stone. The Anglican Evangelical minister David Holloway, in an open letter to Edwards published in the *Church Times* in 1985, identified the period that formed the modern Anglican liberal mind-set:

> So many liberal Protestants seem to me to be inhabiting ... a ghost world long past. Some, indeed, are intellectually still locked into the 'Sixties' (the period when you were at the SCM Press and published *Honest to God*). Thus there is a liberal form of 'fundamentalism'. It is an inability to escape from a fixed 'belief in Science' (with a capital 'S').

It is part of this liberal fundamentalism to insist that lack of absolute clarity or consistency are inimical to certainty of faith in a 'scientific age': thus, in his attack on the *Catechism of the Catholic Church*, Edwards condemns its account of the Resurrection as being 'not related to the questions of our time'. What he means by this is that despite apparent inconsistencies in the gospel texts, the *Catechism* accepts them all as part of the truth. Like Bishop David Jenkins, Edwards wants to claim he believes that the Resurrection is 'true'; but not necessarily that it involves Jesus's physical body. He is alive in the minds and hearts of his followers: that is an idea Edwards believes he can sell in a 'scientific age'. The Catholic teaching, however is that the Resurrection must be a bodily Resurrection, since Christ is God Incarnate; for the Incarnation to be, as it were, phased out at the very point at which it reaches its culmination is to make it a nonsense.

BELIEVING THE MYSTERY

This teaching is, of course, a mystery: but – and here we see the fundamental difference between Catholicism and anything less – for a
Catholic, to believe in a mystery is not necessarily to believe in something uncertain: it is simply to believe in something his mind cannot contain but will accept on trust. This is what Newman meant when he said
that 'a thousand difficulties do not make one doubt'. For Edwards, in
stark contrast, 'The essential Christian faith that "he rose from the dead"
could have been commended more persuasively in our time had there
been a greater acknowledgement of this element of mystery *and therefore of uncertainty*, in the only accounts available to us' [my italics]. Mystery and certainty, in such a view, cannot exist together. Not only that;
we live in an age of uncertainty; *therefore we need an uncertain faith*.
Catholicism is diametrically opposed to both these propositions.

It is precisely the Catholic refusal to allow the *depositum fidei*,
the deposit of faith, to be compromised by passing intellectual fash-
ions, that is one of the essential features of the Catholic mind. There
is here – as in all intellectual integrity – a certain element of bloody-
mindedness. It is this particular refusal that led Edward Norman to
characterize the documents of the Second Vatican Council as being
essentially conservative, 'in the sense that the "mystery" of the
Church was never submerged beneath accommodations to the values
of the secular culture'; 'mystery' here means something sure and giv-
en, not a mere absence of hard evidence: 'conservationist' rather than
'conservative' might be a better word.   ❧

This clash of values is nowhere more marked than when we consider the Papacy itself, surely in this age more than at any previous period
in its history a 'sign of contradiction'. The enemies of the Papacy are as
vocal today within the Catholic Church as without (though in most
Catholic countries they represent only a self-important minority of
malcontents): opposition to the papacy of John Paul II has become,
indeed, the basis of a new élitist ecumenism. Catholic enemies of the
Pope like Hans Küng are heroes of the Anglican establishment. David
Edwards's book begins, significantly, with a letter 'To an unknown
Pope', the one who will succeed John Paul (perhaps he hopes it will be
the Cardinal Archbishop of Milan, also a great Anglican favourite):
Edwards pleads with this unknown Pope to install immediate inter-
communion, to ordain women, and to repudiate the *Catechism of the*

Catholic Church. As John Paul grows older and visibly more bowed by illness and the weight of his office, his enemies await his death impatiently, hoping for better times. One liberal Catholic journalist, in a little restaurant close to St Peter's, was reported as saying that 'Nothing he has done will outlast him. Not the Catechism, not *Veritatis Splendor*, not the document on the ordination of women ... The new man will put aside everything John Paul has done and start over again.'

DIVING BENEATH THE STORM

That is what they hope; but whether it will happen is entirely another question. The longing of these enemies of John Paul's papacy for the installation, even at this late date, of the liberal orthodoxies of the sixties has about it a remoteness from reality that does little to instil confidence in their judgement. There is a new mood now; not for a 'restoration' of the pre-Conciliar Church, but for a rediscovery of the real continuity of the Catholic tradition beneath the chaos of recent decades. I asked Professor J.J. Scarisbrick, the leading historian of the English Reformation, and an active lay Catholic, how he sees the future of the Church. Professor Scarisbrick is under no illusions about the difficulties. 'I believe that a lot of people are confused,' he thinks; 'they can't understand why so many priests are disappearing, why the nuns who used to teach in the convent up the road have disappeared, why so many Catholic practices that were part and parcel of their devotional life have been discontinued. But the Church will pass through this time of confusion. If I look at what is happening in many parts of the world from a merely human perspective, I wouldn't put my money on it. But the Church has been written off before by those who look at things from a merely human perspective. I know – I know – that Our Lord's promise will be kept: that against his Church the gates of Hell will not prevail.'

It is precisely here that we can locate what has always been, for those Anglicans who in the end convert to Rome, the turning point in their journey. As one Anglican clergyman put it to me, 'Whatever difficulties Rome may be going through, there's one thing Our Lord did not say: "Thou art Peter, and on this rock I will build my Church of England".' Those Anglicans who form the reservoir from which many of the converts of the coming decades will be drawn know much more about the Catholic Church than most English or American Roman

Catholics suspect. They are well aware of the tensions and conflicts of modern Catholicism. But they perceive much more clearly than some Catholics do where the difference lies between an Anglican liberalism whose final point of development can only be a full-blown secularism, and a Catholic liberalism whose intention is not to dismantle tradition as a working principle, but to cleanse it of what it perceives – rightly or wrongly – as accretions or aberrant historical developments, especially in the way in which authority in the Church is exercised.

In the end, that is to say, Catholic-minded Anglicans are often much more clearly aware of the essential unity of Catholicism, only a few fathoms beneath the *Sturm und Drang* of the post-Conciliar Church. Today's Roman Catholics have not been used to handling life in a confused and contumacious Church: and many, particularly the traditionally minded, find it depressing in the extreme. Anglican converts have lived in a Church divided in an infinitely more fundamental way for over 400 years, and do not see what all the fuss is about: what they tend to perceive first when they become Catholics are the fundamental principles within Catholicism which bind Catholics together, even when they themselves suppose they are divided.

CHAPTER NINE

THE WEIGHT
OF HISTORY

*Is it possible that, after all, we shall come to think that Catholic eman-
cipation has turned out to be a mistake?*
Ferdinand Mount, *The Spectator*, 29 January 1994

IN JANUARY 1994, The Duchess of Kent – after the Queen and the
Queen Mother perhaps the best-loved member of the Royal family –
was received into the Catholic Church. It was (it could hardly have been
otherwise) an occasion of deep satisfaction for most English Catholics.
It was not only that this devout and lovable woman had come home;
there was also a real feeling that with the conversion of a major Royal,
history too had, in some sense, come full circle. *The Tablet*'s cover
illustration that week conveyed the heightened atmosphere of the
time. Two historical tableaux were shown: next to Cardinal Hume welcoming the Duchess into the Church stood Elizabeth I condemning St
Edmund Campion to a martyr's death. It was as though in some way the
rejection and marginalization of the past was being undone; but there
was also, perhaps, a hope among many that what the English and Welsh
Catholic martyrs died for was coming to a kind of fruition, that a Royal
conversion had surely to be the harbinger of something wider than
itself.

The Duchess's conversion elicited a by now familiar exchange of
public declarations, designed to discourage any such interpretation.
The Archbishops of Canterbury and York declared that it was 'the personal decision of a devout Christian on a spiritual journey'. Such journeys, continued the Archbishops, 'quite commonly lead individuals
across the denominational boundaries ...' The statement concluded by

insisting that the relationship between Anglicans and Roman Catholics was 'warmer and more co-operative than ever before'.

From Cardinal Hume, there emerged a complementary statement, similarly designed to discourage the inference that anything with more than a merely private significance had taken place: 'We must', he said, 'respect a person's conscience in these matters, and I know that the Duchess recognizes how much she owes to the Church of England.'

Other Catholics felt they had no such obligation to be tactful. Most tactless of all, perhaps, was the veteran journalist Paul Johnson. 'Is the cause', he wrote in his column in *The Spectator*, 'for which St Thomas More died on Tower Hill, St Edmund Campion was hanged, drawn and quartered at Tyburn, Cardinal Newman preached, Cardinal Manning fought and schemed, and a host of great writers – Belloc and Chesterton, Maurice Baring and Evelyn Waugh, Christopher Dawson and Ronald Knox – devoted their splendid talents, now at last in sight of victory?'

It was that word, 'victory', which sparked off the furious article by the editor of the *Times Literary Supplement*, Ferdinand Mount, – also in *The Spectator* – which inaugurated the strange affair of the 'Popish plot'. The ecumenical improvements of the post-Vatican II era were, it seemed, all a characteristically Romish deceit: or so Mount affected to believe. 'Victory,' he exclaimed: 'Ah, so there was a war on, after all. The ambitions for the conversion of England were never abandoned, never even modified, but only expressed *sotto voce* for tactical reasons.' 'There is', noted Mount, 'no disguising the note of stifled excitement in the pronouncements of Catholic spokesmen and journalists.' Among the journalists, he mentioned the novelist Piers Paul Read, and the present writer: '"The Church of England is finished" cries Mr William Oddie with all the exuberance of a recent convert.' (I have been unable to trace this quotation in anything I have written.)

THE ESTABLISHMENT STRIKES BACK

Mount's onslaught was followed the next day by an attack in *The Times*, produced by a previously unknown Oxford chaplain, Tim Bradshaw (who turned out to be a former colleague of the Archbishop of Canterbury, Dr George Carey). There had, wrote Bradshaw, been a 'consistent onslaught' on the Church of England, 'carried out by Roman Catholic journalists, notably Paul Johnson, William Oddie, and Clifford

Longley' (Longley promptly responded with a writ for libel). The message was that 'Anglicanism should be replaced by Romanism [an interesting reversion to the polemical vocabulary of an earlier generation] as the nation's primary expression of Church Life.' This, said Bradshaw, was the aim of 'a powerful corps of right-wing journalists committed regularly to write corrosive articles'.

Even stranger – 'A huge media campaign is under way'. This underlined Mount's assessment, that on this issue 'it is the Pope's big guns who dominate the media'. Other articles followed in other newspapers, conveying more or less the same message; but none of them mentioned more than about half a dozen names, mostly freelance writers: apart from those already mentioned, these included Cristina Odone, editor of the *Catholic Herald*; Auberon Waugh, prolific columnist and son of the novelist Evelyn Waugh; and William Rees-Mogg, formerly editor of *The Times*. Most of them who had met did so rarely; there was absolutely no plot.

But the word 'plot' was not used unadvisedly: it was calculated to send a frisson down the average Englishman's historical memory. 'There is a papist plot by a group of writers to undermine the Church of England,' trumpeted the *Times* headline writer above Bradshaw's article, which was given the headline 'Anglicans fear the Catholics who conspire'. The affair of the 'conspiracy' of the Papist journalists showed, if it showed nothing else, how deeply rooted were the anti-Catholic instincts lying just beneath the surface of English (and probably English-speaking) culture. It was all calculated to stir up half-forgotten inherited feelings that – as Charles Moore put it, on the eve of his own conversion, 'there is something creepy about Roman Catholics'.

This perceived creepiness was hard to define, but it included the idea that Catholics were not quite English, that what they got up to was exotic and dangerous, that they had a double loyalty, even that they were part of an international conspiracy (as Dominic Lawson, the Jewish editor of the *Spectator* later pointed out, if you were to replace the word 'Catholic' in Mount's article by the word 'Jewish', it would read remarkably like a case of classic anti-Semitism). Catholics were mistrusted for their reserve; at the same time, they were now given the strong impression that they would be tolerated only if they kept their Catholicism to themselves: 'It would be much nicer,' Mount ended his article, 'if ... some of our best friends could continue to be the affable and self-effacing papists we used to know.' It was tantamount to a warning that the papists should return to the ghetto from which they were beginning to emerge.

CLOSED IN WITH HIGH WALLS

In a sermon preached in 1852, seven years after his own conversion, John Henry Newman recalled his youthful impressions of Catholic life as being exemplified by 'an old-fashioned house of gloomy appearance, closed in with high walls, with an iron gate, and yews, and the report attaching to it that "Roman Catholics" lived there; but who they were, or what they did, or what was meant by calling them Roman Catholics, no one could tell – though it had an unpleasant sound.' The feeling that there was 'something creepy' about Roman Catholics could be explained to some extent by their defensive withdrawal from the English mainstream. But it had to do also with a consistently applied polemic against Catholicism itself, one which conveyed that Catholics were diffident about their beliefs, not because of any fear of intolerance, but because of their religion's devious and insinuating character. A classic example of this phenomenon is to be found in the controversy which led Newman himself to write his great classic of conversion, the *Apologia pro Vita Sua*.

The circumstances were these. Charles Kingsley (author of *The Water Babies*) had written, in a review of J.A. Froude's *History of England* (itself a good example of the persistently anti-Roman bias of English historiography), that 'Truth, for its own sake, had never been a virtue with the Roman clergy. Father Newman informs us that it need not, and on the whole ought not to be; that cunning is the weapon which heaven has given to the saints wherewith to withstand the brute male force of the wicked world which marries and is given in marriage. Whether his notion is doctrinally correct, it is at least historically so.'

Newman's indignant reply was, in one way, a landmark in the post-Reformation history of Catholicism in England: for the first time, a major Catholic intellectual figure had not only defended his Church, but had gained massively in public stature by doing so. Nevertheless, the contemporary response was almost unanimous in refusing to extend to Newman's religion the admiration it lavished on Newman himself. He tended to be seen as a tragic figure, a 'fallen angel, but still an angel' in the words of one reviewer. There was a widespread feeling that, though Kingsley had picked on the wrong target in Newman, his attack on Romanism for its cunning and dishonesty was far from unjustified. The staunchly protestant *North British Review* for instance, was exceptional only in the vigour of its tone:

If the Romish doctrines regarding equivocation remained as abstract doctrines, there would perhaps be little to be said against them. But, unfortunately, in intercourse with Protestants, they start at once into active and most mischievous life ... the Romanist finds no difficulty in regarding Protestants as the swine before whom pearls are not to be cast ... who are habitually to be treated, on religious subjects at least, with 'economy' ... all the many forms of simulation and dissimulation are allowable in dealing with the outer barbarians; nay, they are positively praiseworthy, if used with the design of 'saving a soul'; in other words, of making a proselyte ... many a family throughout the land can sadly testify that this is the Romish practice.

This notion was at the core of Anglo-Saxon anti-popery, and it was to remain so at a more or less conscious level, for the next hundred years and more. The Catholic Church, it was widely supposed, used fraud and superstition, even physical force, to perpetuate itself: young women for instance, it was widely believed, were imprisoned against their will in convents. The nineteenth century saw the growth of a violent anti-Catholic popular literature. Some of it, as Edward Norman notes, 'like *The Awful Disclosures of Maria Monk*, published in 1836, were of North American origin, indicating the successful emigration of the English "No Popery" popular culture'.

This hostility persisted into the twentieth century: as Adrian Hastings puts it, writing of the twenties, Catholics, in religious and even in political terms, 'were felt and felt themselves to stand extraordinarily apart, the object of profound latent suspicion able to burst forth from time to time ... in an almost paranoid gust of popular hostility, evoking memories of gunpowder, Titus Oates and the Gordon Riots'.

THE END OF THE ELIZABETHAN SETTLEMENT

Much had changed since then. Nevertheless, Mount's article – with its only half-joking opening question 'Is it possible that we shall come to think that Catholic Emancipation has turned out to be a mistake?' – was an indication that, for some at least, the old antagonisms were not dead but sleeping. Certainly, the imagery of popular anti-popery lay easily to hand, only lightly buried beneath the surface topsoil of more recent civilities. Those papist writers on church affairs who so much as publicly alluded to Anglicanism's current difficulties (and since it was of an Established Church they were writing, it was something they were not only entitled but almost duty-bound to do) now became fair game: the purpose of all conspiracy theories is to find scapegoats when things go wrong. The *Guardian*'s account of the affair was written by the ecumenically minded crypto-Anglican, the 'liberal' Catholic Peter Stanford. 'The Guy Fawkes of this conspiracy to turn England Catholic', wrote Stanford, 'is historian and left-to-right political convert Paul Johnson. Aspiring [sic] to the role of Titus Oates are William Oddie ... and Lord Rees-Mogg, who has turned his column in *The Times* over to an assault on every vestige of Anglicanism.' (Titus Oates, of course, was part of an anti-*Catholic* conspiracy.)

What the affair of the supposedly conspiring papist hacks showed most clearly was that the Anglican Establishment and its apologists were now badly rattled – for the articles complained of (Johnson, perhaps, apart) hardly bore the construction placed on them. What they did reflect (and not only Catholic journalists had arrived at the same conclusion) was a sense widespread at this time that a fundamental historical shift was under way, in which current ecclesiastical controversies were only one element. If the papists, after all this time, were coming out from behind their high walls, perhaps much else was changing, too.

Certainly, such notions were in the air: and it was not Catholics alone who had put them there. At the press conference given by Cardinal Hume to launch the 1993 Low Week statement, a non-Catholic journalist had asked Cardinal Hume if current events marked the end of the Elizabethan settlement of religion: 'Could be,' the Cardinal had succinctly replied, after a very brief pause for thought. He took good care to say no more. The Elizabethan settlement, the national mythology that had grown out of it, and its historical reinforcements with the 'glorious revolution', the penal laws and much else besides, had not merely put the papists in their place: they had laid down the foundations of the Englishman's national self-consciousness. The Elizabethan settlement and all that flowed from it was the foundation, not only for the Established Church but of English patriotism *contra mundum*: thus, a lot more was at stake here than the change of allegiance of a few hundred spiky clergymen and their followers.

The Elizabethan settlement, followed by a long history of popular anti-popery – often deliberately induced – created something else: not only the political and social marginalization of English Catholics but also the ingrained separatism of the English Catholic mind. It needs to be added that from this enforced marginalization came also much that was most admirable about the English Catholic tradition. The English Reformation of the sixteenth century, as the Anglican historian Edward Norman argues,

> left the Catholics in ... an excluded condition, cut off from the vital Protestant culture in which the modern State in this country was born and developed. What is most unusual about their subsequent history is that it did not follow the patterns so familiar in their condition. The English Catholic 'recusants' – those who refused to conform to the laws of the unitary Protestant establishment – did not develop sectarian qualities, did not become political radicals ... did not deviate from orthodoxy, and did not, above all, quietly slide back into a comfortable acquiescence with the new order. Theirs is a noble history of enormous self-sacrifice for higher purposes, and of a rooted determination to preserve both their English virtue and their religious allegiance in a sensible and clear balance.

REASSESSMENT OR *RECONQUISTA*?

The 'excluded condition' of English Catholics may have had some impressive results; it was the result, nevertheless, of a persistent injustice in English life which could ultimately be justified intellectually in only one way: by arguing that the English Reformation *as it actually took place* was a necessary event, which expressed the popular will, and was the inevitable response to the corruption and remoteness of the Catholic Church as the Middle Ages drew to a close.

This had been the historiographical orthodoxy until very recently. But by an interesting coincidence, this orthodoxy, which had been looking increasingly insecure for over a decade, finally collapsed at about this time with the publication of Dr Eammonn Duffy's best-selling historical blockbuster, *The Stripping of the Altars*. It was the feeling that Paul Johnson's exuberant triumphalism was the expression of a more widely based, and solidly founded, intellectual reappraisal of the roots of modern English life that really hit a raw nerve for Anglican intellectuals like Ferdinand Mount. 'Nowhere', he protested, 'is the desire for *reconquista* more evident than in present-day Catholic historiography':

> Distinguished historians like J.J. Scarisbrick and Eammonn Duffy have made considerable headway in convincing their non-Catholic colleagues that throughout the Reformation the English people clung passionately to the old religion which was being taken from them by a minority of fanatical Protestant radicals. By this means, the intervening centuries of fierce popular anti-popery are neatly stepped over, and the Roman Church re-established not only as the one genuinely Catholic church but also as the church of true-born Englishmen, which is soon to come into its own again.

The difficulty for Mount – as he realized himself – was that Duffy's thesis was supported, not merely by other Catholic historians, but by non-Catholic historians too. It was based on painstaking scholarship: it was irresistibly becoming the new consensus because it had every appearance of having been the truth all along. The old historical orthodoxy had been imposed after the struggles of the sixteenth and seventeenth centuries had ended in the apparently final defeat of the Catholic cause: the view that the pre-Reformation Church in England had been remote from the spiritual needs of the people, that it had become decadent and worldly, and that the Reformation was an irresistible popular movement, now collapsed overnight in the face of a huge mass of evidence to the contrary.

As Eammonn Duffy himself explained in *The Stripping of the Altars*: 'Late medieval Christianity exerted an enormously strong, diverse, and vigorous hold over the imagination and loyalty of the people up to the very moment of the Reformation. Traditional religion had about it no particular marks of exhaustion or decay, and indeed in a whole host of ways, from the multiplication of vernacular religious books to adaptations within the national and regional cult of the saints, was showing itself well able to meet new needs and new conditions.'

Dr Duffy shows that in England at any rate, the Reformation was brutally imposed as an act of state upon a reluctant people. Chesterton's characterization of the English Reformation as a 'revolt of the rich against the poor', with the suppression of the religion of the poor as a consolidation of that revolt, had always been dismissed as papist polemics: now it appeared to be vindicated.

THE CLAIMS OF THE PAST

The Reformation attack, for instance, on prayer for the departed, with the suppression of the guilds of all souls and the seizing of their property and Mass stipends, was in Eammonn Duffy's words, 'more than a polemic against a "false" metaphysical belief: it was an attempt to redefine the boundaries of human community, and, in an act of exorcism, to limit the claims of the past and the people of the past, on the people of the present'. It was, in short, to complete the dispossession of the people from their spiritual patrimony by washing away their collective spiritual memory. Anglicanism – first in England and then in North America and the white Dominions – was never to be (except, from the nineteenth century, in some Anglo-Catholic and Evangelical parishes) the religion of the poor as well as the comfortable and the educated.

Does all this matter now? There is today a certain reaction within the Catholic Church against what is dismissed as a mere historicist romanticism, sometimes exemplified by pointing to the convert novelist Evelyn Waugh's acquired recusant notions about English Catholic history. There is also the feeling that to harp on the past is to disinter old resentments, that it is something less than eirenic in an ecumenical age. The difficulty is that the past is not merely where we have come from, it is what we are. For a nation or a people or a community, its history – or at least, how it perceives its history – is what defines it. We can (indeed, we must) set aside the resentments of the past: but we forget it at our peril. Those who have been dispossessed, who have lost the memory of their origins – as, for example, the descendants of the slaves of North America have done – will often go to extreme lengths to rediscover their 'roots': this is why it is now politically incorrect usage to refer to black Americans as anything but African Americans.

This rediscovery of 'the claims of the past and the people of the past' can be very powerfully experienced by converts to Catholicism: for religious conversion is not a merely private matter, it is to leave one community in order to become part of another. One undergoes, that is to say, not merely a spiritual and religious conversion, but a shift in one's sense of historical identity. One becomes aware, by personal experience, of the truth of the old adage that it is the victors who write the history of the events in which they have been victorious: for one of the effects, in England, of leaving the Church of England to become a Roman Catholic is that one leaves a group which has been in recent centuries dominant and joins one which has been subordinated, even oppressed by it.

One's historical perspective, in other words, is *de facto*, to some extent at least, transformed. It occurs to one that the 'Glorious Revolution' was nothing of the kind; one perceives Elizabeth I not as 'Gloriana' but as an unpopular and ruthless dictator whose glamorous image was constructed, exactly like Stalin's cult of personality, by recruiting artists and writers to build it up, and whose power, like Stalin's, was sustained by means of a vast network of spies and informers not wholly dissimilar to the KGB. Elizabethan Jesuits are no longer the devious agents of a foreign power, but heroes of the faith: one could go on.

INHERITED RESENTMENTS

An historical perspective of this kind will not normally be felt as vividly as this. Most English cradle Catholics are not especially indignant about the privileges of the Establishment, even when, perhaps, they should be: as in the case, for instance, of the exclusion of non-Anglicans from most college fellowships in theology at Oxford and Cambridge, or the more pointed and specific disqualification of Catholics or their spouses from the succession to the throne. Nevertheless there is, inevitably, among English cradle Catholics, an inherited sense of exclusion and injustice which in many of them, and perhaps most, hardly manifests itself at all at a conscious level, certainly not as anything like an active sense of bitterness or rancour. It exists, nevertheless.

It may be worth considering whether this was an element in the deep suspicion shown by some Catholics before (and, as we shall see, after) Low Week 1993 towards the idea of making special pastoral arrangements for Anglican converts. For, without necessarily realizing that this is what they were doing, the Anglican dissidents – for all their insistence that they were suppliants – were proposing to abandon the dominant ecclesiastical culture (at the point at which it was visibly losing its dominance) for the historically subordinate culture (at the point at which it appeared to be throwing off its subordination).

It was simply not understood that the Anglo-Catholics were themselves part of a religious subculture which had consistently suffered marginalization, even persecution (including the imprisonment of some of its clergy), at the hands of the Anglican authorities. It simply appeared to some Catholics that having decided to leave the privileges of the Establishment, they now required other privileges to compensate them for what they had lost, privileges which were not necessarily to be granted to born Catholics. One of these privileges most bitterly resented by some Catholic clergy was the dispensation from the celibacy laws granted to some former Anglican clergy who wished to be ordained to the Catholic priesthood.

how come?

It is necessary to say that such resentments were very far from being the dominant sentiment among Catholics towards the prospective converts. But that they existed has, I suggest, to be seen as one important contributing factor in the radical scaling down of the Roman Option which took place, during the latter part of March and the early weeks of April 1993, as Cardinal Hume and his inner group of bishops prepared for the traditional Low Week Conference of all the English and Welsh bishops.

WHAT DID YOU DIE FOR?

After the package had been announced, a group of dissident Anglican clergy went to see one Catholic bishop to see how he interpreted the new dispensation. It soon emerged, not only that he did not regard Catholic Anglicanism as a legitimate phenomenon, but that a recusant – almost a revanchist – psychology was being allowed to have a very clear influence over the way in which their case was being assessed. 'He seemed to snatch a holy glee', remembered one of those present, 'from pointing out that when the Pope went to Canterbury, in spite of promptings from Dr Runcie, he never once referred to him as St Augustine's successor.' Referring to a recent occasion on which the local Anglican bishop had claimed that the Church of England was the ancient Catholic Church of the land, the same Catholic bishop told the assembled dissident clergy that he had gone afterwards to the tomb of one of the English Catholic martyrs. 'What did you die for?' he had asked him. The message was plain: 'It was', said my informant, 'all said jocularly; but said, nevertheless.'

It was a chilling experience for this particular group, perhaps. But, in one sense, the very existence of such feelings among English Catholics, never far from the surface of consciousness, indicated the real sincerity of those bishops whose feelings about the Roman Option were more positive, and who were determined – as Low Week 1993 approached – that old resentments should not be allowed to negate the possibility of a creative response to current events. The bishops' Low Week statement, to which we must now turn our attention, had to reconcile two very different priorities. The first was to create a new and potentially developing situation, in which it would be possible to begin to meet the challenge of the times. The second was to calm the insecurities and antagonisms, both of Catholic liberals (anxious that post-Conciliar Catholicism should not be undermined) and of conservatives, rightly concerned that the faith for which their forebears had suffered and died should not be compromised.

PART THREE

CHAPTER TEN

TWO STEPS FORWARD, ONE STEP BACK

ON FRIDAY 26 April, 1993, Cardinal Hume announced the English and Welsh Catholic bishops' first collective reaction to the Anglican approaches which had been inaugurated by Dr Graham Leonard less than six months before.

Seated at a long table, flanked by bishops Murphy O'Connor, Clarke, and Nicholls, and faced by a packed press conference complete with television cameras and representatives of the world's press, Cardinal Hume expounded a three page document, and answered questions for over an hour. Afterwards, I went to lunch with three experienced and senior religious affairs correspondents from Fleet Street and the BBC. The only thing we were all agreed on was that the Cardinal had just given a brilliant and subtle performance; what we were much less sure about was what it was, exactly, that he had just announced.

The real question was this: had the Cardinal come to bury the Roman Option or to praise it? You could read it either way. A cynic might have said that people saw in the bishops' statement what they wanted to see: he might even have suggested that this interesting document had been carefully drafted so as to make it possible for him to do precisely that. Whether you were an Anglican or a Catholic, your description of the Roman Option as it now appeared to have emerged often depended on how you *hoped* it would emerge. The (Anglican) Bishop of Oxford – who had taken a distinctly unsympathetic line with his own dissidents – described it with undisguised satisfaction as 'a real douche of cold water from Rome'; Dr Graham Leonard (still an Anglican bishop, but soon to begin his own move towards reception and eventual ordination as a Catholic priest) saw it as 'so pastoral, sensitive and positive that it brings deep satisfaction and real joy'. Which was it in fact: a douche of cold water, or 'pastoral, sensitive and positive'?

AN ESSAY IN AMBIGUITY

The answer is that it was both. The idea of a prelature – or any other sort of parallel Anglican Catholic entity – was ruled out: certainly for the foreseeable future. There was to be no Pastoral Provision on the American model. There was to be no Anglican rite. But groups could be received: the old model of individual 'submissions' only was, to that extent, superseded, though at the moment of reception, each member of the group would make his own profession of faith. There would be a reordination of clergy wishing to become Catholic priests: but it would be made clear that their previous ministry was now receiving its fulfilment and not its negation. In brief: things had moved forward, but it was not, yet at least, the breakthrough that many had hoped for.

The greatest disappointment for some Anglicans was the apparent abandonment of the notion that a way needed to be found in which the cultural and liturgical riches of Anglicanism (many of which themselves had Catholic origins) might be brought back into the Catholic mainstream. There was, many of them found, something chilling about the paragraph which paid lip service to this idea but which also seemed to rule out the essential condition which might have given it meaning: the establishment of parishes of Anglican tradition in communion with Rome, fully accepting the Magisterium and the authority of the local Catholic bishop but preserving their own cultural heritage:

> The aim for those who seek to enter into full communion with the Catholic Church must be their eventual total integration into the life of the Catholic community. As pastors we give a ready understanding to those who approach us and we value the riches of the Anglican spiritual heritage which they bring with them.

But what could that mean? What spiritual heritage? What riches? Were these not now to be digested by the dissolving acids of 'total integration', a process which would completely and designedly obliterate this heritage?

At the press conference, one journalist pressed for an answer. Bishop Clarke enthusiastically described what he saw as the most important of these riches: the way in which the Anglican clergy instinctively saw themselves as having a pastoral responsibility to the whole of English society. But this was, of course, an essentially Catholic attitude inherited from the Middle Ages, one which the English Catholic clergy (cut off from these roots) ironically did not share: their attitude to ministry was, one might even argue, in that sense at least, not Catholic at all but sectarian, concerned pastorally not with the whole of society but with their own sometimes inward-looking community. Here, in fact, was a demonstration of the way in which the dissidents had a cultural heritage which *needed* to be brought into modern English Catholicism, not simply for the continuing spiritual sustenance of the new converts, but to illuminate certain cultural blindnesses of the contemporary English Catholic Church itself: it was, or could have been, a repatriation of part of the English Catholic tradition which had been forcibly destroyed in the parent Church. It might have operated rather like the replanting in France of French vine stocks taken to America, which had escaped the blight of phylloxera which had partially wiped out the vineyards of their country of origin. That was certainly a metaphor which could be applied to the converts' attitude to ministry: but was there not a wider sense in which a carefully selective but full-hearted cultural and liturgical transplantation of the Catholic element in Anglicanism's ancient heritage might have enriched English Catholicism by supplying what perforce it so notably lacked: deep roots in the mainstream of English life and history?

That phrase in the Low Week statement, 'eventual total integration into the life of the Catholic community' was, quite simply, seen by too many Anglicans (particularly among the laity) as a stipulation that they must leave the mainstream English tradition and enter a Catholic ghetto which was itself not typical of Catholicism anywhere else. And for some of those who had been privy to the Westminster conversations (with their wholly different mind-set) the question was irresistible: what had happened to 'united not absorbed'? When the Cardinal was asked at the Low Week press conference (by the present author) whether this phrase could be used to describe the bishops' proposals, he explained that it had been originally intended to describe the future reunion of Canterbury and Rome, not the selective reception of one Anglican tradition. True: but as we have seen, he was the one who had raised the hopes of the Anglican representatives at the Westminster conversations by repeatedly describing the Roman Option in this way, a description duly recorded in the official minutes of more than one of the meetings. The assumption among those who knew this was that the Cardinal had not been allowed to have his way by some fellow bishops. But there was more. The record shows that the phrase had been introduced into the current discussions 'from Rome': it was not the only indication (as we shall see) that the mind of 'Rome' was very much less cautious than the collective mind of the Catholic bishops of England and Wales.

There was, nevertheless, enough in the statement to make it possible to argue that a future development towards this end had not been wholly ruled out. The bishops spoke of 'those who wish to become Catholics, whether *as part of a group* or individually' (my emphasis). These would 'follow a process of reception which includes an appropriate catechesis leading to the rite of reception, namely, individual profession of faith, reception into full communion, reconciliation [confession], Confirmation and Eucharist.' Nothing unexpected there. But –

> For those who approach us *as a group* we envisage the possibility of some temporary pastoral arrangements which will help them, after their reception, to become fully integrated into the local Catholic community. *This is a matter for further consideration and decision at a later date* ... [my emphasis].

What was temporary? Who was to say, in a Church whose watchword was that it thought in centuries not decades? The Cardinal himself made a point of stressing that 'total integration' was qualified by the adjective 'eventual'. The real point was that the statement laid down principles rather than concrete operational details: the bishops who wished to could use the statement in a dynamic and creative way which might lead to substantial developments for the future: the log-jam of 'individuals only' (or as it had been firmly explained to one Anglican priest – only twelve months before the synodical decision to ordain women – 'no coach parties') had been broken.

It was noted, too, that the statement had several aims. Obviously, to make proposals for the pastoral care of the aspiring Anglo-Catholics. But there were not only hopes to satisfy, but anxieties to address. First, those of the Anglican bishops. It would not do if the English Catholic

Church were to appear unduly predatory; nevertheless, the signal had to be reiterated as tactfully as possible that relationships could no longer be what they had been in the past. So, there was due recognition of 'the progress made in developing ecumenical relations with the Church of England in recent decades', and a commitment to 'continue this dialogue and common effort *in the new circumstances that now obtain*' (my emphasis).

'*TABLE D'HÔTE*, NOT *À LA CARTE*'

But there were other fears that more urgently needed to be allayed. Those Catholics who knew nothing of all this had to be brought into the process. All they had had to go on had been press reports which had often included the wildest kind of speculation. Such reports had nevertheless, in these fevered times, sometimes gained passing credence: one story had been to the effect that the converting Anglicans would not need to believe the whole of Catholic doctrine. The story was extraordinary precisely because it was orthodox Catholic doctrine to which they were most passionately committed; that was why they could no longer stay in the Church of England. But many Roman Catholics did not realize that: many of them thought that the motives of these prospective conversions had something to do with misogyny. That was why Cardinal Hume stressed at the press conference that the converts would be expected to accept the whole of Catholic doctrine, not just the bits they liked – it was, said the Cardinal, '*Table d'hôte*, not *à la carte*'. In fact he was aware that the converts themselves knew that perfectly well and always had. Had not the Anglicans at the Westminster conversations accepted, without the slightest hesitation or hint of dissent, Bishop Leonard's suggestion that the new Catechism of the Catholic Church should be their doctrinal standard? The Catechism had as yet only appeared in French: not all of them had even been able to read it. But this was, of course, the point – they would accept it whatever it said. As Newman had put it, at the moment he had realized that the Catholic Church was 'the oracle of God', all his doctrinal difficulties had fallen away: the Church said it, it was for him to believe it. That was the point at which the Anglican suppliants had arrived: they were not the problem now. It was the fears of the Catholic laity that had to be addressed. Thus, the bishops insisted that 'we are very attentive to the positive interest and to the anxieties of our own Catholic community ... We are confident that all Catholics will show greatness of heart as they work with us in the duty of meeting the need of those who approach us.'

There can be little doubt that the fears, sometimes even the resentments, of some Catholics 'on the ground', some of them clergy, some of them ordinary Catholics in the pew – aggravated by committed opponents of realignment within the Catholic Church – had become a major determining factor in the process which led to the statement which finally emerged from the bishops' deliberations. This was reflected in the pastoral letter from the five English and Welsh Archbishops which was appointed to be read from the pulpit on the fourth Sunday of Easter (2 May) – though some ill-disposed clergy refused to read it. 'We shall', said the Archbishops, 'wish to acknowledge the value of the ministry and life of faith, which those who now seek to join us have already experienced.' However –

> In the light of some fears which have been expressed, let it be clearly understood that this does not mean bargaining with truth, nor a wholesale abandoning of the disciplines of our Church. Nor is compromise sought in what is expected of those seeking full communion with the Catholic Church ... we shall look towards [their] eventual total integration into the Catholic Church. But this is a new situation and we must feel our way forward sensitively, courageously, with understanding and faith.

Anglican Catholics might think that the Low Week statement did not measure up to the scale of their problem or to the historic opportunity with which the Catholic bishops had been presented. It represented definite change, nevertheless. The extent to which things had moved forward can be gauged from the hostility expressed in certain Catholic circles towards what were rightly seen as substantial concessions. The Cardinal had some weeks previously expressed himself as 'terrified now that we are going to turn round and say we do not want these newcomers'. Already there had been some indication of the reality of these fears: during the Low Week meeting a number of glowering Catholics had taken to the media to make it quite clear that they hoped, in the chilling demand of one of them, the broadcaster and London parish priest Father Oliver McTernan, that there should be no general welcome for 'these people'. Now, Father McTernan and four other priests published an open letter to the bishops, volubly protesting against the special pastoral arrangements they had just announced.

Their willingness to contemplate such concessions, said the five priests, was 'deeply disturbing'. Any such arrangements, they claimed, would be 'deeply divisive of our communities', though they did not explain why this should be so (nor have any such divisions ever emerged). They asserted that 'many' were 'disheartened' by the readiness to contemplate special arrangements for converts, when 'many of our own people are suffering ... the consequence of major pastoral problems ...' Father McTernan and his friends were vague as to what they meant by 'major pastoral problems' (though the context made it likely that they were talking about priests who had resiled from their vow of celibacy in order to marry and now wanted to practise their priesthood again). But it was difficult to see why the existence of pastoral problems for others should be a disincentive to trying to solve another kind of problem, that of the disaffected Anglicans. It was difficult to avoid the impression that their objections came from simple old-fashioned sectarianism: the important lesson of this episode, however, in view of the anxieties that had been expressed, was how little in practice they turned out to represent the general mood among Catholics in the pew, once any anxieties they might have felt had been addressed.

The Anglicans who had been meeting the Cardinal and his small inner group of bishops were determined to avoid any public suggestion that they felt let down; apart from anything else, they refused to give their enemies – particularly certain Anglican bishops and certain Catholic journalists – any more reason for indecent satisfaction at their discomfiture than they had already shown. They wanted too, perhaps, to convince themselves that what they had was more than it seemed. Peter Geldard was to be heard arguing that 'integration' was not necessarily 'absorption'. Forward in Faith issued an enthusiastic endorsement of the Low Week statement. But though they could point with justice to real and substantial changes, particularly in the whole psychology attaching to the process of conversion, their public optimism nevertheless masked a real and bitter disappointment. What was now on offer was very much less than they had been encouraged to believe might be possible in the confidential meetings described in preceding chapters.

About a month after the bishops' Low Week meeting, the third private 'Westminster conversation', between Anglican representatives

and Catholic bishops, took place, though without one important partic-
ipant, Bishop Leonard, who from this point on withdrew from the
process. The meeting was very different in atmosphere from the two
which had preceded it. The Cardinal was on the defensive, explaining
his difficulties with his own people. The meeting turned into a post
mortem, and an opportunity for the Anglican representatives to com-
plain of the obstructive attitude of some Catholic bishops, which was
already manifesting itself in meetings with Anglican clergy. The meeting makes it clear, nevertheless, that the Cardinal did not regard the
story as complete, and that the handling of Catholic opinion was one
key to future developments. An interesting discussion of current Anglican developments took place: those present, for instance, expressed
their agreement with a controversial statement by the Anglican bishop
of Salisbury that nobody who did not accept women priests should be
ordained in the future.

What the Low Week statement ruled out was clear enough. But
what did it not rule out? In theory at least, one essential element in the
Roman Option was still possible: the staying together of a parish with
its pastor during the process of reception and even (as in America) afterwards: nothing had been specified as to the length of time it would take
after his reception for an Anglican clergyman to become a Catholic
priest. (Cardinal Hume, when asked after the bishops' November meeting how long this period needed to be was to answer with one of his
telling throw-away lines: 'It took Manning a week.') In theory, what
was still possible was something like the American 'Pastoral Provision', without the Anglican rite. By this and other shifts, hopes for the
communal reception of parishes with their own clergy, and for the possibility that clergy and people might continue together afterwards, were
kept alive in the aftermath of the Low Week statement.

THE IMPORTANCE OF THE GROUP

Why was this aspiration so deeply felt? Why was it so important to the
Anglican dissidents for it to be an option to be received corporately,
with their pastor? One important part of the answer was given in an
article published that summer by one of them, Father Tony Pinchin, in
the *Catholic Herald*: 'The dynamism of any group,' he wrote, 'is more
than the sum of its members. The priest belongs in the equation as part

of the group's life of celebration, evangelism and pastoral care.' I asked
one ex-Anglican priest who later brought a large group (about two-
thirds) of his people whether fewer would have come with him if they
had not been received as a group. 'The interesting thing', he replied, 'is
that not all the people I had down to come actually came. They would
all have come if we could have stayed in the building. What amazes me
was the people who joined the group who left. I would say that the
group dynamic doubled the size of the group.'

It is, after all, a thoroughly Conciliar theological perception. Christian faith is essentially corporate, not private: the Lord's Prayer does not
begin 'My Father', but 'Our Father'. The Church exists in the first place
because individuals are not strong enough to make their pilgrimage
through life alone. Many of the laity could not envisage any change as
important as this being made alone, either.

That was the point. Many of the potentially defecting clergy who
later made the decision, with heavy hearts, to stay in the Church of
England, would have left for Rome alone if they could have set aside
their responsibility to their own people. The purpose of the Roman
Option as it was originally conceived was to make it possible for them
to bring their people with them. For the pastor and his people to prepare
for reception together (this was a development of the next three months
and beyond) obviously went some of the way. But the American experience – limited but real – strongly suggests that the optimum conditions
for maximizing lay conversions obtain when an Anglican parish – or a
group within it – is allowed to become a Catholic parish, and its pastor
stays with it, becoming its parish priest under the new dispensation.

A comparison of two groups of former Anglicans makes the point
clearly enough: the Episcopal parish of St Mary the Virgin, Arlington,
Texas (received under the American Pastoral Provision) and a group
from the parish of St John's, Waltham Green, in West London. Both
these groups were received into the Catholic Church at about the same
time – the summer of 1994.

On 29 June Allan Hawkins was ordained a Catholic priest in the lux-
uriantly unAnglican Cathedral of Fort Worth, Texas. It was his second
ordination: he had been ordained in England over thirty years before by
Bishop Robert Wright Stopford, later Bishop of London, then Bishop of
Peterborough. Bishop Stopford might well have been bemused by Allan
Hawkins's second ordination: but he would have been astonished by
the presence at the ceremony of the entire Anglican congregation of

which he had been rector for over eleven years, every member of which (with only one exception) had been received with him into the Catholic Church only three weeks earlier.

It had been a long and exacting process, which had begun three years before. Part of the delay had been caused by the very long wait for the 'rescript' from Rome – the document which gives permission for the ordination of a married former clergyman. But the long wait was by no means a negative experience, and this time had been spent as one of spiritual preparation and catechization for the entire parish. During the whole of this period, Father Hawkins continued to celebrate – as an Anglican priest still – the Anglican liturgy (with Catholic adjustments) authorized by the Pope for the Pastoral Provision.

About a year before his reception and ordination, in the summer of 1993, Father Hawkins was asked to give some idea of how the Pastoral Provision worked, by one of the bishops then preparing the guidelines for the implementation of the Low Week statement in England and Wales. Father Hawkins (two years into the process) was anxious to dispel any impression that the reception of such groups was at all disruptive of the life of the local church: 'The outcome has been', he wrote, 'the establishment of parishes which have slipped quietly and happily into the every-day life of their respective dioceses, where they are regarded neither as oddities nor as competitors. They are simply one more enriching element in the whole Catholic scene.' He was also careful to address the concern of the English and Welsh Catholic bishops that there should be no multiplication of ecclesial entities within the Church. He insisted that the 'Anglican use' clergy of the Pastoral Provision

are, in fact, ordained to the Latin Rite. So we understand ourselves – and we regard our distinctive liturgical heritage simply as a minor (though we would say culturally and historically important) variant or sub-division of that rite. I cannot stress strongly enough that it is very important to us to be fully integrated into the life and mission of the local diocese, looking to the local ordinary as our Father in God.

At the time of its reception into the Catholic Church about a year later, the parish, having held together faithfully, numbered around 120. Father Hawkins was in no doubt of the spiritual value of their common experience. 'Of course,' he told me at the time, 'it was always possible for us to have been received into the Catholic Church as individuals. But the common journey strengthened us. Like the people of Israel crossing the desert, we have at last arrived at our true home.'

Three days later, across the Atlantic, the Revd Martyn Webster, Vicar of St John's, Waltham Green for 10 years, together with his curate, the Revd David Bell, and twenty-four of their people were received together into the Catholic Church in Westminster Cathedral. It was the last occasion on which they were to worship together. Father Bell and Father Webster now reverted to the lay state and began, alone, their long preparation for the Catholic priesthood. The laity scattered, to become 'totally integrated' into various different Catholic congregations.

Which was better for those involved? It was and remains a moot point; certainly, as one who became a Catholic (though with my family) by 'individual submission', I have nothing but positive feelings about the process of being 'fully integrated' into a Catholic congregation. But what, in the Waltham Green parish, of those who might have been drawn in if the group had stayed together? Perhaps this would not have been the result. But perhaps it might: three years after its corporate reception, the parish of St Mary the Virgin, Arlington, had grown from 120 to 400. About half of those who joined later were former Episcopalians. Some, a small minority, were cradle Catholics who preferred the liturgy. Others were lapsed Southern Baptists who (like the former Episcopalians) for cultural reasons would have found entry into the mainstream Catholic Church – which in their area might be heavily dominated by Spanish-speaking immigrants – difficult: this was an interesting example of the Conciliar principle of inculturation at work, one with obvious relevance to certain areas in some British cities, notably London and Liverpool. It was a striking vindication of a suggestion Father Hawkins had made in his letter to an English Catholic bishop about twelve months before his parish was finally received, and about three months after the Low Week statement:

> ... a holy, wise and scholarly priest – a personal friend, and a friend to my parish – said recently that he believed that my parish (and, by implication, all such 'Anglican use' communities) have received a providential vocation. That mission, he suggested, is to be an 'accessible door' into the Catholic Church for many who come from Anglican and Reformation traditions, and who may find the normal 'doorway' very difficult for cultural or

other reasons. We found this idea, presented to us during Lent this year, to be moving and challenging, and we have given it much reflection. And, already, experience suggests its validity. Apart from anything else, we think that this argues for the preservation of the 'common identity' in some form.

STEPS ARE NOW BEING CONSIDERED

By the time the English Catholic bishops met again in November, the first stage of development of the Roman Option in England was complete, rudimentary though it was in comparison with the Pastoral Provision. As in Low Week, a statement, this time very vigorously written, was published. It strongly rejected the idea of a personal prelature or an American-style Pastoral Provision on the grounds that 'this would only serve to increase the multiplicity of church identities in an unhelpful and confusing manner', though without giving any reasons why this would necessarily be so. Certainly, judging by the statement itself, there was no evidence that any serious study of the Pastoral Provision had been made, since one of the Provision's most striking features had been the entire lack of confusion and friction it had caused in practice. Nevertheless, said the English bishops, their feeling that confusion and friction is what they *would* be faced by amounted to 'a fundamental conviction': it was a conviction, however, which on the face of it, unsupported as it was (then or later) by theology or by rational argument, looked to some of the disappointed Anglican dissidents much more like an unthinking prejudice.

But perhaps that was not the way it was; perhaps the bishops were seeking, rather, to reassure the unthinking prejudices of the likes of Father McTernan. As the Cardinal expounded the November document to the assembled press:

I do not see that in this small island, which we are, that two parallel Catholic Churches would best serve our people. It would divide the local Catholic community. Because if you have different rites going on and things like that it would upset a lot of our priests, I think, well, I know. And so we are not in favour of going down that road. On a provisional basis, to help a community, that's a different matter. [The Pastoral Provision] is an interesting experiment in the States, but I don't think it provides a prototype for us.

But why would the Pastoral Provision – which was nothing like a 'parallel Catholic Church' – 'divide the local Catholic community'? Why, precisely, would it upset 'a lot of our priests'? That surely had to be one question for which the Catholic Anglicans had a right to expect some kind of answer. Would these priests be 'upset' for good and sufficient reasons, or was their opposition a matter of irrational fears or even simple ill-will? Did their feelings reflect well or badly on their Christian charity and zeal for souls? Was their thinking, to put it another way, Catholic or sectarian? It was clear that Cardinal Hume had received representations from some of his clergy. But what were they worried about? It would upset a lot of priests, said the Cardinal, 'if you have different rites going on and things like that': but why?

In most major cities, many Anglo-Catholics were already using the Roman Rite in any case. One difficulty seemed to be the fear that the way the ex-Anglicans would celebrate the liturgy would be so much more attractive than the sometimes trendy, sometimes plain sloppy fashion of too many Roman Catholic clergy, that those who attended existing parishes might flock to them. It was not a fear that events were to bear out in the small number of cases where groups were allowed to stay together: but suppose a number of English cradle Catholics were to discover a preference for Anglican Catholic liturgical ways, rather as some Parisian Catholics prefer an Eastern Catholic liturgy. What of it? Might not that be an entirely benevolent phenomenon? Might it not even prompt some parish priests to celebrate the Mass more worthily?

As I discovered from my *Universe* postbag, quite a few cradle Catholics welcomed this idea, and were disappointed when it fell through. And it would not, in fact, have changed the existing situation radically, since there had already grown up an entirely healthy liturgical pluralism which in some cities allowed Catholics a wide choice. Some who lived in the parishes of, say, Father McTernan in Notting Hill, or Father Richard Hollings in Bayswater preferred to cross Hyde Park to the Brompton Oratory for High Mass or, for that matter, to Westminster Cathedral for a well-disciplined concelebrated liturgy, both in Latin. In Oxford, they might attend a plain modern liturgy at their parish church: or in the city centre they might in the space of a hundred yards choose between the Oratorians at St Aloysius (modern liturgy with flutes or

Latin High Mass), the Benedictines at St Benet's Hall (Latin plainsong), or the Dominicans at Blackfriars (modern concelebrated Mass in the morning, plainsong in English in the evening). 'In this small island' there was already a very considerable (and entirely to be welcomed) 'multiplicity of church identities': how could the addition of a few dozen Pastoral Provision parishes throughout the country, all part of their local dioceses, pose a threat to the stability of the Catholic Church, or even to established nearby Catholic parishes?

And yet, certainly at the local level, that appeared to be the apprehension. I put it to one convert Anglican, now a Catholic priest, who the following year (1994) had brought with him over half his people, that if he had been allowed, like Father Hawkins in Arlington, to stay with them, his parish might have become – as Father Hawkins's had – 'an "accessible door" into the Catholic Church'. He agreed: 'Yes, absolutely.' But:

> one of the reasons we couldn't do it is because we were too much of a threat to the local Catholic parish. It's fear, it's genuine fear. You know, I worked with my local priest in the end and I was very grateful for all he did for me, but I could see that he was nervous about our group, which really shouldn't have been a threat. I kept on saying 'We're no threat, this builds the Catholic church up,' but people don't see it like that.

But perhaps some people did: perhaps, even, some Catholic bishops did. For there is in the November statement evidence of more than one school of thought on the matter. Having firmly, even belligerently, rejected a formally constituted Pastoral Provision, the document then proceeds to describe an informal possibility which appears on the face of it to go a long way towards it:

> In welcoming those pastors who approach us together with a group of parishioners, we wish to state that we respect and esteem the bonds of fellowship that exist within such a group and between the group and its pastor ... Steps are now being considered which will enable a group to stay together for as long as it wishes, not only during a period of enquiry and exploration, and in the process leading up to reception into the Catholic Church, but also if thought fit in particular circumstances, after that

point. The process whereby that group becomes, in practice, fully one with the Roman Catholic local community may indeed be gradual ...

WHAT IS A CATHOLIC?

This raised a question about the theology underlying all this. What did it mean, theologically, to say that a group would become 'in practice, *fully* one with the Roman Catholic local community'? Surely, the very fact that its members after their preparation and reception would be in communion with the Holy See made them automatically part of the local Catholic community in the only way that counted in the end, that is *sub specie aeternitatis*? Were the bishops saying that though now of course they were Catholics in the eyes of God, they would only be *real* Catholics when they had been finally disbanded and absorbed into already existing parishes? But what possible theological grounds could there be for saying that? Was their very sacramental identity regarded as being no more than a mere paper qualification, which would only become functional once they had acquired a certain sociological orientation? And if it was a matter of being welcomed into and joining in with the life of the diocese, St Mary the Virgin, Arlington, had already become enthusiastically one with the local Catholic community at least a year before their reception into the Church.

One parish group asked the priest instructing them, 'What is "being Catholic"?' He had replied, their former pastor told me, that: 'Being Catholic is being in communion with Peter and believing the Catholic faith, and everything else is cultural in the end.' But the bishops seemed to be demanding something else. As the Cardinal explained,

> It's not only just a question of embracing Catholicism, it's not just a question of being fully instructed in what the Catholic faith is ... it's also having a feel for its ethos – that's going to be very different for different people ...

But what was it, this Catholic 'ethos'? Did the Cardinal mean, perhaps, the ethos of *English* Catholicism rather than any other sort of Catholicism? Some former Anglican priests migrated after the decision on women-priests to the French Catholic Church, where they fitted in very happily: they reported that the cultural ethos of their new parishes was in some ways much more like that of an Anglican parish than an English Catholic one. Had what the Cardinal called 'the ethos' of 'the Catholic faith' actually little to do with the faith and more to do with the very particular sociology of Catholicism in England, with its inherited defensiveness and its huge parishes, covering sometimes seven or eight Anglican parishes? This business of becoming 'in practice, fully one' with local Catholics looked to some less like the fundamental existential change of coming into in full communion with the universal Church, and more like a matter of joining a cultural ghetto at precisely the point at which English Catholics should have been finally emerging from the ghetto mentality for good. I put this hypothesis to a former Anglican priest who, having brought with him a large group from his parish had then – at first reluctantly but in the end very happily – left them, in order, as he put it, to 'go native', been ordained a Catholic priest and was now one of the assistant clergy at a large urban Catholic church. His reply is worth quoting at some length:

> One of the things you have to tackle is the inability of the English Roman Catholic mind to get away from empire. These places are like empires, they're not parishes. I mean, you try teaching Vatican II's idea of community, *koinonia*, the people of God, you can't do it because you're dealing, on Sunday here you're dealing with six separate communities, the only common thing is you're worshipping in this particular church building. At eleven, we have 300 people who come here and say Mass in their own language, which is fine but actually the five English Masses are separate entities too; in fact, what you have here are six churches not one. But there's only one priest who collects the money and operates the whole system. One thing I said before we all came was that the model the Anglicans are bringing is actually the model for the future. Because actually the empire's gone. The Catholic Church is struggling in these enormous buildings that people rattle round in just as we experienced as Anglicans. Whereas the group I brought with me – there were seventy or eighty of us – we were an absolutely self-financing self-running church, the perfect Vatican II model, except we didn't have Peter.

It was 'the perfect Vatican II model': but it was not to be allowed to survive. The general intention now was to dissolve such communities in the vasty deeps of the English Catholic ethos. Those who sought to enter into full communion with the Catholic Church were to aim at their own individual 'eventual total integration into the life of the Catholic community'. It was a lot better than nothing; indeed, as nearly all those who proceeded on this path were to discover, it was a lot better than anything they had ever known.

And despite the chilly tone that many Anglicans thought they perceived in the Low Week statement, the reality of how the Roman Option could operate in practice (given a fair wind by the local bishop) was to prove more flexible and very much less bleak. But it was, as yet, a long way short of the Catholic Moment, the *kairos* for the English Church, that some had envisioned. And, quite simply, far too many did not come who should have come and would have come if things had been different; that, in the end, was the bottom line. Five years after the 1992 Synod decision, the official figures were that 240 former Anglican priests had been received into full communion with the Catholic Church, of whom 114 had by that time been ordained as Catholic priests. These figures were almost certainly serious underestimates (some dioceses had not produced any figures at all), and they did not take into account those in the process of being prepared for ordination. But even on the most generous assessment, it could not be said that the real pastoral needs of most of the Catholic-minded Anglicans had been adequately addressed.

That, however, was as far as matters were to be taken in England, for the time being at any rate: it was now to be a matter of seeing how it all worked out. The next major stage in the development of Roman Catholic policy towards Catholic-minded Anglicans had already begun elsewhere: in Rome itself.

CHAPTER ELEVEN

CONVERSATIONS IN ROME

THE DECISION OF the Church of England to ordain women had repercussions far beyond the boundaries of the Provinces of Canterbury and York. Not only did other Provinces of the Anglican Communion soon follow the English example. Just as importantly, this irreversible decision of the Mother Church of world-wide Anglicanism resolved (in part at least – there was still the question of women-bishops to sort out) the problem of 'impaired communion' between Canterbury and those who had already installed this novel ministry.

It also removed the last reason for continued resistance on the part of some dissidents, particularly in North America. Now, Bishop Clarence Pope of Fort Worth, Texas, the leader of the Episcopal Synod of America (ESA) (in some ways the American equivalent of Forward in Faith) made his move. He had been closely in touch with Bishop Leonard for years. He had also been one of those who had negotiated towards what finally emerged as the Pastoral Provision in America: though he had in the end rejected it as inadequate to the situation, the American Roman Option had been the result of discussions between himself (then an Episcopal priest) and other Anglicans with a group of influential Catholics, including Bishop Bernard Law, now Cardinal Archbishop of Boston. Pope and Law now flew together to Rome to see the Pope himself, and to discuss their hopes with Cardinal Joseph Ratzinger (one key to all future developments in this area).

THE UNIVERSAL PRIMACY OF THE HOLY SEE

Law was in favour of developing a scheme which went further than the Pastoral Provision (already more radical than anything the English bishops had agreed to); he was in substantial agreement with Bishop Pope on what needed to be done. Accompanying Pope to the Vatican as his advisers were two of North America's most substantial Anglican theologians: Dr Wayne Hankey and Dr Jeffrey Steenson, who had drawn up a document outlining their aspirations. This was to be the basis for the discussions in Rome.

The discussions took place in the Palace of the Holy Office in Rome, on Tuesday 19 October. The Catholic representatives were Cardinal Ratzinger himself, Cardinal Law, Father Girotti OFM, head of the Disciplinary section of the Congregation of the Doctrine of the Faith (*Doctrina Fidei*) and the Jesuit, Father John Rock, head of the Doctrinal Section of *Doctrina Fidei*.

The Anglican delegation was composed of American Episcopalians, with the exception of the formidable Canadian Anglican theologian Dr Wayne Hankey. Hankey was a professor of philosophy and theology at King's College, Halifax, Nova Scotia, and the author of a major work on St Thomas Aquinas. Like his colleague, Dr Jeffrey Steenson, he had done his doctoral studies at Oxford; he was now on sabbatical, engaged in scholarly work in Rome and acting at the same time as Bishop Pope's representative.

Dr Steenson (having been rector of the prestigious Anglo-Catholic parish of the Good Shepherd, Rosemont, in Philadelphia) was now rector of St Andrew's Church in Fort Worth. The Anglican diocese of Fort Worth was and remains a major centre of resistance to the dominant liberal establishment of PECUSA, and most of the Anglican representatives had some connection with the diocese, which had become something of a safe haven for orthodox clergy from all over the United States.

Bishop Pope began the proceedings by introducing himself. He spoke of his ministries as a priest and then as a bishop. He had come to believe, he said, that Anglicanism was Catholic but not complete: what he and his companions were now seeking was completeness. Anglicans had until now been seeking this completeness through the ARCIC conversations; but it had finally to be recognized that since the events in England of the previous November, and with the general dissolution of Christian faith and order within Anglicanism, there was now no future in the ARCIC process, at least so far as conversations between Rome and official Anglicanism were concerned.

But so far as the Anglicans represented at that meeting were concerned, he argued, it was a different matter. They accepted the criticisms of the ARCIC final report made by Rome and now wished to explore what would have been the consequence if ARCIC had succeeded. All those present were personally committed to union with Peter, they were exploring corporate union with the hope that more might be brought to the fullness of Catholic truth.

After the other Anglican participants had briefly introduced themselves, Cardinal Law asked for some indication of the numbers of those who might be brought in by any proposed Anglican Catholic 'entity'. Bishop Pope said that statistics of this sort were 'like mercury'; but he presented estimates of potential support based on the initial hopes for the ESA: around 250,000. He spoke of the losses to the Episcopal Church over the previous two decades, during which, through 'secularization and apostasy' its membership had fallen from 4.5 million to 2.25 million

The meeting now got down to business. Jeffrey Steenson read out the preparatory document which he and Wayne Hankey had drawn up (see Appendix A, p. 241) and the Catholic representatives commented after each section. The first part was headed 'The Convictions Which Have Brought us Here'. This expressed the belief of those present that 'the fullness of the Catholic Faith requires the universal primacy of the Holy See' and the disillusionment of those Anglicans who had believed that the Anglican Church possessed 'a Catholic heart', but who now found that Anglicanism's 'understanding of "diffused" authority had led it to embrace the unCatholic principle that truth in doctrine and morals can be determined by majority vote in local synods'.

The classical Anglican emphases on Scripture and Tradition had been abandoned; at the same time the Second Vatican Council had made it possible to perceive that these emphases had been preserved by Rome. The attempt to defend an orthodox understanding of Scripture in face of modernist biblical criticism had 'demonstrated how crucial is the teaching office of the Church'.

None of this can have surprised the Catholic representatives; there was nothing new here, though it was well expressed. What now followed, however, began to move beyond the normal analysis underlying Anglo-Catholic approaches to Rome. The final paragraph of this section, in view of Cardinal Ratzinger's reaction, is worth quoting in full:

We believe that a truly historic opportunity now presents itself, namely for the healing of the great Western schism, in a way which few envisioned. The Anglican Church is not the only church of the Reformation to be breaking up, foundering on the rocks of a post-modern secularism it has no power to avoid. We now believe there is little hope that the Anglican Communion, as presently constituted, will ever be able to move toward corporate reunion with the Catholic Church. The hopes we had placed in the official conversations of the Anglican-Roman Catholic International Commission must now find their fulfilment in some other form.

Cardinal Ratzinger expressed himself 'in profound agreement' so far: 'Christ', he expounded,

> created one Church: all Christian life is dynamically led to this One Church. It is ironic that it is now the Roman Magisterium which defends Scripture from being dissolved into the opinion of theologians. Rome has also this problem: that many think of submitting doctrinal matters to the opinion of the majority. Rather, majorities must be in conformity with the Magisterium.

Cardinal Law said he had found the first part of the document 'moving'; it was, he said, 'reflective of Catholic faith'. Father Girotti found it 'clear and precise'.

The second part of the document contained its concrete proposals. These envisaged a very radical development indeed: the establishment under existing Roman canon law of a new jurisdiction, with its own bishop or bishops, which 'might be able at some future time to function internationally, thereby preserving existing relationships amongst members of the Anglican Communion who are seeking to be united with the Holy See'. The scheme envisaged in the initial phase the formation of new congregations as a vehicle 'through which the Catholic Church may embrace her separated sons and daughters': in other words, for new Anglican-Rite parishes to be established not only for disaffected Anglicans, but also for their counterparts in all the increasingly radical liberal Protestant churches. It was to be nothing less than an extra-territorial missionary diocese.

The first paragraph of this section – paragraph 5 – deals with one of the concrete difficulties of establishing a new Anglican Catholic entity (one which, indeed had already been addressed in the Westminster conversations in England): what to do about the fact that Anglican Catholics were uncertain of precisely what form of liturgy to use: 'We are divided among ourselves about which liturgical and devotional forms are the best instruments for conveying Christian truth and shaping our liturgical lives.' Many Anglicans (like Father Hawkins in Arlington) were happy to use modern Anglican liturgical texts (always with the exception of the liturgy's central prayer, the canon of the Mass). Others (particularly in North America) preferred a traditional language liturgy: for, 'Although we have found it difficult to define precisely, the Book of Common Prayer is the cornerstone of that tradition of worship and piety Pope Paul VI termed "a worthy patrimony".'

Cardinal Ratzinger's reaction was that this would have to be resolved somehow: 'There must be a common reflection with the Holy See on which of the elements mentioned in paragraph five are to be preserved. Agreement must be reached because the particular structure must have a spiritual identity.' Oddly, perhaps, Cardinal Law does not appear at this point to have mentioned the liturgy already authorized by the Pope for use by the Pastoral Provision in America (of which he was the 'director'); perhaps this was because of Bishop Pope's rejection of the Pastoral Provision some fifteen years earlier. There was a political difficulty here; the clergy of the Pastoral Provision were not entirely sure they wanted to be drawn into a new 'entity', valuing as they did their membership of their own territorial dioceses. All that would have to be sorted out if the present initiative ever bore fruit.

THE HEART OF THE MATTER

Now, the discussion approached the heart of the matter: if there was to be a 'particular structure' (and that seemed already to be taken for granted) what was its purpose to be and how was it envisaged that that purpose would be achieved? It was here that the Anglicans under Bishop Pope were impelled by a vision more radical than anything thus far approached in England: 'Our prayer has been', the document continues,

that out of the present confused state of Anglicanism might emerge a compelling evangelical vision for our future. It must certainly be more than the preservation of the distinctive features

of Anglican Church culture ... We desire that our return to union
with Peter will enable us to contribute to the healing of the
Western Schism, by means of an apostolate uniquely dedicated
to Christian unity, as a vehicle through which the Catholic
Church may embrace her separated sons and daughters and augment the resources for her work of evangelization. We envision
the formation of congregations and ministries in the United
States and Canada with this particular mission in mind.

'This', commented Cardinal Law, clearly identifying himself with Bishop Pope's project, 'is at the heart of our enterprise.' Bishop Pope took the
opportunity to reiterate a central principle (equally relevant to the situation in England): 'This', he said, 'is why we are not proceeding individually and personally.' Cardinal Ratzinger endorsed this approach,
asserting that 'Our first duty is to bring the Gospel to people.' The hope
that more might be brought, he went on, was the 'justification' for the
creation of a new ecclesial structure.

The discussion now proceeded to the technicalities of how such a
structure might be set up. But first, the Anglican discussion document
establishes the reasons for doing so. In spite of being separated from the
Holy See, Anglicans had always understood themselves to be a part of
Western Catholicism: 'We belong to the Latin Church because we come
from her.' Over 450 years there had developed within Anglicanism
expressions of ecclesial life which 'although incomplete, God has nevertheless used to attract and nourish many devout and committed
Christians'. This tradition still had the power to awaken a yearning for
'the full riches of the Catholic faith'. But it had to be secured: 'It is for
this reason that we seek a distinct jurisdictional entity within the Latin
Church.' This ought to be done in such a way that those who belonged
to such an entity would 'participate in the regular organization of the
Catholic Church'; and in matters of sacramental and clergy discipline,
such a jurisdiction would function in accordance with existing
Catholic canon law.

Cardinal Ratzinger consulted Father Girotti; then he agreed that mixing the two codes of canon law was probably not the right approach. But,
he said, 'we have time' to find the right 'figure'. There were 'some figures
in the new Code of Canon Law' which could be adapted to 'our need'.

The document now approaches the question of what is necessary
for the maintenance of the 'communities' (which it identifies as the

congregations, dioceses, and 'institutes of the spiritual life') of the new structure. It speaks of the preservation of a distinctively Anglican tradition of pastoral care. It is specific in four distinct areas: continuing a married clergy; preserving the Anglican tradition of lay involvement; the provision of separate theological education and training; and the organization of the new structure so that at some time it might be able to function internationally.

For the first time, Cardinal Ratzinger saw a problem. 'If ARCIC had succeeded,' he said, 'Anglican married priests and bishops would have been accepted. However, the fact that we are dealing with a part rather than the whole makes a difference.'

It made 'a difference'; but even now there was no categorical refusal. What the record shows was how 'emphatic' was Cardinal Ratzinger's assertion that all the concrete problems in the way of this enterprise could be overcome. 'The essential thing', he insisted, 'is the common faith. Because of this common faith between us, there will be solutions to the concrete problems.'

The meeting now approached its final conclusions. The Anglicans insisted that they were seeking reconciliation with the Catholic Church, not simply because they were reacting against the liberalization of their own churches, but because they believed it was the will of Christ.

The fact remained, however, that it was this liberalization which had made the current discussions necessary and possible. Rome's attitude to other Western Churches had now undergone a sea-change. Ecumenical dialogue had to continue: but it could no longer be a determining priority, and it no longer justified a hands-off attitude towards Catholic-minded Anglican dissidents. As Cardinal Law put it, 'Countering the objection from the ecumenical interest is the fact that there is no hope of union now this way. So, these ecumenical dialogues have no primacy of place, though we must continue them because we must continue dialogue with other Christians.'

The discussions now moved to the immediate question of how the current process was to continue, for there seemed to be no question in anyone's mind by now that these discussions were about the concrete practicalities of further progress, and that the essentials of what the Anglican delegation had requested were to be granted. The record makes it clear that the senior Catholic participants in the discussion were not merely well disposed towards these proposals but positively enthusiastic about them.

Cardinal Ratzinger consulted briefly with Father Girotti; the meeting was told that the Pope had personally determined that these matters fell within the jurisdiction of *Doctrina Fidei*. That meant that they could proceed without further delays. Cardinal Ratzinger said that he would inform the Holy Father informally about their discussion, and would set his own staff to work on the problems involved. Cardinal Law proposed that the process should be: first, the drawing up of guidelines by Cardinal Ratzinger; then, there should be a mixed Anglican/Catholic commission, then 'back to Cardinal Ratzinger' for the final plan.

It was, or so there was every reason to suppose, the green light. Bishop Pope and his companions were received in audience the following day by Pope John Paul II, who embraced Pope, then cryptically pointed to him and then to himself, with the words 'in communion'. Bishop Pope returned to Fort Worth, well satisfied, to await events.

The following month, there were more discussions about the Anglican question for Cardinal Ratzinger: this time it was about England. Cardinal Hume and his inner steering group of English Catholic bishops arrived to see Cardinal Ratzinger and Cardinal Cassidy. There were practical details to discuss, including the question of speeding up the often sluggish business of issuing the necessary dispensation of married former clergy from the vow of celibacy (by having the process carried out in England rather than in Rome): this was to become known as the 'fast track'. Other subjects of discussion included the proposed liturgical additions to the ordination Mass, acknowledging the reality and value of a man's previous ministry. The meeting was fruitful; there was going to be no objection to the English bishops' proposals from Rome, except, possibly for a feeling – expressed or not – that they might have gone a little further than they did: as Cardinal Ratzinger had commented after the Low Week statement, 'What are the English Bishops afraid of?'

By the end of the year 1993, nevertheless, there had been, even in England, very considerable movement in the thinking of the Roman Catholic Church about its pastoral response to Catholic-minded Anglicans. Despite the gulf between the aspirations of many within the English Anglo-Catholic constituency and the reality of what turned out in the event to be politically feasible at the time, the unthinkable had not only been thought: it had even been, up to a certain point, enacted. Low Week was not a green light: but it was not red, either; the statements that emerged in April and November had been designed to open the road but not to allow the traffic to become so dense that it might frighten the horses. By the end of the year it could be plausibly argued by enthusiasts for the process that further developments in England seemed not only possible but likely; and by opponents that the Cardinal 'had been pulled back from the edge of the precipice'. The Low Week statement had seemed discouraging to many potential converts: but from the November meeting, though it was definite in what it ruled out, there emanated warmer vibrations. All this was intentional. As Bishop Nicholls had put it in November, 'One of the shifts that you can see from Low Week to this November statement is the way the Low Week statement was addressed substantially to the Catholic community whereas this statement is addressed substantially to those who have approached us.'

The contrast between the English Catholic approach and the American was total. The English and Welsh bishops were cautious, arguably too cautious. But there was a balance to be struck in a situation of great delicacy, and Cardinal Hume – though himself clearly more visionary than they in his approach – had involved his brother bishops from the beginning. Cardinal Law of Boston, by contrast, had gone straight to Rome, apparently without bringing the matter to the attention of the American conference of bishops at all at this stage. When (before Allan Hawkins's ordination in June 1994) I asked the Catholic bishop of Fort Worth his opinion of the previous October's revolutionary discussions in Rome involving Clarence Pope (still in office as his Episcopalian opposite number) he told me that he knew nothing at all about them. This could not have happened in England. But which approach was more effective in the end? That will be the question, though nobody yet knows when it will be possible to ask it, let alone what the answer will turn out to be.

At the end of his conversations with Cardinal Ratzinger, Bishop Pope had returned to Fort Worth with the clear impression that all he had to do now was wait for Rome to act. Pope was discretion itself, and was saying nothing about the discussions (nor at this stage was anybody else). But what he wanted was no secret among those who knew his mind: and it was noticed that he was smiling a good deal. He had had a long period of ill-health; suddenly, he was full of energy and optimism.

THE LONG SILENCE

Then began the long silence. The ball was in Rome's court; but it did not seem any longer to be in play. Letters went unanswered. It was as though none of it had ever happened. As the months went on, Bishop Pope's optimism began to wane. The long silence from Rome continued; one rumour was that during their visit the previous November the English bishops had expressed strong resistance to the formation of a new jurisdiction in America because of its possible effects in England. This was one rumour: but nobody really knew. Another whisper around the Vatican was that there had been dissension within *Doctrina Fidei* and that Cardinal Ratzinger had himself been 'pulled back from the precipice' by prelates who – unlike Ratzinger, who was a thinking conservative and therefore capable of radical thought – were mere reactionaries and therefore opposed to all change whatever it might be.

Then, after about nine months, there were signs that things had started moving again. Pope announced his individual conversion, not waiting for the fruition of his plans. 'I come with no strings attached and no conditions,' he told the *Dallas Morning News*. 'This is a spiritual pilgrimage and I believe it to be under the direction and guidance of the Holy Spirit.' On 1 February 1995, he was received into the Catholic Church. His reception, it now seems, was very far from warm in some Catholic circles; and he was deeply unhappy for this and a number of other reasons. After a bare six months as a Roman Catholic, he returned to the Episcopal Church.

The background of this strange affair is not uninstructive for our wider enquiry. Some of the contributory causes of Bishop Pope's decision soon emerged. One of them was the astonishing behaviour of the Catholic bishop and clergy of Baton Rouge, Louisiana, where Clarence Pope had always planned to live after his retirement as Episcopalian Bishop of Fort Worth, and where he now hoped to exercise his ministry as a Catholic priest. The local Catholic bishop at first agreed to ordain the former Episcopalian bishop as a Catholic priest. Pope John Paul (who, as we have seen, had met Bishop Pope the previous year, and was well acquainted with his personal history) had, without the usual delay, given the special permission needed for former married clergy to be ordained priest, and all seemed to be proceeding smoothly.

But then the Bishop of Baton Rouge did a strange thing: he let it be known that he would entertain the views of his presbyteral council (a council, that is, of local clergy) on the proposed ordination. The moderate centre had little to say: but an unholy alliance soon emerged, of reactionaries opposed to any ordination of married men for whatever reason, and 'liberals' who were opposed to Pope's ordination because they themselves were not allowed to marry. They expressed themselves vociferously, and the bishop backed off and refused to carry out the ordination.

Cardinal Law now offered to ordain Pope himself and to incardinate him in the diocese of Boston, even planning to travel to Baton Rouge to carry out the ordination there. But the local bishop now expressed his uneasiness over any public ordination in the cathedral (on the grounds that it would be controversial): he gave permission instead for an ordination in his own private chapel. Clarence Pope was deeply wounded by this quarantine. It was clear that on his return to his home town as a Catholic priest, he would be isolated not only from his former Episcopalian friends but also – most cruelly – within the Catholic Church itself.

Another factor in his return was his exclusion from any further role in discussions towards the development of an Anglican-Rite identity. It might have seemed obvious to many that, as the English Anglican Catholic Father Geoffrey Kirk put it in a letter to the *Church Times*, if he had hoped for an Anglican jurisdiction within the Catholic Church in North America, 'he grossly miscalculated the mood of the Roman Catholic Church now'. But as we have seen, Clarence Pope had at the time very good reason indeed for expecting that that was Rome's intention and that he would himself play some part in this great adventure.

He was to be bitterly disappointed. As soon as he became a Catholic layman, he was out in the cold. His scheme was discussed by Catholic bishops, but he was told nothing of their deliberations. He was virtually ostracized by the bishop and clergy of his new diocese. On top of all that, he was deeply depressed for purely medical reasons.

The Episcopalian authorities now took a hand: learning how ill and confused Clarence Pope was, the presiding Bishop of the Episcopal Church, Edmund Browning, seized the moment, telephoning Pope repeatedly and tenderly. The clear message was that if he returned all would be forgiven. Bishop Jack Iker of Fort Worth, his co-adjutor (who had been furious at his defection, brutally ejecting him from his office and insisting on his instant departure) joined in these blandishments; and Clarence Pope succumbed.

What are the lessons of this strange affair? Bishop Pope was, perhaps, open to some criticism: it was always unrealistic to suppose that a new convert to the Roman Catholic Church was going, quite so quickly, to play such a leading part in its deliberations: nevertheless, he should at least have been consulted and kept informed about the progress of the initiative whose chief architect, after all, he was. The chief blame, however must rest with the bishop and some of the clergy of Baton Rouge, for a pastoral failure of which they had good cause to feel deeply ashamed.

This was not, of course, typical of how converts are treated: most Anglicans (as I can personally testify) are received into the Catholic Church with enormous warmth and great pastoral care. But there were still, it seemed, within the labyrinthine folds of the Church as human institution, dark cold places, where resentment, suspicion and all uncharitableness yet lurked. This was as true in England as in America: and there can be little doubt that it played some part in the partial deflation of the Roman Option in Low Week, 1993.

But things had changed, nevertheless. What we might call the McTernan/ Baton Rouge syndrome was still in play; but it was no longer able to obstruct the Anglican Catholic instinct towards Rome quite so efficiently as it had in the past. There was a new factor at work now, even though it had not thus far fully emerged into the light of day. This new factor was the willingness (within the limitations of practical politics) of influential voices within the entity known to the world as 'Rome' – whether one interpreted that as the Vatican or the hierarchy of the local church – seriously to rethink traditional attitudes to Catholic-minded but separated ecclesial groups clamouring for corporate pastoral recognition. In two important and quite separate series of conversations during 1993 – in Westminster and then in Rome – there had been at the highest level a willingness to engage in radical thinking towards real historical consequences: these were not seminars, mere intellectual exercises, but practical discussions.

But what had happened then? The new departures for which the prospects seemed so fair had (in both cases unexpectedly and grievously to many of the Anglicans involved) either ground to a halt or been at least partially frustrated. The question for the petitioners – some of them at least – became unavoidable: had it all been a waste of time? Or had these discussions and their aftermath prepared the way, perhaps for historical upheavals yet to come? For the moment, 'Rome', whether in the Vatican City, in Boston, or in Westminster seemed to them to have fallen silent. Had she definitively relapsed into her immemorial inertia once again? Or was she waiting for events to declare the most favourable moment to move forward once more? That was what they could not know.

CHAPTER TWELVE

'AFTER THAT POINT'

I

IN MANY ANGLO-CATHOLICS, the Low Week statement and its aftermath aroused, as we have seen, not merely disappointment but mortification, even resentment. As one Anglican vicar wrote that autumn to the local Catholic parish priest, 'There is considerable and tangible disappointment at what we see as an unimaginative approach by the Roman Catholic Church in this country. High hopes that there might be a "transformation in the Christian landscape" have been dashed. The approach still seems to be (whether fairly or not, this is the impression gained): "If Anglicans wish to become Catholics, then they are welcome to begin the process for reception." How is this different from the situation a year ago?'

Feelings were not wholly unlike those of a man who has always loved a particular woman who – after years of rejection and coldness – has unexpectedly given him reason for hope but has then, after a brief but blissful interval, calmly explained that though his aspirations were always absurd *in that way*, she will always consider him a friend. There were a lot of hurt feelings. 'It did a lot of damage on our side,' another Anglican priest told me. 'The message that everybody picked up was "they don't really want you, chaps". I mean, I don't think anybody wanted flags to be waved. And I think, certainly, nobody expected wild concessions. But I do think that people were thinking that it would grow into something proper and organized and welcoming in a way that it wasn't, was it? I mean, it was half-hearted.'

'BUT ALSO IF THOUGHT FIT'

But to some extent, that depended in which Catholic diocese you happened to find yourself. Over the next two (in some cases three) years, all over the country, clergy explored the possibility envisaged in the November statement, that a group might be enabled 'to stay together for as long as it wishes not only during a period of enquiry and exploration, and in the process leading up to reception into the Catholic Church, *but also if thought fit in particular circumstances, after that point* [my italics]'. Most were unsuccessful. In London, 'after that point' was not being encouraged south of the river in the archdiocese of Southwark (as in most of the country); but in the archdiocese of Westminster things were more hopeful, and there were very limited though real results in setting up parish groups which continued their communal life before, during and after reception.

The experience of these groups is of some importance, and we shall return to it later. Certainly, it could hardly be claimed that the Westminster operation was not 'proper and organized and welcoming': the Archbishop of the diocese – the Cardinal himself – was giving a good deal of his time to making the new initiative work, and, unlike some bishops, he was giving the bishops' agreements on basic principles a maximalist interpretation. The most striking immediate development here was a series of evenings for Anglican clergy seeking to clarify their thoughts, a process generally referred to as 'discernment'; the evenings became known affectionately as the Cardinal's 'Irish country dancing' (his own coinage); around a hundred clergy regularly attended them.

The sessions began, in Archbishop's House, Westminster, at the end of January 1994, and ran through until mid-June. There were fifteen sessions, each lasting an hour, beginning at six p.m. The Cardinal spoke at length at three of the meetings; but normally he appeared at the beginning to introduce a talk by an authority on the subject in hand; this was followed by a discussion, and wholesome refreshments. The sessions covered such topics as Canon Law, Liturgy and Sacraments, Moral Theology, and Ecclesiology. Much of this was familiar territory, though Roman Catholic Canon Law was not a subject many of the assembled clergy knew a lot about. It turned out to be more interesting than they can have anticipated. Father Kevin Eastell described the specialist in Canon Law, Monsignor Ralph Brown, as looking 'like the stereotypical residentiary Canon one would find in most ancient provincial Church of England cathedrals. What distinguishes him is the lightness of touch with which he approaches his subject. With considerable insight and expertise, tinged with precise humour, we were led through the intricacies of Gratian's Decree and the *Corpus Juris Canonici*. It was quite an achievement to bring a potentially dry subject to life, but Mgr Brown achieved it.'

'AN IMMENSELY PASTORAL BISHOP'

The clergy seem to have been generally impressed by the quality of what they heard. The Catholic specialists, for their part, were doing their own discerning, sometimes finding that these potential converts were better informed about the Catholic Church than they had expected. All in all, the evenings were a great success. As Father Eastell recorded later, 'For all Anglican clergy present, the overwhelming impression we retain is the experience of relating to an immensely pastoral bishop in the person of Cardinal Hume. Some of us Anglican "wrinklies" can remember better days when this was normative in the Church of England, before the liberal management episcopal model took over the episcopal bench.'

Cardinal Hume was by no means the only Catholic bishop who was showing evidence of real pastoral solicitude for individual clergy: but he does seem to have been the only one wholeheartedly interested in demonstrating a positive and imaginative attitude (as well as the necessary continuing support and involvement) towards the possibility – envisaged by the bishops' November statement – of keeping parishes together for as long as pastorally necessary after their reception into the Catholic Church, even if that meant a period of some years.

This was not done against the wishes of the local Catholic clergy; undoubtedly this was one of the reasons why even in the archdiocese of Westminster only three parish groups survived as worshipping communities in the same church building beyond the point of reception (though some seven or eight were received together with their clergy). One of these groups survived without clergy: at St Peter and Paul, Enfield Lock, a Roman Catholic Mass centre had been established for some time, under a shared church agreement. A group of the laity were received together with their priests (who then went their own way to prepare for the Catholic priesthood); the convert laity continued to worship in the same building, but now with the Roman Catholic congregation.

The other two parishes were very different from each other, though their stories have certain important similarities, and their example is a vital one for future developments.

The first of these parishes is St Stephen's, Gloucester Road, in central London. Here, the personality of the vicar was important. Father Christopher Colven was a former administrator (and afterwards Master of the Guardians) of the Anglican shrine of our Lady at Walsingham. He was also the superior of the priestly Society of the Holy Cross (SSC), one of the objects of which was reunion with Rome. In this capacity he had been the first Anglican to approach the Cardinal after the Synod decision on women-priests, and, as we have seen, he was one of the participants in the Westminster conversations. But he had to respond also to the situation in his parish.

As the crisis deepened it had become clear to him that the parish was almost entirely of a mind – that they were opposed to what was happening. From the very beginning, Father Colven and nearly the entire congregation determined to try to face up to the situation together. A few left. But the rest stayed, as Father Colven told me,

> to try to find some kind of corporate answer, the idea being that we had worked for unity through the years and it seemed wrong to fragment at that stage. And I talked to the Cardinal all the way through when I saw him about other things and he has been marvellously supportive. But our great godsend was the new Catechism, when that came out: that became the means of our discernment. We spent two years going through it. The Catechism came out in '94: we were about 18 months down the track. We had been talking and meeting in blocs of about four on Wednesday nights, and about sixty people came. And every week we published what we had been talking about so that the whole parish knew what was going on.

On 11 November 1995, exactly three years after the fateful Synod decision, Fr Colven wrote to every member of the parish (see Appendix B, p. 245), formally to announce his own perception that 'to remain outside the full communion of the Roman Catholic Church would be a wilful act on my part,' adding that 'How that personal reconciliation is achieved is very much bound up with the parish community'. It might be, he wrote, that 'there are few who are walking the same path that I am. If that is so, then I must begin to make the decisions that God requires of me. It may be, though, that there are others who share the imperative for wider communion. If they are just a handful, then I will want to discuss with them the way to move towards reconciliation with the Catholic Church ... We worship together in St Stephen's because that is where we believe God has called us to find him through one another. It is not inconceivable that two Eucharistic communities could co-exist in the same building as a living expression of unity in diversity.'

This model depended on the existence of provisions for 'shared church agreements', which were already working well all over the country. In these, two or even more church communities share the same building, worshipping at different times. Father Colven's proposal (made after consultation with the Cardinal and Dr David Hope, then still Bishop of London) was that those who wished to become Roman Catholics should be received corporately; they would then remain at St Stephen's as Roman Catholics. It would still be an Anglican parish; a new vicar would be appointed to care for those who remained, and the new Roman Catholic community would become technically part of the Roman Catholic parish of Our Lady of Victories, Kensington.

The aim would be to retain the congregation's existing bonds as far as possible, even though its members would now form two distinct worshipping communities. It sounds a utopian fantasy, this model for a new ecumenism; but it appears to have worked without a hitch. Forty people said they would definitely become Roman Catholics; many were undecided; only a small group said they would certainly remain in the Church of England. In the event, over 50 were received, out of a normal Sunday congregation of about 120. But this was not a normal parish, situated in the middle of London; many of the Sunday congregation were not regularly attached to St Stephen's. Those who became Catholics with Father Colven were the hard core of the parish, the daily communicants, the churchwardens, most of the Parochial Church Council, 'everybody who had really done anything were the ones who were determined that they had to make the journey'.

'A WAY OF DRAWING PEOPLE IN'

The group was finally received on the Saturday after Easter, 1996, and at the time of writing have lived happily ever since that day under the new arrangement. After reception, Christopher Colven was soon ordained deacon and, after a decent interval, priest; the new arrangements were up and running well before Christmas. Relations between Father Colven and his Anglican successor, Father Reggie Bushell, have been, in Fr Colven's words 'unbelievably peaceful'. Father Colven and his people celebrate their Sunday Mass every Saturday evening (for Roman Catholics, Sunday begins liturgically on the vigil, as do all major feasts).

This has been one factor enabling Father Colven to avoid one pitfall feared by the Catholic bishops: that such ex-Anglican communities would remain tight little groups, never mixing with other Roman Catholics. Sundays are kept free; and St Stephen's having always been the kind of church which draws its congregation from beyond its own parish boundaries, most of the Catholic congregation are now also associated with other Catholic communities closer to their own homes. But the congregation comes into contact with other Roman Catholics in a different way. The Saturday evening congregation has now risen to between 100 and 120 people, mostly from the immediate area: only about one-third of these are now former Anglicans. The majority of the community today tends to be either what Father Colven describes as 'native Roman Catholics', or converts from an earlier stage. The local Catholic clergy (all in thriving parishes) have been, he says, 'very supportive, very very supportive, all of them. I think that they are broad enough to see that within the spectrum of what is happening at the moment that we, perhaps, have a way of drawing people in.'

This led me naturally to my next question. Had his community, like that of Father Hawkins in Arlington, become an 'accessible door' into the Catholic Church? He is clear that this is indeed happening, in two ways: first, 'A number of people have been received and then gone off and we don't see them any more. Some we didn't know, some from the existing congregation.' But another way the St Stephen's Roman Catholics have become an accessible door is in some respects even more interesting: a number of lapsed Catholics have seen it as their way back into the Church: 'Because it's a small community, a number of people who were lapsed for all kinds of reasons have been reconciled: people feel they can get to know one another, relate to one another, that they're part of something and I think in many cases that native Roman Catholics just haven't been used to that: a number of people equally might feel that something more anonymous like the Oratory would be what they need.'

I asked Father Colven if he agreed with other formerly Anglican and now Catholic priests that in some ways many Anglican communities were nearer the Conciliar ideal than some very large urban Catholic parishes. He agreed: 'I think that that's right. I think that there's a particular tradition of pastoral care. I suppose it is based on a smaller community where the group is small enough for the pastors to know their people intimately and to maintain a very close relationship with them, which I think builds a particular sense of community in which people really do have a chance to know one another. I do think there's a particular thing about "the parson" which I wouldn't want to overwork, and in many ways I think the Church of England has used it up, with all its amalgamation of parishes and so on, but at its best I think there was an English tradition of pastoral care based on the parochial system, on small enough units for people to be cared for in a realistic way. In the folk memory it still exists. There is a basic expectation that the priest will be there at moments of need – it's part of many people's perception still.'

The other parish group which has been successfully received into the Catholic Church and has remained together could hardly be more different; this makes the similarities between their experiences all the more striking. St Stephen's is a smart, central London community of the type known as 'eclectic' or 'gathered'; that is, its congregation comes from a wide area. St Matthew's, Bethnal Green, was a traditional East End Anglo-Catholic parish whose people come almost entirely from within the parish boundaries.

Like many other London Anglo-Catholic parishes, the parish had been using the Roman Missal for many years. Its priest, Father Christopher Bedford, had had for some time excellent relations with the local Catholic parish of St Anne's. Even before the decision in November 1992 to ordain women, remembers the parish deacon, Ken Rimini, 'we were all working towards unity with the Roman Catholic Church. We wanted this reconciliation; in the parish we were hoping for it, praying for it.' By January 1993, the PCC were beginning to get feedback from the congregation; by the autumn, Father Bedford was exploring the possibility of the corporate reception of most of the parish with the local area bishop, Victor Guazzelli. Though it was clear enough that most of the parish wanted to become Catholics together, the parish took its time over the decision. One setback was the departure of Father Bedford; Ken Rimini now took over as the parish's leader. As with St Stephen's, there was a lengthy period of discernment. Some parishes failed, thinks Ken Rimini, 'because they jumped in too quickly'. Another problem, he thinks, has been the suspicion of some Catholic clergy: 'There are still some of the older Catholic clergy who find it difficult to accept that you can actually be a convert, we're finding that with some of the cradle Catholics in our parish now, they still look at the ex-Anglicans and see them as ex-Anglicans instead of looking at them and saying these people are now Catholics.'

At Pentecost 1996, most of the parish (about 120 people) were received, remaining in their building under a shared church agreement. The congregation has swelled, the church building being more convenient for some members of the congregation of St Anne's who are cut off from their main parish church by the railway line. But there has been no sense of competition between the two churches: Ken Rimini has worked with the parish priest of St Anne's, so that in effect the St Matthew's Catholic community has come more and more under the aegis of its neighbour. 'We've emphasized to our people', says Ken Rimini, 'that our parish church is St Anne's Church and that St Matthew's is an Anglican parish.' The role of the parish priest, Father Des Hanrahan, has been crucial: 'If we'd handpicked him,' says Ken Rimini, 'we couldn't have done better, he is so sensitive to our situation.' I asked him to summarize what he considers were the essentials for the success of this operation:

First and foremost the congregation. If you haven't got that desire for unity, whatever you do it won't work. In some places the criticism was that it was the clergy pushing the people, here at St Matthew's it was the congregation that was pressurizing the clergy. The Cardinal's been a great help to us, he's been absolutely wonderful. Behind it all there's been the Cardinal. We've had the backing of a wonderful Catholic parish priest, and Bishop Victor. As Anglicans, we had a great parish priest in Father Christopher Bedford. And I came through with the parish, it's been a key role.

HE JUST SAID, 'IT WON'T GO VERY FAR.'

One thing has already emerged clearly: for success in such an operation, there are two essential dimensions – the Anglican and the Catholic – which need to intermesh or at least not to cancel each other out. The Anglican dimension requires a co-operative bishop (for the shared church agreement), a united parish community, careful preparation and good leadership. The Catholic side needs above all both a pastoral and imaginative bishop and supportive local clergy. It is difficult to know how many Anglican parishes there have been in which the desire for unity with Rome and all the other essentials of the Anglican dimension were abundantly present, but whose aspirations were dashed by lack of imagination, by coolness or even, in a few cases, outright hostility on the Roman Catholic side. It is difficult to know exactly, but the numbers are certainly in three figures.

Take one inner-city Anglo-Catholic parish priest I talked to; his experience is duplicated all over the country. 'A group of us,' he told me, 'went to see the local Catholic bishop, who was all enthusiasm and had all the documents from Rome; but he warned me right from the beginning not to get over-excited because in this archdiocese [staying together as a group after reception] was not considered very desirable.'

Why not? 'He never really said why it wasn't desirable. He just said, "It won't go very far." And we were the only group he had on offer, if you see what I mean. And a not insubstantial group – I mean, ninety of us went to see him. He arranged a meeting just outside the parish so that we weren't meeting in our territory or his. It was all done very sensitively. Ninety went, of whom I reckon seventy-five would have gone to Rome. It was virtually the entire communicant body of the parish.'

Could it have been another St Mary the Virgin, Arlington? 'Yes. I mean we are a relatively small parish physically: 4,500 souls in the area. We are roughly 85–90 communicants on a Sunday. And one or two other people from neighbouring parishes. Some have become Roman Catholics individually: the vast majority, including myself, are still there.'

Another priest went with a colleague to see his local bishop, who was 'absolutely charming. I mean he really is a lovely man, and pastorally concerned and so on. But we just did not get the impression that he was prepared to be at all creative about any possibility other than individual conversion.' His parish, too, stayed together on the margins of the Established Church.

I I

It could not be said, especially at first, that stable conditions existed for such parishes to settle down to life in the Church of England content with their lot in the new dispensation, even with the concessions they had been granted. Above all, there was no security for the future. When the Act of Synod authorizing the appointment of the 'flying bishops' was debated and passed during the November sessions, it was made very clear that the new arrangements were not designed for durability, that as one of the dissidents had remarked earlier in the year, it was to be a matter of 'terminal care' rather than a permanent and assured settlement within the new order.

HANDLING THE DISSIDENTS

The Archbishop of York, guiding the measure through the Synod, indicated that the men chosen would not be young and would not be committed to the Forward in Faith agenda. 'Dr Habgood assured the Synod', the *Church Times* reported, 'that only men eligible to be bishops anyway would be selected: men invited by the other bishops, and of wide sympathies. It would also be important that the Church should not appoint men who could be in place for forty years, or who, if needed, could not be moved anywhere else.' The expression 'of wide sympathies' was understood: it meant, someone who is personally opposed to women's ordination but who accepts the way things are; he will work the system without causing any trouble. In fact, the flying bishops, though at first suspected by some Anglo-Catholics of being Establishment men, quickly became committed to their new constituency.

The dissidents had to be handled; but there was no sign that anyone, at least in the Church of England, thought it necessary that their concerns should be understood, even at a theoretical level. Dr Carey was still talking as though all that was needed was for them to pull themselves together; it was a simple matter of facing reality. 'People have got to realize', he said in July (over six months after the fateful decision), 'that the doctrine of the Church of England ... will be that women will be canonically and lawfully ordained.' Then he urged those who had opposed women-priests 'to work with them and support their ministry'.

It was all very difficult for everyone. The victors, too, were beginning to get more than a little irritated – by those who had delayed their triumph for so many years and were now ruining it all, so they thought, by behaving like spoilt children. They were, said Caroline Davis, moderator of the Movement for the Ordination of Women (MOW), 'flouncing around like two-year-olds having tantrums in Tesco'. 'Those who disagree with the decision', wrote the Durham theologian Dr Peter Selby in *The Times*, 'have the right to ask for understanding, and that the safeguards already contained in November's Measure shall be honoured.' But, 'They do not have the right, and must not be given the power, to smother our delight with their depression ... If anyone feels they must leave the Church of England for the Roman Catholic Church, I hope and pray it will be a real homecoming for them.' In other words, if you want to go to Rome, go with our good wishes; but if you stay, accept what has been done. This, safeguards or no safeguards, was what two-thirds of the Church of England understandably thought, whatever they actually said. John Austin Baker, the Bishop of Salisbury, felt that there had been far too much anxiety to help the dissidents stay; ever since the bishops' January meeting in Manchester, said Bishop Baker, he had 'been worried ... that the Church will be tempted to enlarge the category of people we are trying to keep in'.

Not for the last time, he now threw everything into confusion by challenging an Establishment compromise designed to finesse an impossible situation, by pointing out that the situation was indeed impossible and would not be made any less so by a synodical fudge (he was, a year or two later, to drop the same bombshell over the ordination of practising homosexuals). At the end of May, a month after Low Week, he called for a ban on the ordination to the priesthood and the episcopate of anyone opposed to women's ordination on theological principle. It would, he said from the pulpit of his cathedral, be wrong to 'ordain or consecrate in the future someone who does not merely doubt the wisdom or timeliness of such reform, but is convinced that some whom the Church gives him as fellow priests are not priests at all'. A General Synod spokesman described Dr Baker as a 'lone voice' who did not represent the Church's official line. What he had said, however, was difficult to fault logically; it was also what a lot of people – on both sides of the divide over women-priests – thought, but were not saying: that the Church of England was proceeding ineluctably towards a situation which was not only theologically unsustainable but, in the most direct and concrete way, schismatic.

THE LONDON PLAN

In London, poor Dr Hope described Bishop Baker's remarks as 'unhelpful', as indeed, for him, they were. He now announced his 'London plan', a local variant of the national scheme, which dramatically illustrated the way in which the Church of England, with careful deliberation, was institutionalizing a schism. Under the plan, a bishop would be appointed as commissary for the Archbishop of Canterbury, to ordain women in any of the four areas in the diocese where the area bishop was opposed. Where the area bishop was a supporter, traditionalist parishes could opt out of their diocese and transfer to the jurisdiction of the suffragan Bishop of Fulham, then John Klyberg, an opponent of women-priests, who had no area responsibility.

Some bishops supporting women-priests said that concessions had now gone too far; but some dissidents were also hostile, seeing the London Plan as an absurdity, even a sell-out. One distinguished London Anglo-Catholic priest compared the principles underlying his bishop's proposals with those of Vichy France, with Dr Hope cast as Marshal Pétain: 'His intention is somehow to protect his constituency by collaborating with the enemy. But he cannot do that and still represent us. This is something we will never accept; in the end the only real solution is probably to escape over the channel.' The plan's reception by MOW supporters on the ground fully explained these misgivings. A packed congregation at the ultra-liberal church of St James's, Piccadilly, cheered when a woman deacon announced the plan's details. For the point was, explained the Revd Ulla Monberg, that Bishop Hope had decided not to exercise his rights under the legislation either to declare that he would forbid the ordination of women in his diocese or to bar women-priests ordained elsewhere from functioning there. 'This means', said Ms Monberg, 'that next year we may be ordaining women here at St James's.' The official reaction of MOW, for understandable reasons, was somewhat short of ecstatic. Its London branch secretary, Margaret Orr-Deas, said the plan 'sends out bad vibes to women by suggesting that a bishop who ordains them is tainted', correctly adding that 'there is an element of schism'. It was a major victory, nevertheless, and despite a guarded welcome from Forward in Faith it was perceived at the time as a bitter and needless retreat by many London Anglo-Catholics.

Bishop Hope and other traditionalist bishops were now in a theologically anomalous situation. They were against ordaining women in principle. But they would allow others to ordain them, and they would recognize them as priests and allow them to function in their dioceses. But if they recognized their priesthood, why would they not ordain them? It was a strange conception of episcopal authority. As Geoffrey Kirk wrote later,

> For those who did not immediately grasp these contradictions in cold print, the Bishop of London (now Archbishop of York) obligingly played them out in dumb show. Having surrendered his undoubted right to forbid the action, he attended, in his own cathedral, the ordering of women as priests by a representative of the Archbishop of Canterbury (one of his own suffragans), himself engrossed the meanwhile in the writings of the Fathers. That the 'Ordinary' should be present at, and yet be overtly inattentive to, the very rite which characterizes and defines his relationship to the college of priests in his diocese, is powerfully eloquent of the theological disruption which the ordination of women has caused and which the Act of Synod has regularized.

The Act of Synod may have been based on an ecclesiological nonsense: for the dissidents, however, it had its uses, which were very far from what had been intended by those who had enacted it. The Act had been designed to give a breathing space for the 'reception' of the women-priests Measure: 'reception' meant time for the opponents to change their minds and rejoin the Anglican mainstream. What the Church of England's rulers had never seriously considered was the possibility that the dissidents might not change their minds after all, that the reality of women-priests might strengthen rather than dissolving their convictions.

STRENGTHENING THE BRETHREN

Under these circumstances, the new arrangements became a powerful instrument in their hands. As the impossibility of arranging corporate receptions and a continuing common life for groups or parishes in most Roman Catholic dioceses became apparent, many Romeward-inclined Anglican clergy who felt they could not leave their people behind settled down for the long haul. The problem now was to gather those who were opposed, both clergy and laity, as a recognizable body so that they could support each other not to do what the bishops hoped they would do: gradually weaken in their opposition to the new order, and become, little by little, unhappily reabsorbed for want of anything better. The Act of Synod strengthened Forward in Faith's ability not only to define its constituency but to build up its protective barriers. Forward in Faith congregations stayed in their own buildings and used the resources of the Church of England, as they were entitled to do. The important thing was to be able to control the circumstances of their own lives as an increasingly independent ecclesial community. Stephen Parkinson, the lay director of Forward in Faith, put it succinctly but effectively, in the aftermath of a great rally which took place in May 1995, five thousand strong and presided over by the Northern PEV, the Bishop of Beverley, in York Minster:

> What has become clear to us is the necessity to build up a corporate identity in such a way that a subtle but important change comes over our constituency. In the future, surely, our loyalty must be to *each other* rather than to the structures of the establishment ... The reason why those present left the Minster so buoyed-up was because – for an hour or two – they had succeeded in distancing themselves from an Establishment which is intent on belittling us; an Establishment whose vision must surely be that one day there will be no Bishop of Beverley, no Provincial Episcopal Visitors, no Forward in Faith, no one opposed to the ordination of women priests.

By this stage, Forward in Faith had already established its own internal communications and organization. The country had been divided into sixteen deaneries, each made up of two or three of the historic dioceses. Each was presided over by a regional dean, who was the leader of

Forward in Faith in the region committed to his care. It would be his responsibility to ensure that regular clergy chapters met in each diocese for mutual support; he would work in close co-operation with the appropriate Provincial Episcopal Visitor. Forward in Faith also established its own internal disciplines, designed to preserve the dissidents' collective sacramental integrity and to build up their defences against reabsorption. At a National Assembly in September 1994, a Code of Practice was adopted, spelling out general principles for maintaining the impairment of communion between those who did and those who did not recognize the Measure authorizing the Ordination of Women to the Priesthood. It was made clear that this was necessary because it was also thought desirable, even now, to adopt the principle of 'never doing separately anything which can in conscience be done co-operatively'. Nevertheless, there was 'doubt about the validity of the orders conferred' on women 'which requires us to distance ourselves from them'. Similarly, there was to be a distancing from the ministrations of any bishop who ordained women: not because it was intended 'to express doubts about the validity of any of a bishop's sacramental acts other than his priesting of women'; rather, 'Our inability to receive the body of Christ at his hands is to be interpreted as a painful and costly sign of the impairment of communion which his own free action will inevitably have created.' The faithful were enjoined, as a matter of principle, never to

i) Worship regularly in a church where a woman is the incumbent or assistant minister or where women are known to be welcomed as celebrant of the Eucharist, albeit infrequently.
ii) Receive or administer the Holy Communion, from the sacrament reserved in that place, in any parish church, hospital, hospice or other institution where a woman was the incumbent, chaplain or assistant minister.
iii) Commend to the sacramental care of a woman priest anyone close to death.

The 'Agreed Statement on Communion and Code of Practice' was a detailed document covering every circumstance of church life. If the bishops of the Church of England had entertained doubts about the seriousness and the stamina of the dissidents, they must surely have been dispelled by now.

THE MARGINALIZATION CONTINUES

Things were not, of course, as simple as this brief account makes it sound. Three flying bishops, plus the Bishop of Fulham (conveniently, John Broadhurst succeeded John Klyberg in 1996), exercising pastoral care over Forward in Faith parishes – it sounded already like a third province in embryo, gathering beneath its wings all those clergy and laity opposed to women's ordination. But things were not quite so straightforward, particularly at first. A third of the clergy and laity remained opposed: but they were not necessarily tidily gathered together in monochrome parishes. Not all the dissident clergy could get a majority in their PCC to opt for a flying bishop (even though a substantial number – conceivably even a majority – in the congregation might wish to); and there were many dissident laity in parishes where the clergy and many of the parishioners saw nothing wrong in the innovation. That was not the only untidiness: by no means all preponderantly traditionalist parishes were attached to a flying bishop: the original intention, indeed, was that most of them would be catered for within the existing system. Either a diocese would maintain a suffragan bishop who would minister to traditionalists and who would not ordain women. Or a diocesan might borrow such a suffragan from a neighbouring diocese. A few diocesans, survivals from an earlier time – Chichester, Sodor and Man and others – were themselves traditionalists. The PEVs were originally meant, in the description of one of them, Edwin Barnes, Bishop of Richborough, to be 'pluggers of gaps'.

But the gaps became more and more the norm, as liberal diocesans refused to replace traditionalist suffragans. Traditionalist bishops like David Hope in London (then York) and Eric Kemp in Chichester all made a point of appointing at least one woman-ordaining suffragan: but hardline liberals like Richard Harries in Oxford, with the three suffragan sees of Buckingham, Reading and Dorchester at his disposal, refused to reciprocate. This is worth stressing: in no case has a traditionalist suffragan been appointed by a liberal diocesan (Geoffrey Rowell in Basingstoke was actually a left-over from the episcopate of Colin James in Winchester). Whatever might have been promised, or at least implied, by the document which had emerged from the bishops' Manchester meeting in 1993, the reality has been very different.

In effect, the reality on the ground has been that liberals (perhaps not always unwittingly) and traditionalists (with all due deliberation) have in effect connived at the detachment of the dissidents from the structures of mainstream liberal Anglicanism. The natural dynamic of the new order seems to be that traditionalist parishes have been and will continue to be more and more dependent on flying bishops for their pastoral care, since their own diocesans are not prepared to appoint colleagues with whom they disagree. Thus, despite one or two supposedly symbolic appointments like that of David Hope to York, the liberal establishment has in reality continued to marginalize the traditionalists.

The real question is this: Is it such a bad thing that it has? Those liberals who say that, since the Church of England has made up its mind on the divisive question of women-priests, division should now cease, have a real case. The Anglican mainstream needs, as an urgent priority, to establish its own internal coherence; how can it do that if (as the Manchester statement envisaged) the bishops within many dioceses are divided among themselves? But the logic of this reasonable case must now be taken to its inevitable conclusion. The creeping marginalization of the dissidents, in defiance of the spirit of the Manchester agreement, is one thing; their gradual but orderly disengagement would be entirely another, a solution not only more just but more rational. The logical outcome of the situation is that those who wish to separate themselves institutionally from the liberal mainstream should be given every facility to do so, not only for their sake, but – just as much to the point – for that of the liberal mainstream too.

This would appear to be, in any case, the historical dynamic which, whatever the original intentions, has been clearly and irreversibly established. The Act of Synod may have been seen as a temporary expedient by those who cobbled it together under such pressure in 1993; it represented, nevertheless, a radical ecclesiological development which cannot now be disinvented, and whose implications have to be seriously addressed. It is a development which, Bishop Edwin Barnes suggests, is paralleled in the Catholic Church's provision for 'Personal Prelatures', one of the principal aims of which, under the 1983 code of canon law, was to provide pastoral care for groups of people with particular needs. The underlying principle of such a jurisdiction within a Church is that it transcends existing jurisdictions; Bishop Barnes quotes the Catholic authority Pedro Rodriguez, who comments that Personal Prelatures are only possible if 'classical territorialism [is] made flexible by applying the personalist principle'. A Prelature is not a 'particular church' in the same way as a diocese; it has, nevertheless, some of a particular church's characteristics.

THE EMERGENCE OF AN ECCLESIAL ENTITY

There are, of course, certain differences with the Act of Synod; a Roman Catholic prelature would never be established to cope with divergences from the doctrine of the Church, nor would it be conceivable for the prelate to be in full communion with bishops with whom those to whom he ministers consider themselves to be out of communion. In any case, the real point about what seems to be developing within the Church of England is not at this stage its ecclesiological or juridical correctness, but the faithfulness of those involved to the life and witness of the historic tradition. What we can observe among the dissidents appears on the face of it to be the definite emergence of a distinct ecclesial community, which depends on the Provincial Episcopal Visitors for its identity. It is a development which, it needs to be stressed, has to do above all with the growth of a new form of church life, an authentic pastoral reality which has become central to the spiritual lives of those involved, and which they will not now lightly forgo for anything less. I spoke to one Forward in Faith priest who had attempted to take his parish into the Roman Catholic Church and had now been caught up in this new movement. 'The key to what we've got now,' he told me, 'is the bishops. One must not underestimate the extent to which the PEVs have given a real sense of identity and cohesion and confidence and we do look to them considerably.'

I reminded him of the fears originally expressed in certain quarters that the flying bishops would be Establishment figures. His reply was quite clear:

'That's not the case, at all. That has been disproved. What we've found so exciting about the Provincial Episcopal Visitors, and I'm not the only one who has said this, is the completely different and more primitive and apostolic model of episcopacy. When he comes he comes for three or four days. He stays with the clergy. He lives in our vicarages. We have chapter meetings, we have Mass with him. He meets the clergy, he meets their families. There's a real sense in which he's actually living with us as a pastor. It's had some considerable impact, in my view.'

I reminded him that he had once attempted to take his parish to Rome. Did all this mean that in the event of some further Anglican crisis – and some more imaginative response from the Catholic bishops – he would be less likely to try again? He paused, then replied : 'I think it means that Rome has got to have a more creative view of the corporate nature of our present existence.'

It is important to understand that the growth of this new ecclesial identity has by no means put an end to traditionalist Anglican ambitions to establish communion with the Holy See. On the contrary, it is not too much to say that a continuing consciousness of the need to be in communion with the universal Church beyond Anglicanism's boundaries is in present circumstances as urgently felt as ever it was, and possibly more so. It was this, it seems, that prompted Bishop Barnes's possibly slightly unsatisfactory comparison between life under the Act of Synod and a Personal Prelature. 'What now,' he suggests, 'if the PEVs were able to persuade another Church ... that the faith of the traditionalist part of the Church of England was, indeed, recognizably that of the whole Church, and was a distinct prelature, is it unthinkable that such a prelature might enter into a new relationship with that other part of the universal Church while remaining part of the Church of England?'

The quick answer to this question – the question of Anglican orders aside – is that if 'a new relationship' means being in full communion, it is indeed, as far as Rome is concerned, not only unthinkable but a technical impossibility. Nevertheless, this is not a question we can lightly dismiss, and we will have to return to it: for what we really need to ask is why the question is being put at all. There can be little doubt that it is part of a carefully constructed emerging agenda; and this is itself a portent. Bishop John Broadhurst, Chairman of Forward in Faith, puts it in a slightly different form, postulating not a prelature but what looks like a third province of the Church of England:

Is the established Church capable of adopting a federal model, allowing a large group within it to do exactly what it allows some parishes to do? Are liberal Christians generous enough and charitable enough to allow those holding differing views on major issues of faith and order enough room with integrity? Furthermore, will they allow them to establish Unity and Communion with a body outside the Church of England or the State Churches of Scandinavia? My belief is that the answer is 'yes' and orthodox Anglicans ... must work for that day.

There are three questions here. Would the Church of England really allow the formation of a formally constituted third province? Second,

would the other two provinces of the Church of England allow this new
province to enter into communion with an outside body (let us assume
that means Rome)? The third question we have already asked: would
Rome, or Orthodoxy for that matter, agree to such an arrangement while
the new province remained an integral part of the Church of England?

It may seem obvious that the answer to all these questions is in the
negative. Bishop Broadhurst and Forward in Faith, however – and at
least one of the PEVs, perhaps all of them – are proceeding on the working assumption that they can be answered positively. But do they really
think this in their heart of hearts? Or do they have some other scenario,
or scenarios, in mind? And what might those scenarios be? These are
questions to which we must return.

III

Beyond Forward in Faith's protective embankments, the diversion of
the Anglican mainstream has continued on its new course. The clearest
evidence of the shift that has occurred were the results of the General
Synod elections of 1995, which took place three years after the decision
on women-priests.

The smoke and confusion of the women's ordination battlefield had,
for a time at least, cleared away. The prospect of new upheavals over the
translation of women to the episcopate was thought to be far distant,
deferred to a time when the dissidents might have been reduced to a
tiny remnant, faithful but impotent. MOW (despite some grassroots
resistance) had been squared not to start pressing for women-bishops
too soon; they would, it was thought, co-operate in playing the long-
term Establishment game. As the new Synod settled into its first sessions in February 1996, it seemed obvious enough where synodical

power now lay, who were the victors and who the vanquished; an analysis of the election results seemed to justify certain clear inferences about what the future for the Established Church was going to be like. As was easily predictable, the Catholic group had wholly lost its power to block protestantizing legislation such as the Anglican-Methodist reunion scheme of the seventies (or, indeed, any other scheme the group might disapprove of).

THE NEW ISSUES EMERGE

This became evident when one of the early items of business for the new Synod was announced: the speedy ratification – in the form of an Act of Synod – of the Porvoo agreement, which had been concluded between a group of Northern European Protestant Churches including the Church of England. This entailed the recognition, always refused up to this point by the Church of England, of the validity of the orders of Nordic Lutheran Churches who at the Reformation, though they had retained the office of bishop, nevertheless neglected to maintain the historic Apostolic succession, and had therefore not been accepted by the Church of England as true bishops. This meant, in the words of one of the agreement's enthusiasts, 'adopting a more forward-looking and experience-related concept of "apostolicity" – what makes a church an authentic Church. If accepted ... it could provide a basis for a new attitude to the ministry of the Free Churches in this country.' The issues of sacramental integrity involved were thus virtually identical to those of the Anglican-Methodist Unity scheme of the late sixties, when Bishop Graham Leonard had rallied the Catholic constituency in fierce, concerted, and in the end successful resistance.

But the Catholic group in Synod had now no hope of fighting such schemes. They were taken by surprise by the speed of the operation. It was rumoured that the Council for Unity of the General Synod, given the importance of the issues involved, had proposed a slower pace; the Synod's powerful Standing Committee, however, had overruled them. The inference, for some, was that they wanted Porvoo pushed through the new Synod quickly, before any potential opposition had time to organize itself. Forward in Faith elected not to oppose what they had no chance of preventing. Since the ministry of those with what might be thought dubious orders was not exercised on English soil, it would not

have the same practical effect as earlier pan-Protestant schemes; thi
provided a reasonable pretext for not becoming passionately involve
when there was so much else to be getting on with.

There was also the opportunity for mutual support between Catholic
minded Anglicans and Lutherans. When the Agreement came befor
the Synod for its final ratification, Geoffrey Kirk announced in a maid
en speech that though he could not oppose it, neither could he suppor
it. His grounds were that 'the freedoms of conscience which the Act o
Synod [establishing alternative episcopal oversight] enshrined and th
Lambeth Fathers claimed to be in every way necessary to the legitimat
development of doctrine, are not available to many of our sisters an
brothers in the Churches of Norway and Sweden'. On the sacramenta
issues involved he elected to remain silent, though Father Yarnold, vet
eran member of ARCIC and committed ecumenist, pointed them out i
an article in *The Tablet*: Porvoo was one more nail in the coffin of ecu
menical relations between Canterbury and Rome, and it had been rati
fied without a shot fired.

The Catholic group's marginalization had been already clear as th
new Synod met in February 1996. It was not that which most Syno
members had on their minds now. What they hoped for was a less con
tentious future. The real difference now, or so it seemed to many, wa
that Synod members could for the first time in twenty years look for
ward to a period of rebuilding, in which women's ordination had cease
to be an overshadowing and ever-present distraction, a period in whic
the second half of the Decade of Evangelism might be more effectivel
prosecuted than the first. But though one source of contention had – i
was devoutly hoped – now disappeared from the Synod's agenda, anoth
er seemed set to replace it. Just as women's ordination had dominate
the eighties, so homosexual 'rights', from small beginnings, now looke
set to loom ever larger until the millennium and well beyond.

THE NEW ANTAGONISTS

The two issues, indeed, were causally related. Women's ordination ha
prepared the way for the emergence of Christian gay liberation – as ha
been foreseen by the anti-women's ordination lobby, who had looke
across the Atlantic and observed how the ordination of America
women in the seventies had opened a Pandora's box of sexual radicalism

n the American Episcopal Church. Now, the Movement for the Ordination of Women (MOW) officially dissolved itself (though in fact staying quietly in existence); Church of England watchers began to get used
to a new set of initials: LGCM, which stands for Lesbian and Gay Christian Movement.

According to its secretary, the media-friendly London clergyman,
Richard Kirker, LGCM had the support of about 25 per cent of the new
Synod members. George Austin thought the LGCM's real influence
would be higher than that: he reckoned that there were about 20 per
cent hardcore gay rights members, but that they could count on the
support of perhaps another 20 per cent or more. These were composed
among others of so-called 'affirming Catholics' – who one irredentist
Anglo-Catholic of the old school told me believed in 'girls in the sanctu-
ary and boys in bed' – and other fellow travellers. As Kirker pointed out,
in the previous Synod only about ten per cent had supported 'gay
rights'; and it did not seem wholly unlikely that he might well in the
end prove to be right in his claim that just as support for women's ordination grew from small beginnings during the late seventies and eighties, so now would the pressure to 'rethink' Anglican doctrine and
practice towards declared homosexuals, until what LGCM was demanding became practical politics. In the Capital, gay rights candidates
topped the poll in the House of Clergy, both in the London Diocese
itself and south of the river in the Southwark diocese, where the most
successful candidate was the Revd Geoffrey John, formerly Dean of
Divinity at Magdalen, Oxford: the gay party would not be lacking in
persuasive speakers or theological muscle.

This is not to say that they had taken over the Synod. As Kirker
pointed out, though the gay lobby had done well, 'the opposition is also
larger. The middle ground might be squeezed.' According to an analysis
carried out by the *Church Times*, of the elected members who mentioned 'traditional family values' in their election addresses, around 25
per cent actually ran on an openly anti-family values ticket: though
they were, obviously enough, outnumbered by the 75 per cent who
were in favour of them.

It was necessary, nevertheless, to understand how utterly different
the Anglican political landscape had become. The Catholic group had
been halved in strength – many of the most politically effective had
gone to Rome, others had simply become unelectable under the new
dispensation. There was another factor: now women had been safely

ordained, it was no longer thought necessary (by some at least) to keep such misfits as George Austin on board. When the liberal Archbishop John Habgood had begun to mend his fences with traditionalists by appointing him as Archdeacon of York, he arranged for him to keep his seat on the Synod by persuading the other two archdeacons in his diocese to elect him as their Synod representative; now, it was thought safe by his archidiaconal colleagues to renege on what had been an informal condition of his acceptance, and their support was withdrawn. The exclusion of Archdeacon Austin from the Synod after twenty-five years (and thus, not insignificantly, the removal of his voice from the powerful committee responsible for episcopal appointments) was seen by many of his constituency as being symbolic of the new world that traditionalist Anglicans now inhabited. He promptly announced that having been released from the time-consuming business of being a member of the Synod, he would be able in future to devote more time to Forward in Faith – it was a vivid example of how the marginalization of the dissidents led naturally to the building up of their separate corporate identity.

All the dynamics of Anglican power-broking, it seemed, had undergone a radical shift. The great Reformation issues of Bible and Sacraments had, at a stroke, ceased to be what divided the Church of England – those who cared about such things had been shuffled off to the margins to do their own thing. As we have seen, this suited many of them perfectly well. The Anglo-Catholics buckled down to the construction of their church within a church, while conservative Evangelicals, under the banner of Reform (a kind of Protestant version of Forward in Faith), got on with the business of running their own parishes, which were booming while those of the liberal Anglican mainstream often withered on the vine.

'Real' Evangelicals and Catholics had, in fact always despised the Synod, and were quite happy to get on with the Church's true business of winning souls for God. This meant that to some extent the liberal triumph in the Synod elections was a hollow one: for what, some asked, was the point of an assembly which so many of the clergy and laity (arguably the most spiritually vital part of the Church of England) now regarded as an apostate body whose moral authority they did not accept? But even on the Synod itself, the conservatives could not be dismissed. Conservative Evangelicals, for instance, might have their reservations about the corridors of power; but as the gay lobby were uneasily aware, they also had increased their vote, with a swing in some dioceses of around 15 per cent. The Reform Evangelicals had other ways, too, of exercising their influence. They tended to have large rich parishes; withdrawal of their financial support (a movement to do this had been under way for some time) could bring about the bankruptcy of whole dioceses: if the Synod were to show any inclination to conciliate the gay lobby, this threat could very quickly become a devastating reality. The granting of 'gay rights' would certainly lead to an Evangelical withdrawal from mainstream Anglican life, in which financially independent Evangelical parishes would remain formally part of the Church of England while repudiating the authority of the bishops.

The point here is that the demands of the LGCM were and remain very radical indeed; it was not necessary to be a bigot to see them as utterly unacceptable. They included full and public recognition from the bishops that a 'permanent, faithful, stable relationship' of a homosexual couple was as valid as a heterosexual marriage. They demanded the appointment to parishes of openly practising homosexuals. Their ultimate aim is have a liturgy for the solemnization of gay unions included in official Anglican service-books. In the words of Richard Kirker, 'the Church should be able to offer liturgies of commitment by couples to all, irrespective of their sexual orientation.'

DR CAREY COMES INTO HIS OWN

The position of the Archbishop of Canterbury in all this has been crucial, and may well prove decisive. For, though the leadership of Dr George Carey has sustained an unceasing barrage of criticism within the Church of England – one which has needed all his considerable reserves of determination and courage to withstand – it may be that his unexpected choice as Archbishop will turn out to be not, as his enemies (liberal, Anglo-Catholic and conservative Evangelical alike) have assumed, a dreadful blunder, but the only really inspired choice available in these very particular circumstances. The Anglo-Catholic movement will not now – and as I argue in this book, should not ever again, for its own sake and just as importantly for the unity and viability of the New Church of England – return to the mainstream. Dr Carey, like most mainstream Anglicans, has simply not understood their problems; but if he is wise, he will not try to, for his real historic vocation lies elsewhere.

The struggle of the mainstream now is for its own coherence and unity; and Dr Carey may well be the only available Archbishop who could pull it off. He is strongly in favour of women's ordination; so is most of mainstream Anglicanism. He is also, unlike many of his brother bishops and much of the Anglican intelligentsia, very firmly against moral relativism, and he is prepared to take his stand in defence of moral absolutes: in this he is almost certainly supported by most Anglicans in the pew (and by much of the non-churchgoing public beyond).

Dr Carey's genius (and it amounts almost to that) is not for the endless theological bilocation so often supposed to be necessary to keep modern Anglicanism afloat in its present form, but for the kind of simplification of needless complexities which those who are pure in heart so often instinctively achieve. Dr Carey's attack on relativism may not have had the philosophical depth of the Pope's in *Veritatis Splendor* (a document highly praised by Dr Carey); but it has been in its way a considerable success. What will almost certainly be the result, quietly and subtly, is that the Anglican liberal Establishment will over the years attempt to undermine him, as they undermined Dr Donald Coggan twenty years ago when he attempted a not dissimilar operation with his ill-fated 'Call to the Nation'. In 1977, the anonymous Crockford's preface (by David L. Edwards) attempted to cut the then Archbishop down to size – with greater asperity though less famously than Dr Gareth Bennett ten years later – saying *inter alia* that 'it has been possible to think his key statements both splendidly clear and counterproductively simple; both attractively personal and alarmingly naive'.

But Dr Carey's position by the late nineties was in some ways stronger than Dr Coggan's two decades before. For, though Anglican liberalism never seemed stronger than it did on the eve of the vote on women's ordination, it may be that history will record that it was near or even past the peak of its influence. The fight against the ordination of women (in which, ironically, Dr Carey had been on the liberal side) had focused the attention of conservatives, not only on women's ordination but on the whole liberal agenda of which it was part (to much of which Dr Carey was as obdurately opposed as they were); and the rise of gay liberation as the next item on that agenda consolidated the opposition to any further general movement in that direction. The Synod may have supposed, erroneously, that the Anglo-Catholics would settle down happily with the ordination of women once they had become used to the idea. But they will enter into no such fantastical conjecture about the Evangelicals' peaceful acceptance of the ordination of openly practising homosexuals.

The chances are that this line will now be held, that though there will be embarrassing debates in the Synod which will not help the Church of England's reputation, the gay lobby will never gain the kind of dominance in the Synod chamber or the corridors of power that the women-priests lobby achieved. Demonstrations – particularly one involving the person of Dr Carey himself – have not helped the cause of gay radicalism. Anglicans now have a longing for unity; that is the new factor in the equation on which Dr Carey will be able more and more to rely. In a moment of discouragement he once indicated that he was considering early retirement: he should now reconsider this, for he has a great and historic task to bring to completion. He should now address what could be for him his true vocation: the long overdue work of uniting in one fold, not only the emerging tradition of a New Anglicanism but the whole English Protestant tradition.

CONCLUSION

LET MY PEOPLE GO

I believe that the Church of England has a key role to play. They must take a strong lead. They must make a generous offer. It's going to be an act of Grace that cracks this one ... Why can't they just open the doors, offer us room, allow us to be to them what the Jesuits, Dominicans, Franciscans and Benedictines are to the Roman Catholic Church?
Leslie Griffiths, President of the Methodist Conference, February 1995

IN OCTOBER 1994, the weekly *Methodist Recorder* revealed that preliminary talks had taken place involving a small group which included the Archbishops of both York and Canterbury and the Revd Leslie Griffiths, President of the Methodist Conference. They had discussed the interim report of the Anglican-Methodist International Commission, published the previous year; and they had decided to appoint a larger group with representatives from both Churches to discuss on what terms 'talks about talks' towards unity might begin once more after an interval of twenty-five years.

Before the talks themselves began, Leslie Griffiths got a few home truths off his chest in his regular column in the *Methodist Recorder*. The gist of his remarks was that if any progress was to be made, it was the Church of England which had to make the running. The collapse of the process a quarter of a century before had been deeply distressing for all those on both sides who had wanted it to succeed. Archbishop Michael Ramsey had been grief-stricken (and had never forgiven Bishop Graham Leonard for his part in frustrating the scheme). But the Anglicans had other fish to fry ecumenically: it was the era of Archbishop Ramsey's visit to Rome and the setting up of the Anglican-Roman

Catholic International Commission, which in the end, it really was thought by many, would lead inevitably to full corporate reunion between Canterbury and Rome. For Methodism in England there were no new adventures. They had actually brought themselves to the point at which their conference had made the decision to put an end to the English Methodist Church if the scheme went through: they would have been not, as Pope Paul was to say to the Anglicans, 'united not absorbed', but simply absorbed. It had been a terrible and courageous act of corporate self-immolation, a kind of death before a new life in a new Church: and their sacrificial act had – or so it seemed to them – been thrown back in their faces. They had suffered a kind of death without resurrection. Even now, a quarter of a century later, wrote Leslie Griffiths, 'We've never really got over the trauma of being rejected as we were.'

This laid a very particular responsibility of leadership in the new process on the Anglican authorities, he wrote early in 1995:

> Even the most ardent ecumenical enthusiasts among us don't feel we have the heart to go back to the drawing board with the Church of England. We don't have the energy any more. In any case, we'd secretly be wondering if the Anglicans could deliver at the end of the day ... 25 years after the the 1969 great rejection was surely a timely moment for the C of E to put out feelers again. They'd got through their struggle to ordain women. For the moment Rome had put them on the back burner. The Porvoo agreement ... seems to hold out new possibilities for a further reconciliation with us Methodists ... But no word seemed to be coming ...

But now the process had started again: it was, it seemed, indeed the right moment. So the question now arises: why is there no sense of growing anticipation, why (at the time of this book's publication it is nearly three years since the subject was broached again) does it all appear to be moving so slowly? The talks themselves began in March 1995, with further talks in December, at St Stephen's House. Nevertheless, the impression so far is that given the momentous character of what is being talked about, there is not exactly a rising sense of excitement. The question has to be this: is the Church of England really exercising the leadership Leslie Griffiths was asking for, or is it playing for time? And if it is, why might that be? Is it because the Anglican authorities themselves fear, not so much that they will be unable to 'deliver at the end of the day' (since they certainly have the synodical votes to do that handsomely), but that they will harden the alienation of the dissident minority from the New Anglican mainstream? And if the answer to that question is in the affirmative, are we to draw the inference that the Establishment seriously believes there is any hope that this constituency might yet *cease* to be alienated, that there might even now be a change of heart? If so, they are playing a dangerous game: for if they now raise the expectation of the English Methodists yet again and then play a waiting game, the cause of reunion could be damaged irreparably, perhaps this time for ever – and for nothing, since the dissidents will never budge an inch. The Anglican authorities, says Leslie Griffiths, 'must take a strong lead. They must make a generous offer.' This is surely a matter in which priorities have to be weighed and decisive leadership given: and the time it all takes will become important.

Certainly, the English Anglican establishment is with cool deliberation playing such a political waiting game over another issue which ought surely now to be regarded as a major Anglican priority: the resolution of the ecclesiological anomaly whereby a woman may be ordained to the priesthood of the Church of England but not to its episcopate. In effect, women have been ordained to a kind of second-class, or at least disabled, priesthood. Here, the reasons for delay are more overtly acknowledged. It is to give more time for the 'reception' of women's ordination to the priesthood, which being translated means an extended period in which it is hoped opponents might change their minds. The leaders of the women's ordination movement have been persuaded not to mount any concerted challenge, in the forlorn hope that this might happen. But the real question is for how much longer the large numbers of women already ordained can be persuaded to accept what they must see not only as an anomaly but as a real injustice.

The mood among Anglican women clergy, five years after the decision to allow their ordination as priests, was not one of unalloyed contentment over the way things had worked out in practice. At a fringe meeting for the supporters of women's ordination held at the 1996 summer Synod at York University, one observer had sensed 'an overwhelming feeling of disappointment, and even lack of direction'. There was a general sense that having ordained women, the Church of England did not know what to do with them. As Stephen Trott, famous for having started a clergy section in a major British Trades Union, put it, 'Many of those ordained since 1993 have previously served many years as deaconesses, then as deacons, and have considerable experience of ministry and pastoral gifts which they long to see taken up and used effectively by the Church, which seems now to be almost embarrassed as to how to deploy its new resource.' Women, argued the Evangelical minister John Pearce, Rector of Limehouse, were 'getting a very raw deal. Indeed, in one diocese known to me, women are only offered the jobs that no one else will take ...'

Himself a member of the minority 'integrity', John Pearce thought that the logic of the present situation was that the Church of England should 'get on with the job' and ordain women as bishops; 'for the two-thirds majority,' he wrote, 'there is no reason whatsoever why women should not be consecrated at once. Only misogyny prevents this – just as it prevents women from being given good jobs in the parochial ministry.'

This was a growing view among the dissidents: that the majority should 'get on with the job'. Women-bishops were like the sword of Damocles: better have the crisis now and bring it to a head one way or another, rather than wait for attrition and old age to take their toll and have the move imposed just as the existing safeguards crumble. As John Broadhurst argued (before his translation to Fulham), 'the only reputable argument against women bishops in a church which already has women priests is the argument of provisionality':

> ... the church is not sure whether women can be priests and is waiting to see if it is God's will ... However, I believe [provisionality] has always been a dishonest argument made by those who want the opponents to die out quietly. We will not! They should follow their convictions and accept the consequences which is granting us that alternative episcopal oversight or parallel jurisdiction that we have always said was the consequence of ordaining women. *A church cannot live peacefully, or purposefully, when large numbers reject the ministry of many of its clergy* [My italics].

This last assertion would equally describe the consequence of any new Anglican-Methodist unity scheme along the lines of the last one. And any new scheme would surely have to be on the basis, for the

Methodists themselves, of 'no retreat'. It is hardly to be supposed that Methodist ministers would submit to reordination by Anglican bishops after the recognition in the Porvoo agreement of Lutheran clergy who by traditional Anglican standards are certainly not episcopally ordained. The issues of sacramental integrity are therefore identical with those of twenty-five years ago; they are also much the same as those so often rehearsed during the controversy over women's ordination.

The two great ecclesiological developments (women-bishops and reunion with English Methodism) which it is now the Church of England's manifest destiny to achieve – and which for the spiritual well-being, even safety, of those concerned need to be concluded within a foreseeable time-scale – both entail the same condition for their calm and peaceful conclusion: a final settlement with the dissident Anglican minority which it feels to be equitable and pleasing to God.

HOPE DEFERRED

There are several possible outcomes, once it is understood that there can be no going back now, *and that all these issues have to be resolved sooner rather than later*. It is vital that it should be understood by the Anglican majority that it is unrealistic to suppose that women-bishops can be delayed for as long as it would take for opposition to them to die out. After a quarter of a century, one-third of the priests in the Lutheran Church of Sweden remain opposed to the ordination of women, for identical reasons to those advanced by the English-speaking dissidents. If anything, the opposition in England is even more determined and it is well prepared for the long haul. And, quite simply, the line cannot be held against women-bishops for that long: this is a consummation whose time has come.

Much the same has to be said about Anglican-Methodist reunion. Now talks have begun once more they must come to their logical conclusion sooner rather than later. The issues have been long rehearsed; and as the Bible and Shakespeare say, 'hope deferred maketh the heart sick'. The Methodists cannot be fobbed off for ever. And this too has implications for the Anglican traditionalists.

All this brings us back to the three questions we asked in the last chapter about the dissidents' ecclesiological demands and aspirations, at least as they are currently formulated (though whether these formulations correspond to their real assessment of what is possible or their actual long-term goals is certainly a question worth asking). First, is it conceivable that the Church of England would actually allow the formation of a formally constituted and permanent parallel jurisdiction? Second, would the two existing provinces of the Church of England allow this independently governed ecclesial entity to enter into communion with an outside body (let us assume that means Rome)? The third question is even more to the point: would Rome, or Orthodoxy for that matter, agree to such an arrangement while the new province remained an integral part of the Church of England?

Let us, for the sake of argument, examine the hypothesis that the answer to the first question is in the affirmative: let us suppose that the bishops of the Church of England were to erect what would be in effect a third province of the Church of England. What then? The first thing to note is that it would make very little difference in practice. Those parishes who would opt for such a jurisdiction would for the most part be the same as those which have already either opted for a flying bishop or become affiliated with Forward in Faith, or both. Future episcopal appointments would be made independently. There would be precisely the same condition of 'impaired communion' between the new jurisdiction and the Provinces of Canterbury and York as there was between the American Episcopal Church and the Church of England before women's ordination in England: but since such an impaired relationship already exists, nothing much would change there. The new entity would need its own theological college (St Stephen's House would do nicely). It would elect its own members to the General Synod; its bishops would attend the Lambeth Conference. In short, with one or two adjustments, things would go on in practice very much as before: the Act of Synod made it possible for the dissidents to erect their own informal jurisdiction anyway; what would really change would be that this entity would be recognized and its future secured.

What, then, about the second and third questions: would the New Anglican mainstream permit its third province to establish communion with some part of the wider Church (let us say with Rome)? And would it be possible for some part of the wider Church to establish communion with the third province without being in communion with the rest of the Church of England?

The straightforward answer is that though the Church of England might well permit it, the Roman Catholic Church would certainly refuse formally to establish full communion with such a body. The concept of partial or impaired *communio in sacris* (in the sense widely adopted within Anglicanism to cope with the problems attendant on women's ordination) is unknown to Catholic ecclesiology. Churches which are in communion with other Churches are in communion with all those within them: selectively to establish communion with part of another Church would be to say that that Church is not one but two separate bodies which are not in communion with each other. It is inconceivable that the Catholic Church would make such a determination in the case of different jurisdictions within the same Church.

This brings us to the second hypothetical scenario, which seems to me in any case altogether more likely to come to the point of being tested. As in the first scenario, the Anglican Establishment is brought to the point at which it has to proceed sooner rather than later to the consecration of women to the episcopate; but it refuses to grant the dissidents the autonomous jurisdiction they regard as an essential minimum settlement. The first result of this would be that the PEVs and the Bishop of Fulham would declare themselves to be out of communion with all other bishops in the Church of England: that is their declared position. So would the clergy and laity within their constituency. What would the Anglican bishops do then? They would be faced by four bishops in office and between two and three hundred Forward in Faith parishes in possession of their buildings. They would be faced also by at least 1,200 clergy affiliated to Forward in Faith, supported by up to 2,000 more who would be opposed to women-bishops, some of whom might not actually declare themselves out of communion with their bishops (though many would), but all of whom would give moral support to those who did.

Under these circumstances, the bishops of the Establishment would have two options. They might take a tough line, abrogating the Act of Synod and the London Plan, removing recognition from the pastoral function of the PEVs and the Bishop of Fulham, and withdrawing their stipends, and attempting to take possession of the Church buildings occupied by Forward in Faith clergy.

They might attempt such a thing, but if they did they would inevitably be forced into a retreat. The parishes would withdraw their contributions to their own dioceses and pay them into a central fund from which they would support their bishops and clergy directly. In many, perhaps most of the parishes, the vicar would have the parson's freehold, and so could not be removed without costly and uncertain recourse to both

3rd Province cannot be
Anglican + PORVOO + Methodism !!

the ecclesiastical and secular courts. Those clergy ('priests-in-charge') without the parson's freehold would have the right to remain until the end of their five-year terms, and would then resist their expulsion, supported by their people, who would occupy their churches and clergy houses in their defence. There would be many *causes célèbres*, in which the Establishment would appear as a heartless oppressor of faith and integrity. The simple fact is that the Church of England could not afford a policy of such ruthlessness, either financially or morally and also because it really is not nasty or brutal enough, and would have no stomach for the work.

There would be a stand-off. The dissident entity would now have become to all intents and purposes an independent Church. Its faith would be orthodox and clearly enunciated. It would be against all its instincts to attempt to survive alone, cut off from the fellowship of the wider Church: and it would therefore attempt to establish a relationship with that part of the Church nearest to its own heritage and instincts, the Latin Church of the West. What then would be the attitude of the English Roman Catholic Church?

The answer is almost certainly that there would be no question of establishing full communion with such a body, for several reasons. First, there would be the old obstacle of Anglican orders. Second, it would be seen by the Church of England – reasonably or unreasonably – as a hostile act. But suppose both these difficulties could be overcome: there would still be the overriding difficulty that in the case of full communion with such a body there would be established, in effect, a Uniate church independent of the local hierarchy: a scenario which as we have seen is guaranteed to trigger off all the alarm bells in the English Catholic Church. But might there be a less clear cut temporary solution? There is an interim state which is something less than full communion in which, nevertheless, there exists something rather like it, a state in which something called 'Eucharistic hospitality' is permitted between two bodies which recognize each other's orders and have determined that they share a common faith. The faithful of one communion may receive the sacraments of the other where they are recognized; the priests of one may in case of urgent need celebrate the Eucharist at the other's altars. Such a relationship exists, for example, between the Polish National Church and the Roman Catholic Church in America, where it is seen as part of a continuing process of convergence which may end with the re-establishment of full communion.

Might such a relationship be possible for the new entity? Suppose that the English Catholic hierarchy were faced by a clearly constituted ecclesial entity, asking for the occasional exchange of sacramental hospitality, whose faith was in all essentials identical with theirs, *and who were in a position to establish with all necessary proofs that all its clergy were validly ordained in a Catholic sense?*

What then? The answer might seem to be that the question could not arise, since (*Apostolicae Curae* having made the matter clear beyond peradventure) no Anglican orders could be recognized in this way. But what if Forward in Faith were to pre-empt this answer? The status of their orders and sacraments has in any case become a live issue for the dissidents themselves. As Bishop Broadhurst put it in *Quo Vaditis* (1996), a collection of essays by Anglican and Lutheran dissidents, 'if a majority of Christendom rejects our orders in what sense are our sacraments sure and certain signs?' The participation of Old Catholic bishops in most Church of England Ordinations since the twenties was supposed to have settled the question, but it has not. And indeed, as Bishop Broadhurst continues, '... it is difficult to see how it could. What is the nature of the ministry in a church containing those who ... assert Christ is objectively present alongside those who believe any presence is purely subjective? ... I am firmly convinced that this issue is one that affects our corporate psyche and disables our Church.' 'Surely,' Bishop Broadhurst goes on, 'it is time to seize the nettle and sort out the question.' These last are interesting words: given the record of Forward in Faith in the matter of concrete ecclesial building works, for constructing rather than simply for talking, what might they portend? His answer is plain enough: 'Conditional ordination by the Old Catholics, or others, would not demean us, rather it would clearly demonstrate that we are in earnest in the search for unity and truth. We would be firmly on a path of convergence.'

How would the Catholic Church react? Though they might not like the existence of an undoubted and authentic ecclesial entity, possessing both Catholic faith and Catholic order and over which they had no control, it is hard to see how the English Catholic bishops could actually deny that such a development would indeed constitute 'a path of convergence'. Any open recognition of such a body, however, would be another matter, for one simple and overriding reason if for no other: the wholly undue deference (which goes far beyond any reasonable conception of ecumenical courtesy) which English Roman Catholic bishops continue to pay to the bishops of the Established Church. 'Why is it,' one dissident Anglican priest complained to me, 'that on no subject except sexual ethics and particularly abortion are the Roman Catholic bishops in England and Wales ever the principal speakers on any platform? Why do they push an often second-rate Anglican bishop forward? It isn't as though, as it might have been said at one stage, on the whole the calibre of Anglican bishops is higher than that of Roman bishops. They're a pretty dull bunch now. You could have excused it if they were the sort of people you'd naturally put forward in a particular circumstance in this country – "a man of his education", and that sort of thing – but they're not.'

This almost servile deference extends to the Established Church as an institution. As long as the Church of England stood in its way, or for as long, indeed, as there was the slightest suspicion that the Anglican bishops might not like a close relationship with the dissident entity to develop, such a body would be treated by the Catholic Church in England if not as a pariah, certainly with great circumspection. And this undue deference is a factor in any conceivable solution of this problem: it makes Anglican co-operation even more essential than it would be anyway.

One key to any further progress towards Realignment is thus the Church of England's own self-perception. Neither essential element in the 'two bloc' scenario which I have outlined (the convergence of those of the Catholic mind in communion with Rome, at the same time as a parallel convergence of those of the Reformed tradition in communion with Canterbury) can be established until the Church of England has faced a moment of truth. It has to understand the logical consequence of women's ordination: *that it has opened up a future for Anglicanism which is radically different from its past.* Anglican pluralism can no longer contain the Catholic tradition; and this tradition is now a major obstacle blocking the realization of what have become the Church of England's deepest instincts. Quite simply, it is not in the interests of the New Anglicanism to attempt to frustrate the inevitable historical logic of what its dissident Catholic minority is now seeking to achieve.

It seems unlikely on the face of it that the bishops and Synod of the Established Church will come to realize this without a period of conflict. In the end, however, the logic of history will prevail, and an exhausted Church of England will come to see what it should have accepted already, that it cannot move forward until it has allowed these people to take to the boats. What then will be the response of the

English Catholic bishops? Will they respond generously and this time with more vision and imagination than they showed in Low Week 1992?

What would such a response need to embody? I do not believe that the ecclesial entity that Forward in Faith has created is intended, even by them, as a permanent structure: it is a provisional solution, a desert encampment. They know very well, despite their rhetoric, that there will be no third province within the Church of England; nor does it seem at all likely that they are so cut off from reality that their ambition is to create a Uniate church. What, then, should the Catholic bishops be prepared to offer? I recorded in the last chapter a conversation with a Forward in Faith priest who had attempted to take his parish to Rome, had been repulsed by his local Catholic bishop, and had settled down to life in communion with his Provincial Episcopal Visitor. For him, the essential in any solution was that 'Rome has got to have a more creative view of the corporate nature of our present existence.'

His present existence is not in fact something he can hold on to within the Church of England. The present situation is provisional, not permanent. It is, to look at it in a more positive way, dynamic rather than static. As Geoffrey Kirk told me, 'The truth is that everybody knows that we are in an in-between time. That a holding operation has been achieved':

> The holding operation might not even have been necessary had the original Roman proposals made a Roman Option that was viable, and gradual. It had to be viable in terms of what an Anglican worshipping community is like, gradual in the sense that you could opt into it over a period of time. Parishes could opt into it, groups could opt into it, over a period of time. In other words, it had to be a mopping up operation, conducted with a certain amount of patience.

A PARTICULAR QUALITY

The fact is that the procedures for such a 'mopping up operation' had already been devised and authorized for use with Anglicans elsewhere. The 'Pastoral Provision' authorized for American Anglicans at the beginning of the eighties could have then and still could now provide the basis for such an operation. Under Canon 372, it will be recalled, it was envisaged that 'there may be established in a given territory particular Churches distinguished by the rite of the faithful *or by some other similar quality*.' In many dissident parishes, the Rite used was not an important consideration: it was a matter of their particular ethos and shared history – that was the 'particular quality' that distinguished them, and they had been through a good deal to preserve it from wilful destruction.

The Pastoral Provision was discussed by the English Catholic bishops at their meeting in November 1993. Cardinal Hume's summary, at the press conference which followed, of the reasons why the Pastoral Provision had been rejected by the Bishops' Conference is worth repeating here, since it has to be said, with the very greatest respect (an expression I do not employ lightly), that not one of the reasons the Cardinal adduced stands up to any kind of scrutiny; and I strongly suspect that he was not very convinced by them himself:

> The first thing is that the United States situation is very different from ours: fifty million Catholics, two million Episcopalians. In this country it is the other way round. And so we begin with a different kind of numbers game. And of course the United States is slightly larger than this country. Also, experience of the Pastoral Provision in the United States is fairly limited. Roughly 49 married priests, who actually exercise the Latin Rite and aren't in parishes and the number of parishes is five, the largest of which is 150, so it's not a big enterprise. And therefore I feel there's not enough experience for us to be able to build on it. And then, a very important point, the difference between the United States Episcopalians and ourselves: there's no question of church buildings. They can bring their buildings with them; [English Anglicans] can't.

The first claim here is that we have in this country 'a different kind of numbers game' from that across the Atlantic – a huge American Catholic Church and a tiny American Anglican Church, with the numbers reversed in England. But that is not of course the case: in terms of actual church attendance, the numbers in England are similar, with the Catholic Church slightly ahead for most of the last few decades. But the way the 'numbers game' is described here is significant nevertheless:

what the Cardinal seems to be expressing is less the reality of the case than the fears of the bishops. The message here seems to be that in America there is no chance whatever that the Catholic church could be swamped by the numbers of potential converts: but the Pastoral Provision in England might make it possible that quite substantial numbers would come, and *we therefore rule it out.*

This fear, it ought to be said first (and it undoubtedly exists in some quarters), is unworthy. It is the underlying vocation of the bishops to gather souls for God, especially if they are in a condition of particular spiritual need or danger. But it is also unreal: the Catholic Church will not be swamped or destabilized. Forward in Faith has affiliated with it, in round numbers, some 250 parishes (nearly all presently under some form of alternative episcopal oversight) and 1,200 clergy. Sources within Forward in Faith estimate that in around 200 of these parishes nearly all the congregation (as at St Matthew's, Bethnal Green) or a substantial part (as at St Stephen's, Gloucester Road) would come if the circumstances were right. Of the clergy, around 800 would come if they could bring all or a group of their people with them under some such arrangement as the Pastoral Provision.

To take the clergy first: it will be noted that there are more clergy than parishes, reflecting the large part of the constituency who are in parishes where Catholic-minded laity do not form a majority. Many of these lay people could be expected to come together in groups to form new Pastoral Provision parishes (Forward in Faith has already begun to establish 'Mass centres' outside the parish system – the first of these being in the Church of Christ the King, formerly the home of the London University Anglican chaplaincy). Many of these clergy would probably become in the end part of the general pool of clergy in their dioceses. The result would be that (if we add the former Anglican clergy ordained since 1993) there would be 1,000 more Catholic priests in England, an increase of about 25 per cent. This would take place gradually, probably over as much as a decade. Would this 'swamp' the Catholic Church? Or would it provide it with a much needed increase of pastorally expert clergy at a time when there is a crisis in vocations to the priesthood?

Much the same can be said about the parishes and parish groups. They would be spread over the country and received gradually; there would be, after reception, a constant process of osmosis into the wider Catholic community. They pose no threat whatsoever to the stability of the English Catholic Church. As Geoffrey Kirk said to me, 'They don't realize, the English Roman bishops, how much the convert Anglican clergy would be on their side in integrating the people with their dioceses.'

The next argument against the Pastoral Provision is similar to the first. It is that the Pastoral Provision is designed for a much larger country than England. Unlike America, where all the churches are built much further away from each other than they are here, some of our churches are built quite close together. Is that the argument? It is difficult to see what else it might be. But given good will, there is absolutely no reason why Catholic churches quite close together should not co-exist perfectly happily. The existence of ill-will from some Catholic clergy is not a valid argument: it is their ill-will that would be the problem, not the Pastoral Provision. In fact, no one has ever found any such ill-will wherever the Pastoral Provision has been tried. In Arlington, Father Hawkins's church is a mere fifty yards away from the nearest existing Catholic church, in Texan terms practically an annexe. There has never been the slightest problem.

Then we are told that since the experience of the Provision is so limited, it does not give us a model that we could use. But the fact that a limited experiment is successful is not thought by a scientist to be a reason not to repeat it: on the contrary, he repeats it over and over again to see if it can be falsified. So far this experiment has not been falsified, and in the Cardinal's own diocese, two very similar experiments have met with considerable success. The point is that the Pastoral Provision is not a monolithic and utopian plan whose failure (like some ecclesiastical ground-nuts scheme) would be a total and costly disaster: it is, rather, a flexible long-term process which can be continually monitored, adjusted and if necessary selectively terminated. It is not a parallel jurisdiction, though there is a director and a co-ordinator: such parishes are firmly part of their diocese and under the authority of the local bishop.

The final argument is that in America, Episcopalians can bring their buildings and that this is impossible for English Anglicans. But the Pastoral Provision does not depend on bringing buildings, and some parish groups have had to make other arrangements, such as being given a time-slot for Mass in an existing Catholic church building. Furthermore, if parishes can continue to use their buildings (as in England they can unless the local Catholic clergy object) they do not need actually to bring them and on the whole it is probably better if they do not. Shared

hurch agreements are one of the great ecumenical successes of the last
wenty years, not least because they have the great benefit of being
ost-effective for all concerned. The Anglicans, other matters being set-
led, would put nothing in the way of concluding such agreements
wherever they were requested: they do not want even more of a major
problem which is already large enough, that of maintaining alone
under-used but much loved church buildings.

GROWING INTO COHERENCE

The question of buildings is not without importance in a more than
merely practical way. One eminent convert is wont to say that Anglicans have a disproportionate love of their buildings, that 'as long as they
don't have to give up their parish churches, they would become Bud-
dhists'. The success of shared church agreements is a practical illustration of the way in which defensive and exclusivist attitudes can be
broken down, once we decide to stop protecting what we have by simply holding on to it, come what may.

But these agreements are more than merely illustrative, they are
symbolic. Church buildings are constructed to be inclusive of those
within them, they are the place where the community gathers; they
also exclude those who are not part of the community. A shared church
agreement changes and expands the meaning of the building. It remains
a place where the community meets and defines itself: but not where
one community defines itself in a defensive or protectionist way
against another. Walls are inclusive; they are also defensive (and sometimes in the past, in a purely physical way, they have needed to be). A
community which opens this protective and defining space to another
community is lowering its defences. The walls now include two communities which remain distinct but whose difference from each other is
not now seen as a threat, because distinctiveness is protected by mutual respect. A congregation which divides on a matter of fundamental
principle, as did that of St Stephen's, Gloucester Road, can nevertheless
maintain the bonds of fellowship even though they are now members of
different Churches.

This brings us back to where we started. 'We have prayed for Christian unity and now it could be happening: a realignment of English
Christianity so as to bring us closer together, in two blocs, instead of

lots of blocs,' said Cardinal Hume in February 1993. But Realignment has been understood since as an essentially divisive process, largely because of our ingrained habits of seeing religion as a way of keeping things as they are. Realignment should be understood as a way in which the two main Christian traditions in England – and ultimately in the other English-speaking countries whose Christianity derives partly or entirely from the English experience – could become more internally coherent without losing the variousness which is the sign of spiritual life. A movement of Catholic-minded Anglicans into the Catholic Church, in a gradual and manageable way over time, paralleled by a convergence of Methodists and Free Churchmen around the Church of England – all this would be part of the same process. Two great Christian traditions, the Catholic and the Reformed, growing into ever greater internal coherence, the wounds of the past finally healing; and then, one day, possibly in as little as a century or two, errors and apostasies having fallen away like dead skin-cells, the union of all Christian people: that is the ultimate vision that Realignment opens up now.

What is striking about Realignment is not how utterly unlikely such a thing is, but how close it is to the internal logic of movements already well under way. What hinders it is a whole series of incoherencies, a log-jam of ecclesial blockages whose release would allow the process to flow onwards to its natural conclusion. Anglican Catholicism has stood in the way of Anglican-Methodist reunion: not because of any settled bloody-mindedness on the part of Anglo-Catholics but because their own fundamental principles were being threatened from within their own Church. There is only one future for them now which is stable and secure: a future in communion with the Holy See. But that homeward return is now being blocked for most of them as once they blocked the return of the Methodists, not only by the spiritual protectionism of the Catholic bishops but by the lack of vision of the Anglican bishops, who continue erroneously to suppose that it is in their own interests to do everything they can to detain those they would be better off without, and who would be happier and more fulfilled elsewhere.

'What we have, we hold,' is an attitude deeply held, both by English Catholic and English Anglican bishops. English Roman Catholic possessiveness has its roots deep in the tribal history of recusant and immigrant Catholicism. It is time for English Catholics to understand that this is an historical turning point whose time ought now to have come, but which they can block or at least delay if they retreat once more into the ghetto. The point is that the Catholic tradition can no longer be maintained simply by protecting its own boundaries. Mass attendance is falling. Already the Catholic Church in England is retreating, because it has denied for too long its own deepest nature, which is not simply to bury its faith safely in the ground in order to conserve it for those born into it, but to proclaim it from the housetops, to gather a harvest of souls for Christ, to convert the world. The Catholic prayer for the conversion of England is rarely said today: when the Cardinal referred to it as he called for Realignment in February 1993 he was widely criticized and had to withdraw. 'Why', the Pope asked after Low Week 1993, 'are the English bishops so unapostolic?' It is a hard judgement; but it was not difficult to see why he asked the question.

There is in any case no need to be defensive, to repel boarders, in the case of Catholic-minded Anglicans. The extreme caution manifested in the 1993 Low Week statement reflected an ignorance of the motives and intentions – as well as the spiritual character – of this movement for reunion with Rome. Bishop Crispian Hollis's suspicion, reported by Peter Hebblethwaite, was that 'the Anglo-Catholic party has acted as a political faction, using bluff and pressure to get its own way'; and his inference was that it would carry on with its divisive tactics if any kind of corporate solution was offered. 'It cannot be allowed to do that in a Catholic context. Back to the individual solution.'

The assumption that Catholic Anglicans would carry on with their quarrelsome ways after reception into the Catholic Church showed a complete lack of understanding of what it was that had made them so difficult in the first place. Roman Catholic experience of the Anglican clergy who have so far come is that those who as Anglicans showed the greatest and most effective resistance to the Establishment have turned out to be the most loyal and obedient Catholic clergy. There was no reason why they should not; they now had, for themselves at least, what they had always longed for in their hearts, communion with the Holy See. Nor is there any reason to suppose that a pragmatic and flexible corporate solution on the lines of the Pastoral Provision would lead to former Anglicans acting within the Catholic Church 'as a political faction'; at this stage, even to state the fear is surely to show its intrinsic absurdity.

Despite the deliberately limited operation of the Roman Option in its first half-decade, it has become clear that the fears and insecurities of many of the Catholic bishops have been dispelled by events. Even bishops who in the early stages gained the reputation for being unhelpful to Anglican clergy offering themselves for the Catholic priesthood, seemed after a year or two to relax, to realize that they could let down their guard. Many Catholic bishops underwent, in the words of one of them, a 'very steep learning curve' about the beliefs and capacities of the Anglican clergy with whom they now had to deal. In the seminaries where they went for training and discernment, teaching staff were sometimes astonished by how little they had to do. Above all, the ministerial experience and qualities of the former Anglicans came into their own once they were operating once more as pastors.

hopeful
X

BRINGING THEM AT LAST SAFE HOME

One of the lessons of history is that real changes, historical 'realignments' of this kind, tend to happen not – as it can seem in retrospect – at a given moment, but in a series of convulsions which finally bring the process to critical mass. Between upheavals, it can seem that the immediate crisis has been contained and that the *status quo ante* has been preserved. But all the time, on the ground, the process of change is relentlessly proceeding and pressure is building up towards the final and definitive crisis.

The Low Week statement of the Catholic bishops was presented, as it had to be, as the only possible final outcome of the discussions that had preceded it: the public speculation that had surrounded the Westminster conversations was now dismissed as the kind of thing which occurs only in the minds of those who do not know how these things are done. But how, in the end, it was decided they should be done was not the inevitable way of doing them. A corporate solution was not then and is not now unthinkable: for, as we have seen, the unthinkable had already been thought and given credence at the highest level; *and it will be thought again*. Like the Porvoo agreement, the Low Week statement will be seen by History not as a final settlement but as the beginning of a continuing movement.

With Porvoo, there was formally established a shift of theological principle over how the Church of England understands Apostolic order, a movement taking it definitively away from a supernatural Catholic understanding and towards a functionalist Protestant understanding of the nature of ministry and sacraments. In concrete historical terms, it

heresy

heralded the eventual union of English Anglicanism with Methodism and with the United Reformed tradition (itself a union of Congregationalists and Presbyterians).

With the Low Week statement, we may yet prove to have witnessed the first tentative movement towards the reunion of the Roman Catholic Church with what Aidan Nichols in his book *The Panther and the Hind* called 'Anglicanism selectively defined'.

These things will happen if they are not prevented from happening. It is my submission that it is the natural course of events that they should. All the conditions for them to happen still obtained in the Roman Catholic and Anglican Churches in England, five years after the General Synod vote of November 1992 (and will endure for a generation). The concessions allowed in England by the Catholic bishops had been limited: they enabled, nevertheless, a series of experiments and clarifications to unfold which little by little stilled the fears and suspicions of many, including some of the most obdurate opponents, thus preparing the way for a more effective and comprehensive settlement.

In the Church of England, the problem posed by a large dissident minority had not been solved but had grown more intractable. The minority had not, as it was supposed they would, withdrawn their objections to the ordination of women and become reabsorbed into the life of the Church of England. They had on the contrary been consolidated into a separate and identifiable constituency, with its own bishops and internal communications.

Thus, when the next convulsion within Anglicanism supervenes, the Roman Catholic bishops will find that the pastoral challenge with which they are faced will be both more clearly defined and on a very much greater scale than that of the period 1992–3. But they will also find that events have removed many of the crippling fears and anxieties of the Roman Option's initial phase, enabling them – given courage and vision – boldly to respond to the *kairos*, to God's moment. Will they be prepared? There remains at the time of writing some time left; but the sands are running out.

The same question can be put to the Anglican Bishops. Will they be prepared? Will they have the vision to accommodate the Anglican Catholics in an orderly manner, to understand that their separation (and in the end almost certainly their exodus) is necessary if the Church of England is to be empowered to fulfil its historic vocation in uniting the Churches of the Reformation?

The answer is that probably there will have to be at least one more major emergency before they can be brought to this point. The process of Realignment would be so much simpler if Anglicans, Free Churchmen and Roman Catholics would simply sit round a table and make rational decisions. But that is not how great historical movements proceed, at least, not at first. The great peace treaties are ratified only after major convulsions. There will be further, and deeper crises: that is how the great clarifications of Christian history unfold. Events will be infinitely more complicated than any of the simple scenarios I have outlined. There will be more pain and more healing, more petty stupidity and more inspired vision; ancestral insecurities and resentments will again manifest themselves on the Church's unimpressive human face: but in the end all this will be cast aside by the glorious Grace of God, sweeping through his people and bringing them at last safe home.

APPENDIX A

(see pp. 180 ff)

AN APPROACH TO THE HOLY SEE BY CERTAIN MEMBERS OF THE ANGLICAN CHURCH

The Convictions which have Brought Us Here

1. Above all else, we have come to the conviction that the fullness of the Catholic Faith requires the ministry of Peter and his successors, which is expressed in the universal primacy of the Roman See. Our understanding is in accordance with the teaching of *Lumen Gentium*: 'although many elements of sanctification and of truth can be found outside of [the Catholic Church's] visible structure, these elements, however, as gifts properly belonging to the Church of Christ, possess an inner dynamism toward Catholic unity.' It is imperative that we now act on this conviction.

2. We began our ministries in the Anglican Church confident that it did indeed possess a Catholic heart, and we have drawn much strength from the doctrinal and spiritual writings of our principal theologians. We found in the classical Anglican theological method – fidelity to the Scriptures and the Fathers – a means of union with the life and doctrine of the undivided Church. We believed that this method, together with our threefold ministerial order, was a sufficient basis to assert an underlying Catholic character within Anglicanism. But experience has shown us that our church is no longer capable of maintaining fidelity to the Bible and patristic tradition. Its understanding of 'diffused' authority has led it to embrace the unCatholic principle that truth in doctrine and morals can be determined by majority vote in local synods.

3.   The Second Vatican Council, particularly in its teachings on Scripture and Tradition, has opened an important door for us theologically. It has enabled us to make an informed and conscientious decision, proceeding out of our own theological principles, to seek reconciliation with the Catholic Church. How ironical it seems to us, that one of the central pillars of the Reformation – the authority of Scripture – is upheld by the Pope in his teaching at a time when much of contemporary Protestantism has effectively abandoned it! The consequence of our attempting to recover an orthodox interpretation of Scripture in the face of modern historical critical scholarship has demonstrated how crucial is the teaching office of the Church for the maintenance of the Faith. And the deeply patristic spirit of Vatican II has led us to see in the Roman Communion what we sought and held dear in our own.

4.   We believe that a truly historic opportunity now presents itself, namely for the healing of the great Western Schism, in a way which few envisioned. The Anglican Church is not the only church of the Reformation to be breaking up, foundering on the rocks of a post-modern secularism it has no power to avoid. We now believe there is little hope that the Anglican Communion, as presently constituted, will ever be able to move toward corporate reunion with the Catholic Church. The hopes we had placed in the official conversations of the Anglican-Roman Catholic International Commission must now find their fulfilment in some other form.

WHAT DO WE SEEK?

5.   As Anglicans, we are unable to approach the Catholic Church completely united about what is fundamental and worth preserving of our tradition. We are divided among ourselves about which liturgical and devotional forms are the best instruments for conveying Christian truth and shaping our ecclesial life. In consequence, we seek guidance about which of these elements should be brought forward into the Catholic Church. For some of us this is not an overriding issue: the liturgical movement has brought about a real convergence of liturgical forms in our respective communities, so that in many respects (e.g., lectionary, liturgical texts, and ritual) there is already a common observance. But for others, particularly for many of the laity, it is the Book of Common Prayer which defines the chief characteristics of Anglican

church life. Although we have found it difficult to describe precisely, the Book of Common Prayer is the cornerstone of that tradition of worship and piety Pope Paul VI termed 'a worthy patrimony'.

6. Our prayer has been that out of the present confused state of Anglicanism might emerge a compelling evangelical vision for our future. It must certainly be more than the preservation of the distinctive features of Anglican Church culture (i.e., its liturgical, devotional, and musical heritage), as worthy an undertaking as this may be. We desire that our return to union with Peter will enable us to contribute to the healing of the Western Schism, by means of an apostolate uniquely dedicated to Christian unity, as a vehicle through which the Catholic Church may embrace her separated sons and daughters and augment the resources for her work of evangelization. We envision the formation of congregations and ministries in the United States and Canada with this particular mission in mind.

7. We belong to the Latin Church because we have come from her. In spite of being separated from the Holy See, we have always understood ourselves to be a part of Western Catholicism. The Anglican tradition is Augustinian in its foundations and formed in relation to Western scholasticism and Western modernity. Throughout its 450 years, however, there have developed within Anglicanism unique expressions of vibrant ecclesial life which, although incomplete, God has nevertheless used to attract and nourish many devout and committed Christians. We believe that these Anglican elements still have power to awaken in people a yearning for the full riches of the Catholic faith, but that they must be properly secured under true apostolic authority. It is for this reason that we seek a distinct jurisdictional identity within the Latin Church. Our prayer is that existing ecclesial bonds might be preserved, augmented, and developed in such a way that we might be permitted corporately to contribute to the mission and ministry of the Catholic Church. We hope that this structure would also be established so as to make it possible for us to participate in the regular organization of the Catholic Church. In matters of sacramental and clergy discipline, we wish to function in accordance with the provisions of the existing codes of Catholic Canon Law.

8. In a secularized society hostile to Christian spiritual life, communities preserving essentials of that life are to be treasured and gathered in, not scattered. This is what we seek for our communities (congregations, dioceses, and institutes of the spiritual life), which have

continued faithful and even grown in the midst of an apostasizing ecclesial structure. What do we believe is necessary for preserving and extending these communities and giving them a place in the mission of the Catholic Church?

i) Preserving our tradition of pastoral care with its emphasis on the priest as pastor and teacher. This congregationally-oriented and pastoral style of Anglican priestly ministry has been especially characteristic of the North American Anglican churches.

ii) Continuing our discipline of a married clergy and voluntary celibacy. This is an important element of the distinctive clerical style within our communities, identifying the pastors with the life of the communities they serve.

iii) Encouraging those aspects of lay involvement which have been traditional in Anglican experience, but in a manner which is consistent with Catholic teaching.

iv) Providing the means of educating clergy and lay leaders for this proposed jurisdiction.

v) Organizing this new structure so that it might be able at some future time to function internationally, thereby preserving existing relationships amongst members of the Anglican Communion who are seeking to be united with the Holy See.

9. In conclusion, we seek reconciliation with the Catholic Church because we have come to believe this is the will of Christ, not simply because we are reacting against liberalizing policies in our own churches. We believe that developments within Anglicanism are moving it inexorably away from the Gospel of Christ, particularly in the way it now insists that *koinonia* must be the primary theological category, from which truth is subsequently discerned. We believe that Christ's constitution for the Church begins with Truth (John 17:17), from which the Church's mission and unity springs. Hence we have come to Peter ...

APPENDIX B

(see pp. 194 ff)

FROM: CANON CHRISTOPHER COLVEN
TO ALL ASSOCIATED WITH SAINT STEPHEN'S,
GLOUCESTER ROAD

Commenting on the 11 November 1992 decision by the General Synod of the Church of England to allow the ordination of women priests, the present Archbishop of York said: 'Nothing can ever again be the same.' The legislative mills of the Church of England grind slowly, and it was not until the summer of 1994 that the first of such ordinations took place. During this period, the General Synod also debated and approved the Porvoo Declaration which opens the way to a new level of communion between the Church of England and the Lutheran Churches of the Baltic region: in so doing, it chose to re-define the notion of Apostolic Succession in such a way that the Nordic Churches (some of whom make no claim to continuity beyond the Reformation period) could share in authoritative episcopal ministry.

For some of us, these decisions have brought into question the claim of the Church of England to be an authentic, national expression of the One, Holy, Catholic and Apostolic Church of Christ. Unilateral actions do not sit well with universal claims. Some of our congregation have felt that they could no longer walk with us, and they have made the decisions that were right for them. Each of them left a gap in our community, but their going was with our affection and prayer. The prophecy of Isaiah says: 'In returning and rest you shall be saved: in quietness and trust shall be your strength' (30:15). In that spirit, we have deliberately committed ourselves to a thoughtful process as we seek to know how to respond to the evolving situation. During Lent 1994 we looked at the meaning of 'discernment', and we discovered how it is possible to come to an understanding of God's will, and to find reassurance in our attempts to do what he asks of us.

The publication of the English version of the Catechism of the Catholic Church in the Spring of 1994 gave us an opportunity to look at this contemporary expression of Catholic faith and practice. After discussion with the church council and at the parish's annual general meeting, we began an exploration which will come to an end around Advent this year. Through nearly thirty weekly sessions we have looked at our own personal beliefs against the backcloth of the official teaching of the Roman Catholic Church. I hope that each of us has experienced a new confidence in believing as we have gone back to the Scriptural and Patristic sources, and recognized that our faith has a coherent and confident pattern. What I pray the Catechism has given us is a shared matrix of thought and expression.

During these past three years there have been many external pressures placed on us as a parish. The attention of the media has not helped, as the simplistic sound-bite is more readily consumed than the necessarily nuanced position of a community seeking, patiently and quietly, to discern the will of its Master. For many years Saint Stephen's has had a high profile within the Catholic Movement in Anglicanism, and this has meant that our journey has attracted interest and expectancies from outside. I believe that we have come through this long period of discernment a stronger community: there are honest differences of theological emphasis among us, but the fundamental concern that each person should be valued, and their opinions respected, has not, I trust and hope, been compromised.

In everything that I have said or written through the years, I have tried to build on this fundamental principle of unity. In our Catechism exploration we have discovered that there is no aspect of our faith which can be viewed other than through the prism of the Blessed Trinity. At the heart of the Christian revelation is the God who exists as One, in Diversity. The command of Jesus to his disciples was that in their own relationships with one another they should manifest such a degree of unity that the rest of the world would understand the nature of the Triune God. For Christians to exist in intimate communion with each other is not a matter of pragmatism – it is a reflection of the profoundest theological truth. We are called to exist as one, because God is One.

'May they all be one, Father, may they be one in us, as you are in me, and I am in you' (John 17:21). Two contemporary Orthodox writers reflect on Jesus's words thus: 'The essence of the Church is the divine life unveiling itself in creatures: it is the deification of the creature in the strength of the Incarnation and Pentecost' (Paul Evdokimov), and: 'The Church is an image of the Holy Trinity' (Vladimir Lossky).

Our shared concern has been to try to find ways in which Saint Stephen's can be true to Jesus's prayer. Now the time is coming when the process of discernment needs to be drawn towards its conclusion. As individuals, and as individuals within a community, we need to clarify our direction. Perhaps it will help, at this stage, to underline the fact that Saint Stephen's is a parish church within the Diocese of London and that, as far as one can reasonably see into the future, it will remain so. Given the small size of the parish boundaries, and the restructuring of the London Diocese, it might be that Saint Stephen's will be drawn into a new relationship with one or more of its neighbours, but whatever form its future takes, Church of England sacraments will continue to be administered to Church of England people within its walls. Those who genuinely feel that God requires them to remain as Anglicans must have no worries that Saint Stephen's will continue to offer a ministry to them.

I owe it to you to explain the position I have reached. I was brought up to love the Church of England as a legitimate part of the whole Church – with Archbishop Michael Ramsey, I always believed that Anglicanism was 'transitional', and that it was destined to re-find its original unity within the context of the Catholic Church. I was excited by the work of the Anglican/Roman Catholic dialogue (ARCIC), and continue to believe that its agreed statements are models of ecumenical method. I truly believed that by the year 2000 we should see a *rapprochement* whereby 'sister churches' were once more in communion, and that, together, Anglicans and Roman Catholics, while maintaining the individuality of their cultures, would set about the evangelization of this nation. It has been a great sadness to see that dream disappear into the mist, and to witness the Church of England define itself increasingly with the churches of the Reformation.

Those of us who believe that the truth of Christianity is inseparably bound up with the Catholic faith, and who cannot separate the authentic transmission of that faith from the unity of Saint Peter and the Apostles with their successors, are caught into a dilemma. While we believed that there was a dynamic towards the Church of England regaining Apostolic unity, we could, and did, serve it with full hearts: but now that there is no longer any hope of such a corporate reconciliation, the Gospel imperative is still to seek the way to unity which is open to us. In the sixth century Pope Pelagius wrote to the Emperor Justinian: 'If anyone is divided from the apostolic sees, it cannot be doubted that he is in schism, and is trying to raise up an altar against the universal Church': fourteen hundred years later the situation may be very different, but Pelagius' point still needs to be answered.

A number of Anglicans have found their resolution by turning to Eastern Orthodoxy for apostolic communion. While I respect the Orthodox churches, I believe that for Christians in the West, their natural centre of unity can only be Rome – 'The only see which makes any claim to universal primacy is the see of Rome, the city where Peter and Paul died' (ARCIC agreed statement on Authority). In the face of the growing secularism of British society ecumenism cannot be viewed as a luxury: it is at the heart of the proclamation of the Good News of salvation. In the changed situation which we now face, I feel that I can do no other than carry on the journey towards full communion with the Roman Catholic Church.

There are two other areas of concern that have brought me to the conviction that it would be wrong to remain separated from the Apostolic See. Membership of the General Synod showed me a face of the Church of England I had not seen before: so much of the agenda was concerned with 'issues', and the purpose of what was virtually a party political system seemed to be the securing of bare majorities rather than genuine consensus. A local church, exercising an autonomy in matters of doctrine, worship and ethics, without any wider safeguards, lays itself open to constant strife and division and also the culs-de-sac of wrong belief. I think that the Church of England has locked itself into an issue-dominated future, and I cannot, in all honesty, encourage new Christians to be part of such an agenda.

My second area of concern is the explosion which is taking place in the understanding of human genetics. We are only making the first tentative steps towards understanding so much more about the human person in physiological and psychological terms. With the dawning of the new millennium so much that we have only dreamed about will become possible in terms of human engineering. If this new knowledge is to be harnessed for the good of the universe – and not to lead to chaos – there will need to be clear ethical parameters. I believe that the only hope we have of articulating a Christian voice which will be able to defend the integrity of the human person must be one with recognized universal claim. Just as it was Saint Peter who first expressed the Apostles' faith in Jesus as the Son of God, so his successors will be charged with developing the ethical values of Christianity in the face of the revolution in scientific experimentation. The Church gathered around Peter can be the only credible guarantee that we shall not slip into a new holocaust.

So what am I trying to say? I am clear in my own mind that to remain outside the full communion of the Roman Catholic Church would be a wilful act on my part. How that personal reconciliation is achieved is very much bound up with the parish community. Since I accepted the 'cure of souls' at Saint Stephen's nine years ago, I have tried to maintain a unity in diversity – at a parish level to apply Jesus's prayer for our one-ness. The tensions of the Church of England have obviously been echoed within our own walls, but we have held together as a community and have witnessed steady growth and holiness of life.

Through the years I have attempted to teach the Christian faith without allowing 'issues' to undermine its coherence – though I have also tried to build a measured response to the wider debates, chiefly through what has been written in the parish magazine month by month. I hope that you have come to understand my approach to the Gospel: but as your parish priest I have very deliberately never sought to ascertain what views you might have as individuals. You know what I think and believe – in only a few cases can I say the same of you.

A couple of years ago I used the image of a Palestinian shepherd leading his sheep from the front (in distinction to those in the West who tend to chivvy along their charges from behind). I said then that at some stage I would look over my shoulder and see if any were still following my lead. It might well be that there are few who are walking the same path as I am. If that is so, then I must begin to make the decisions that God requires of me. It may be, though, that there are others who share the imperative for wider communion. If they are just a handful, then I will want to discuss with them the right way to move towards reconciliation with the Catholic Church. What I am asking is that through the coming days and weeks any individuals who might share my goals, or who are perhaps unclear as to the future, should talk to me. I will set aside as much time as I can to be available to come to see you, or for you to come to me.

If the number of those wanting to move into the wider unity proves significant, then another scenario opens up. The Lord told a parable about new wine in new wineskins, and perhaps, just perhaps, there might be a way in which we can establish a model of local ecumenism which could have wider consequences. We worship together in Saint Stephen's because that is where we believe God has called us to find Him through one another. It is not inconceivable that two Eucharistic communities could co-exist in the same building as a living expression of unity in diversity.

In other more polarized times, the idea of a group of Anglicans moving into communion with the Roman Catholic Church while maintaining the highest degree of fellowship with their brothers and sisters who had remained within the Church of England, would have been difficult to envisage. But need that necessarily be so any longer? To a divided world and a polarized church the model of Christians recognizing legitimate difference and yet remaining as friends has much to commend it. Is this just a pipe-dream which would be pulled apart by external pressures and inherited prejudices? Possibly so. But it is only through 'dreaming dreams' that we leave ourselves open to what the Holy Spirit might be saying – and the 'sin against the Holy Spirit' is the one sin that Scripture (Matthew 12:32) tells us the Father will not forgive.

Up and down the country there are a number of examples of 'shared church' agreements. In these, two (or even more) distinct Christian communities enter into an understanding whereby their Eucharist is celebrated at different times in the same building. In our own case, those who were members of the Church of England would retain full title to the church building and all its resources, while covenanting with those who had entered full communion with the Roman Catholic Church to allow a continued presence. If this idea were to find any favour among us, the situation at Saint Stephen's would be unique in that we would not be differing churches coming together under one roof, but a single family trying to make sense of the reality of impaired communion, while demonstrating the fundamental ties which link the Baptized. 'My dear people, let us love one another, since love comes from God' (1 John 4:7).

Can I ask everyone to pray very hard through these coming weeks. What I have suggested above is only the embryo of an idea: it would take a great act of faith, and enormous gentleness and sensitivity, to bring it to any kind of birth. Whatever does, or does not, happen, there is no question that those who want to remain as members of the Church of England within Saint Stephen's will do so. There is also no question that a form of sharing agreement could only be entered into if there were a clear consensus on the part of the congregation that this was a right direction to take. There is much to be excited about: perhaps, like Mother Teresa of Calcutta, we are being invited to 'do something beautiful for God'.

Pray for me, as I pray for you.

Christopher Colven

Feast of St Martin of Tours – 11 November 1995

APPENDIX C

The translation (attributed to the reformer, Miles Coverdale) of the Roman Canon, as it was authorized by Pope John Paul II for use in America by Anglican Rite Parishes of the Pastoral Provision

EUCHARISTIC PRAYER

The priest begins the Eucharistic prayer.

The people remain standing. The Celebrant, whether bishop or priest, faces them and sings or says:

	The Lord be with you.
People	And with thy spirit.
Celebrant	Lift up your hearts.
People	We lift them up unto the Lord.
Celebrant	Let us give thanks unto our Lord God.
People	It is meet and right so to do.

Then, facing the Holy Table, the Celebrant proceeds:

It is very meet, right and our bounden duty, that we should at all times, and in all places, give thanks unto thee, O Lord, holy Father almighty, everlasting God.

Here a Proper Preface is sung or said on all Sundays, and on other occasions as appointed.

If no Proper Preface be appointed, then the Celebrant continues:

Therefore with Angels and Archangels, and with all the company of heaven, we laud and magnify thy glorious Name: evermore praising thee, and saying,

Celebrant and People
Holy, holy, holy, Lord God of Hosts:
Heaven and earth are full of thy glory.
Glory be to thee, O Lord Most High.
Blessed is he that cometh in the name of the Lord.
Hosanna in the highest.

EUCHARISTIC PRAYER I
(OLD ENGLISH CANON)

In this Eucharistic prayer the words in brackets may be omitted.
The priest, with hands extended, says:

Celebrant alone
Most merciful Father, we humbly pray thee, through Jesus Christ
thy Son our Lord,
He joins his hands and, making the sign of the cross once over both
bread and chalice, says:
And we ask, that thou accept and bless † these gifts, these presents,
these holy and unspoiled sacrifices.
With hands extended, he continues:
We offer them unto thee, first, for thy holy catholic Church; that thou
vouchsafe to keep it in peace, to guard, unite, and govern it throughout
the whole world; together with thy servant N. our Pope and N. our Bishop and all the faithful guardians of the catholic and apostolic faith.

Commemoration of the Living
Celebrant or one Concelebrant
Remember, O Lord, thy servants and handmaids N. and N.
He prays for them briefly with hands joined. Then, with hands
extended, he continues:
and all who here around us stand, whose faith is known unto thee
and their steadfastness manifest, on whose behalf we offer unto thee, or
who themselves offer unto thee, this sacrifice of praise, for themselves,
and for all who are theirs; for the redemption of their souls, for the hope
of their salvation and safety; and who offer their prayers unto thee, the
eternal God, the living and the true.

Celebrant or one Concelebrant

*United in one communion, we venerate the memory, first of the glorious ever Virgin Mary, Mother of our God and Lord Jesus Christ, of Joseph her spouse; as also of the blessed Apostles and Martyrs, Peter and Paul, Andrew, [James, John, Thomas, James, Philip, Bartholomew, Matthew, Simon and Thaddaeus; Linus, Cletus, Clement, Xystus, Cornelius, Cyprian, Lawrence, Chrysogomus, John and Paul, Cosmas and Damian] and of all thy Saints: grant that by their merits and prayers we may in all things be defended with the help of thy protection.

[Through the same Christ our Lord. Amen.]

With hands outstretched over the offerings, he says:

Celebrant with Concelebrants

Vouchsafe, O God, we beseech thee, in all things to make this oblation blessed, approved and accepted, a perfect and worthy offering; that it may become for us the Body and Blood of thy dearly beloved Son, Jesus Christ.

He joins his hands.

The words of the Lord in the following formulas should be spoken clearly and distinctly, as their meaning demands.

Who the day before he suffered

* *On Maundy Thursday he says*: Who the day before he suffered to save us and all men, that is today,

He takes the bread and, raising it a little above the altar, continues:
took bread into his holy and venerable hands,

He looks upward.

and with eyes lifted up to heaven, unto thee, God, his almighty Father, giving thanks to thee, he blessed, broke and gave it to his disciples, saying:

He bows slightly.

Take this, all of you, and eat it: this is my body which will be given up for you.

He shows the consecrated host to the people, places it on the paten, and genuflects in adoration. Then he continues:

Likewise, after supper,

He takes the chalice, and, raising it a little above the altar, continues:
taking also this goodly chalice into his holy and venerable hands, again giving thanks to thee, he blessed, and gave it to his disciples, saying:

He bows slightly.

Take this, all of you, and drink from it: this is the cup of my blood, the blood of the new and everlasting covenant. It will be shed for you and for all so that sins may be forgiven.

Do this in memory of me.

He shows the chalice to the people, places it on the corporal, and genuflects in adoration, then he sings or says:

Therefore we proclaim the mystery of faith:

People with Celebrant and Concelebrants
Christ has died, Christ is risen, Christ will come again.
Then with hands extended, the priest says:

Celebrant with Concelebrants
Wherefore, O Lord, we thy servants, and thy holy people also, remembering the blessed passion of the same Christ thy Son our Lord, as also his resurrection from the dead, and his glorious ascension into heaven; do offer unto thine excellent majesty of thine own gifts and bounty, the pure victim, the holy victim, the immaculate victim, the holy Bread of eternal life, and the Chalice of everlasting salvation.

With hands extended, he continues:

Celebrant alone
*We beseech thee then, O Lord, graciously to accept this oblation from us thy servants, and from thy whole family: order thou our days in thy peace, and bid us to be delivered from eternal damnation, and to be numbered in the fold of thine elect.

[Through Christ our Lord.]

Vouchsafe to look upon them with a merciful and pleasant countenance; and to accept them, even as thou didst vouchsafe to accept the gifts of thy servant Abel the Righteous, and the sacrifice of our Patriarch Abraham; and the holy sacrifice the immaculate victim, which thy high priest Melchisedech offered unto thee.

Bowing, with hands joined, he continues:

We humbly beseech thee, almighty God, command these offerings to be brought by the hands of thy holy Angel to thine altar on high, in sight of thy divine majesty; that all we who at this partaking of the altar shall receive the most sacred Body and Blood of thy Son

He stands up straight and makes the sign of the cross, saying:

may be fulfilled with all heavenly benediction and grace.
[Through the same Christ our Lord. Amen.]

Commemoration of the Dead
With hands extended, he says:

Celebrant or one Concelebrant
Remember also, O Lord, thy servants N. and N., who have gone
before us sealed with the seal of faith, and who sleep the sleep of peace.
*The priest prays for them briefly with joined hands. Then, with
hands extended, he continues:*
To them, O Lord, and to all that rest in Christ, we beseech thee to
grant the abode of refreshing, of light, and of peace.
[Through the same Christ our Lord.]
The priest strikes his breast with the right hand, saying:
To us sinners also, thy servants, who hope in the multitude of thy
mercies,
With hands extended, he continues:
vouchsafe to grant some part and fellowship with thy holy Apostles
and Martyrs; with John, Stephen, Matthias, Barnabas, [Ignatius,
Alexander, Marcellinus, Peter, Felicitas, Perpetua, Agatha, Lucy,
Agnes, Cecilia, Anastasis] and with all thy Saints, within whose fellow-
ship, we beseech thee, admit us, not weighing our merit, but granting us
forgiveness;
He joins his hands and continues:

Celebrant alone
through Jesus Christ our Lord, through whom, O Lord, thou dost
ever create all these good things; dost sanctify, quicken, bless, and
bestow them upon us;
*He takes the chalice and the paten with the host and, lifting them
up, sings or says:*

Celebrant alone or with Concelebrants
By whom, and with whom, and in whom, in the unity of the Holy
Ghost, all honour and glory be unto thee, O Father Almighty, world
without end. Amen.

YOUR NUMBER ONE STOP

ONE MORE CHAPTER

FOR PAGETURNING BOOKS

One More Chapter is an
award-winning global
division of HarperCollins.

Sign up to our newsletter to get our
latest eBook deals and stay up to date
with our weekly Book Club!
<u>Subscribe here.</u>

Meet the team at
<u>www.onemorechapter.com</u>

Follow us!
🐦 <u>@OneMoreChapter_</u>
📘 <u>@OneMoreChapter</u>
📷 <u>@onemorechapterhc</u>

Do you write unputdownable fiction?
We love to hear from new voices.
Find out how to submit your novel at
<u>www.onemorechapter.com/submissions</u>